Sinn Féin Women

SINN FÉIN WOMEN

Footnoted Foot Soldiers and Women of No Importance

Margaret Keiley-Listermann

AN IMPRINT OF ABC-CLIO, LLC
Santa Barbara, California • Denver, Colorado • Oxford, England

Library of Congress Cataloging-in-Publication Data

Keiley-Listermann, Margaret.
　Sinn Féin women : footnoted soldiers and women of no importance /
Margaret Keiley-Listermann.
　　　p. cm.
　Includes bibliographical references and index.
　ISBN 978-1-84645-015-0 (hard copy : alk. paper) — ISBN 978-0-313-09740-9
(e-book)　1. Sinn Féin—History.　2. Women—Political activity—Ireland—History.
3. Ireland—Politics and government—20th century.　4. Northern Ireland—Politics and
government.　I. Title.
　JN1571.5.S56K45　2010
　324.2415'083082—dc22　　　2010023172

ISBN: 978-1-84645-015-0
EISBN: 978-0-313-09740-9

14　13　12　11　10　　1　2　3　4　5

This book is also available on the World Wide Web as an eBook.
Visit www.abc-clio.com for details.

Praeger
An Imprint of ABC-CLIO, LLC

ABC-CLIO, LLC
130 Cremona Drive, P.O. Box 1911
Santa Barbara, California 93116-1911

This book is printed on acid-free paper ∞

Manufactured in the United States of America

CONTENTS

LIST OF ILLUSTRATIONS

LIST OF TABLES AND FIGURES

PREFACE

I remember clearly a newspaper article with a picture of Gerry Adams and Martin McGuinness standing outside Stormont Castle in 1997. I had just begun my doctoral studies at the University of Alabama, and what caught my eye was that there were a couple of women standing behind them. Their identities were unknown to me, but I thought it was interesting . . . perhaps because their frames were out of focus and their names uncredited. Ten years later, I would find myself interviewing one of them at Sinn Féin headquarters in Dublin.

As I completed my dissertation on Sinn Féin and the peace process, my curiosity about these women grew. Why is it that we know the male figures in Irish history but—aside from the occasional reference to the Countess Markievicz and her pistol or Maud Gonne and her writer (Yeats)—we knew very little about the women who shaped the drive for an Irish Republic? Certainly, anyone familiar with an Irish woman knows her sharp mind, razor wit, and strength of character. Why was it that history perpetuated the frailty of a softer gender when the inner strength of the Irish women I met seemed to permeate social and cultural reality?

And so I began a journey to learn more about these women that history left behind and the media left uncredited.

I proposed a gargantuan task—to provide an overview of the role that women had played in the development of Sinn Féin across the span of the 20th century. I knew the National Archives in Dublin and the Linenhall Library in Belfast well; I had spent the better part of my dissertation in them. And so, I would return, but this time, I sought to learn the stories of the community by conducting a series of personal interviews and informal conversations with the women whom I began to learn more about.

I am deeply appreciative that Sinn Féin granted me five formal interviews. This superior access to elected political figures and key party members facilitated this groundbreaking project, which combined a centenary overview of Sinn Féin with profiles of Republican women within that century.

In turn, this book contains the first notable analysis of Margaret Buckley's presidency within Sinn Féin.

That said, there were certain limitations on this study; in particular, the women selected for portraits were designed to profile a representative mosaic of different roles, personalities, and characters. There will be some discussion about the women included here that were not members of Sinn Féin and those who later left the party. In such cases, the embodiment of the spirit of "sinn féin" and the contribution to party development was the impetus for their inclusion. Likewise, there were many women that I learned about, even came to know, along the way that simply could not be included. This book should be viewed as a sincere attempt to recognize the efforts that women have made to the political party of Sinn Féin and to place them within the folds of otherwise well-documented Irish history. It is my hope that future scholars will further this work by telling the stories of all Sinn Féin women.

ACKNOWLEDGMENTS

On May 14, 2007, I was sitting in a church pew among 500 some odd women in Atlanta, Georgia. Celebrating the 90th anniversary of the founding of the Junior League of Atlanta, my family and I listened to the organization's president describe the important role that women have played in serving the Atlanta community by lobbying for a child endangerment statute in Georgia, sewing baby blankets for Grady Healthcare Systems, starting the Atlanta Speech School, and partnering with over 40 community agencies to impact the needs of women and children in my city. She quoted former Justice Sandra Day O'Connor in saying that "[w]e don't accomplish anything in this world alone . . . and whatever happens is the result of the whole tapestry of one's life and all the weavings of individual threads from one to another that creates something."[1] In honoring my great-grandmother Robyn Young Peeples, the Junior League of Atlanta leadership called its cofounder's family to stand. My grandmother Robyn Walsh rose, then my mother Robyn Keiley, and then I stood to join them. Standing among these dedicated volunteers who have woven their threads into the tapestry of community service, I could not help but think of the women in Sinn Féin and how they too have weaved a tapestry with their lives.

The Sinn Féin tapestry is a collective product of individual threads, frayed by oppression and hardship, intertwined into hopes for their community. Although some threads are more visible than others, the artistic result relies on the contributions of all, whether acknowledged or not. Here within, some of those threads are revealed in the hope that a few individual stories will bring the needed dimension to appreciate the colors and textures of the Republican tapestry.

This book is dedicated to the many women I have met along my journeys, but especially to the two who launched me into this world with the confidence that all girls should have . . . to the two strongest women I have known, my mother and my grandmother. They taught me to listen, to learn, and to be the best daughter, wife, and mother that I could be.

Many thanks to Praeger/Greenwood Press for acknowledging the need for a book on Irish Republican women, and to the Writers' Institute at Georgia Perimeter College for allowing the time to be prioritized for this project. To my colleagues at Georgia Gwinnett College, I thank you for the inspiration I needed to complete this endeavor.

Much gratitude is owed to the advice and feedback from the American Conference for Irish Studies and the Georgia Political Science Association. To Dr. Barbara Chotiner at the University of Alabama, thank you for showing me how inspiring a female professor could be.

This book would not have been possible without the direction of the Sinn Féin, especially Dawn Doyle, Eoin Ó Broin, and Chrissie McAuley. Special thanks to Chrissie for her time, which is tirelessly spent to improve the conditions of women and men in Ireland. Thank you to Eibhlín Glenholmes, Martina Anderson, Mary Lou McDonald, and Caitríona Ruane for granting interviews and allowing me to share in retelling their stories. These women are a genuine testament to the role that women have played in achieving a better Ireland.

Special thanks to Ruairí Ó Brádaigh and the women of Republican Sinn Féin for generously granting me their time, which allowed for Margaret Buckley's story to be told.

With great appreciation, I would like to acknowledge the efforts of Belfast photographer Kelly Morris. She believed in this project and in me when it was needed most, and through her passionate efforts, captured the light that best reflected the rich texture of the Sinn Féin tapestry. Kelly's wonderful photography of the interview subjects in this book has brought these women to life; she lives in Belfast where she is raising her beautiful son.

Finally, I am forever indebted to my family, including my four children, who sacrificed time with me in order that this story might be told. When friends and family kept asking me how I, a mother of four, full-time professor, and committed community activist, had time to write a book, I would remember that it is my hope that this book will share some of the her-story of Sinn Féin women and that they will be removed from the footnotes of Irish history.

INTRODUCTION: FOOTNOTED FOOT SOLDIERS

Everyone, Republican or otherwise has their own particular part to play. No part is too great or too small, no one is too old or too young to do something.

—Bobby Sands

It is somehow fitting to begin a journey of a hundred years with the insight expressed by Bobby Sands, the first to die on hunger strike on May 5, 1981. The 25th year commemorations were held in 2006, with many visitors from around the world descending upon Ireland to pay respects to a man and his cause. His words recognize the truth that bore the idea for this book—that everyone has a role to play in the cause of an independent Ireland. Although he did not reference the gender of those who should play a part, it is clearly understood that Republican women should play a part too. Disrupting the tendency to overlook the Republican women who, for now over a century, have been united in purpose though often divided in means, this book seeks to acknowledge the part, no matter great or small, that Sinn Féin women have played in Irish independence. It should not go without mention that 25 years after Bobby Sands won his historic seat in Westminster Parliament, it was a woman—Michelle Gildernew—who won the seat back for Sinn Féin. Sinn Féin women have been awaiting political equality and representative parity for almost a century, since Countess Markievicz was elected as the first woman in Westminster Parliament in 1918.

Even though the role of women within Sinn Féin has been consistent and persistent, many historical books seem to be unaware of the contributions of women in the struggle for Irish independence. Whilst the important events in Irish history are retold with the precision worthy of mythical legends, the legacy of Republican women seems to be reduced to an obscure footnote. In this book, deconstructing the images of Irish women and demonstrating the significant responsibilities of a female foot soldier within Sinn Féin will profile a general overview of the duties performed by the Republican woman.

IRISH "HER-STORY"

Modern Irish history seemingly has two themes—that of a struggle for independent nationhood and a complicated entanglement of political intrigue. Everyone has a story, a story repeated time and time again in the homes across Ireland and in Irish immigrant homes worldwide. The Big Fellow (Michael Collins) and the Long Fellow (Eamon de Valera) are recalled as if they were friends, perhaps even family. Though Bobby Sands has become a mythical legend, our stories still capture the humanity of his story. It is a constant paradox how people, events, and places are so keenly remembered, and yet how distorted these memories can become. The controversial divide of historical accuracy competing with myth-historical revisionism leaves the scholar with an additional thought—how is the Irish woman being portrayed in modern Irish history? The glaring omission of the contributions of women at significant moments in Irish history—as well as the consistent social and political contributions—is apparent. Women have been relegated to the footnotes and parenthetical references of history.

What is the Irish "her-story?" Culturally, the Irish woman is often portrayed as strong, defiant, gregarious, perhaps even androgynous or quiet suffering, temperate, moral, and nurturing. The fiery tempered or sanctimonious characterization minimizes the breadth of roles and duties an Irish woman has performed. Women have been land reformers, linguistic and cultural revivalists, armed soldiers, logistical and strategic military support, casualties, prisoners, members of Dáil Eireann and various city councils, suffragettes, authors, activists, hunger strikers, assassination targets, homemakers, and top-tier members of national government. Why then, when the Easter Rising is recounted, are the Revolutionary women— many more than just Countess Markievicz—who took up arms along their brothers, fathers, and husbands, relegated to a footnote?

Female scholars have recently been seeking to address the historical oversight of Irish women in their own history. In the 1990s, there was a rush of biographic profiles of Kathleen Clarke, Maud Gonne, Hanna Sheehy-Skeffington, and Linda Kearns.[2] Similarly, the Revolutionary women have increasingly caught the attention of academia.[3] Finally, a new fresh look at Irish female nationalists has begun to surface in some innovative approaches. Identifying the "oversight" of substantial contributions made by women in Irish history, four studies stand apart as recommended reading— Margaret Ward's *Unmanageable Revolutionaries* (1995) and *Irish Women and Nationalism: Soldiers, New Women and Wicked Hags* with Louise Ryan (2004), Silvia Calamiti's *The Trouble We've Seen* (2002) and Sinéad Mc-Coole's *No Ordinary Women* (2003).

THE INDELIBLE IRISH IDENTITY QUESTION IN IRISH POLITICS

Ireland is often referred to as a patriarchal society with stereotyped images of the Irish woman, unless one examines the development of women's rights within the Republican movement. Whether overt or covert, these Republican women have been seen as agents of rebellion and social action. Strong, determined, and principled, Republican women have played an integral role in the political development of an independent Ireland. In a centennial review of the legacy of the women of Sinn Féin, this book seeks to raise awareness of the footnoted foot soldiers and their lasting contributions.

Long before 1905 when Sinn Féin (the political party) was founded, Republican women were tending two fires—one at home and one on the political battlefield. As early advocates for land reform and cultural revival, the Republican women intermingled with some very common historical male figures. During the important years of 1879 to 1905, nationalist women became land reformers, cultural activists, and Irish linguists.

Under the weight of colonial domination, Michael Davitt and Charles Stewart Parnell founded the Irish Land League in 1879. The Irish Parliamentary Party (IPP) then advocated the Home Rule movement as a solution to the aggressive and oppressive landowners. Recognizing the power of collective thought and action, the British government quickly passed the Coercion Act of 1881. The act outlawed the Land League and forced its leaders into prison, house arrest, or hiding. However, the founding of the Irish Ladies Land League by Anne Deane and Beatrice Walshe saved the land reform movement. Since the Coercion Act had identified "land reformers" as subversives and the male leaders were imprisoned, the Ladies Land League, through a gender bias in the penal system, found itself outside the jurisdiction of the act and, thus, carried on the land reform initiative. And at the national helm of the Ladies Land League was Parnell's sister Anne.

As these women rose to prominence, another revival was underfoot. Co-inciding with protests of the impending visit of Queen Victoria to Ireland in 1900, cultural activist Maud Gonne founded the Inghinidhe na hÉire-ann (Daughters of Ireland) to promote Irish language, drama, and writing. By 1908, the Daughters of Ireland were publishing a newspaper, *Bean na hEireann,* edited by Helena Molony. The Countess Constance Markievicz also joined both Sinn Féin and the Daughters of Ireland that year. She subsequently founded the Fianna Éireann in 1909 to provide weapons instruction for school aged boys. A girl's branch of the Fianna also briefly popped up in Belfast.

In 1901, Máire de Buitléir, a vocal proponent for Irish culture, had written an article entitled "Womanhood and Nationhood" in the *United Irishman.* Her close association with the newspaper owner, Arthur Griffith, led her to suggest a name for his new organization—Sinn Féin (we ourselves). Her passionate command of the Irish language furthered the development of the Irish national identity with her suggestions that Irish women, as guardians of the homestead, could teach language, dance, and song to the children of Ireland. Women, according to Buitléir, would be the chief nation builders in the Gaelic Revival. Although parochial and perhaps plain in contrast to the colorful feminist suffragette Hanna Sheehy-Skeffington, Máire de Buitléir married Irish language with Irish culture, and hence a sense of nation, with the Republican movement. An independent Ireland, however, would only be realized after a comprehensive call to arms—one that women as well as men heeded.

The Irish Republican Brotherhood (IRB) was founded in the 1850s to seek the unequivocal withdrawal of the British Crown—to establish a 32-county republic. James Larkin, by contrast, founded the Irish Citizen Army (ICA), in 1913, as a response to a labor union dispute. It was a group of men and women devoted to socialist values and workers' rights. When Larkin left for America in 1914, James Connolly took over as president and became embroiled with "Fenians" (the IRB). Among the earliest active ICA members were the Countess and Hanna Sheehy-Skeffington, founder of the Irish Women's Franchise League and wife of 1916 martyr Francis Sheehy-Skeffington.

James Connolly, along with the women and men who supported the Irish Citizen Army, recognized the inherent link between women's suffrage, socialism, and Irish self-determination. His strong sentiments about equality—regardless of economic status or gender—and unconventional gender roles, including a woman learning how to handle a gun, permeated the development of the modern Irish Republican movement. Also founded in 1913, the Irish Volunteers were an armed paramilitary force who shared the ICA's goal of enforcing the pending Home Rule Bill. Prominent members included Patrick Pearse, Roger Casement, Bulmer Hobson, and Erskine Childers. Erskine's wife Mollie Osgood Childers assisted him in smuggling weapons into Howth from Germany on the *Asgard* boat in 1914. The Ladies Auxiliary of the Volunteers became known in 1914 as Cumann na mBan and boasted a membership roster that included the Countess, Maud Gonne, Elizabeth O'Farrell, Mary MacSwiney, Ada English, Helena Molony, Winifred Carney, and Margaret Skinnider—the lone female casualty of the Easter Rising.

The Easter Rebellion of 1916 merged many strains of Irish nationalism and republicanism into one moment of resistance. The women of Sinn Féin, frequently also members of the Irish Citizen Army Cumann na mBan and Inghinidhe na hÉireann, were actively engaged in the rebellion. They were not simply relegated to just traditional combat support roles such as nurses or food suppliers. Many of them were armed and engaged in active fire exchanges. The Countess served as second in command at St. Stephen's Green. She was so devoted that she only surrendered after the British were able to produce Patrick Pearse's surrender letter. Although she was sentenced to death for her role in the rebellion, Countess Constance Markievicz was later pardoned, in part due to her gender. She went on to become the first elected woman to Westminster Parliament, though she did not take her seat since she had run as a Sinn Féin abstentionist candidate. Many of the women who participated in the Easter Rising also went on to positions of power, including Belfast-born Winifred Carney, who was elected to her city council.

Largely due in part to the highly visible franchise activism of Hanna Sheehy-Skeffington, Sinn Féin adopted an official party policy of gender equality in 1917. Women over 30 years of age in Ireland got the right to vote in 1918, and all women were granted universal suffrage in 1921. This was seven years before British women got the right to vote. Political and constitutional issues plagued Ireland during the Anglo-Irish War and then the Irish Civil War, but when the smoke settled, the Irish Republican woman was ready to step to the forefront of Irish politics and society.

From actively debating in Dáil Éireann to campaigning for women's rights, the Sinn Féin woman forged a new agenda toward an independent Ireland based on equality of religion, gender, and politics. Though many of her efforts went unrealized, the only woman to be Sinn Féin president, Margaret Buckley, served from 1937 to 1950. It is certainly interesting that there is a significant lack of biographical literature on the only female Sinn Féin president, but she was a Daughter of Ireland, Dáil Court judge, Minister for Home Affairs, and author of *The Jangle of the Keys* (1938). A strong opponent of the Anglo-Irish Treaty negotiated by Arthur Griffith and Michael Collins, Buckley was ultimately jailed for treaty opposition and went on a hunger strike while in jail. Once released, she spent her presidency trying to resolve differences between Sinn Féin and the Irish Republican Army (merged with the Irish Volunteers and most of the Irish Citizen Army in 1917). Her presidency also faced the challenge of a formal partitioning of the North of Ireland and a full independent, southern republic.

The North remained a part of the United Kingdom, and throughout the 1950s and 1960s, the conditions for Catholics deteriorated under a modern Protestant ascendancy. In the midst of civil unrest across Northern Ireland, Sinn Féin women used their voice to broadcast the plight of those most crippled by the siege. One such activist was Mary Nelis, a "pregnant petitioner" from Derry. She joined Sinn Féin after the British troops arrived in the Creggan. The civil rights activist recalls how the experience impacted her and her 10 children:

> When I look back at dividing lines and where things have changed in my life, it was the day that the British Army came on the streets. Because then we lived not in a ghetto, but in a concentration camp, with check points in and out, and soldiers raiding our houses, and children who were growing up being arrested and taken into interrogation centers and picked up and shot dead. It was a war situation. People euphemistically describe it as "troubles." But it we were in a war [sic]. I can't think of any other way to describe it. You know, if you're living in a housing estate and the only way you can get in is through a check point with soldiers frisking you down, searching your shopping bags, and a guerrilla army is on the streets shooting at them, and they're shooting back. . . . And your children are going to school and getting smothered in CS gas and lying down vomiting in the streets—that's how we lived for years. We never slept. It was really very difficult times and there's nothing romantic or nice about it.[4]

Civil rights activists combined a moral imperative for equality with a passionate use of limited resources. This female ingenuity vocally called attention to discrimination, violence, and hazards using creative sanitary napkins soaked in a solution as "masks" for the CS gas, constructing Molotov cocktails at home, and banging garbage lids on the street to signal to neighbors for collective action. As the tension rose and the now infamous events of Free Derry (1969), internment (1971), and Bloody Sunday (1972) occurred, Republican women became the voice of the movement. In some cases, this was a result of imprisoned brothers, fathers, husbands, and sons. Female advocates formed organizations like the Relatives Action Committee that assisted the families of H-Block prisoners. The criminalization of Republicans put the men behind bars and the women out front.

Although some Republican women were detained or interned, many Sinn Féin women rose in the ranks of the party while the men—like Bobby Sands, Danny Morrison, Tom Hartley, Martin McGuinness, and Gerry Adams—served time in the cages. By the 1970s, Máire Drumm was the vice president of Sinn Féin. During a brief period, she stepped up to serve as the acting president when the president was jailed. This, unfortunately, made her a target. Loyalists assassinated her while she lay in a hospital bed in 1976.

Widespread civil violence resulted in increased security by the British government throughout the 1970s and 1980s. Some Republican women ended up on the inside of the prison system, being subjected to strip searches and prolonged detainment under the Prevention of Terrorism Act and Emergency Powers Act. Women on the inside participated in the no-wash (or dirty) campaigns for special category prisoner rights. In 1980, there were a total of 10 prisoners carefully selected by Sinn Féin to represent the seven male signatories of the Easter Proclamation and the female participation in the Rising. Women were quite aware of the strategic value of awakening social consciousness with a hunger strike. They were also quite experienced. The first female hunger strike known in modern Ireland had been in 1900 for female suffrage. Familiar with the strategy of hunger strikes, the Irish woman had participated in other organized strikes in 1923, 1940, 1974, and 1976 to demonstrate political protest. The three women who joined their Republican brothers in 1980 were Mary Doyle, Mairead Nugent, and Mairéad Farrell. All three women had been convicted of IRA membership or activity and were serving their sentence in the Armagh Jail. After Brendan Hughes began the strike in the Blocks in October of that year, the women joined on December 1, 1980.

The 1980 hunger strike was ended under the false assumption that special category status had been renewed. The men were ordered to stand down on December 17, 1980. They had been striking for 53 days. Suspicious of a British acquiesce, the women remained on strike another 24 hours longer (for a total of 18 days on hunger strike). Historical lore seems to obscure the 1980 hunger strike, in light of the deadly outcome of the 1981 strike lead by Bobby Sands, but Sinn Féin continually reasserts the significance of the 1980 strike and publicly acknowledges the female participation in it.

In the 1980's there were two hunger strikes. The first began in October 1980 and ended in December 1980 without loss of life. There were ten prisoners on hunger strike, seven in the H-Blocks *and three women in Armagh jail* [emphasis from the author].

The second hunger strike began in March 1981, five years after the British government withdrew political status from the prisoners. The second hunger strike claimed the lives of ten republican prisoners:

Bobby Sands, Francis Hughes, Raymond McCreesh, Patsy O'Hara, Joe McDonnell, Martin Hurson, Tom McElwee, Kevin Lynch, Kieran Doherty and Michael Devine.[5]

Mairéad Farrell was later released and resumed Republican status on the outside. In 1988, she was one of the Gibraltar Three—shot at close range by British authorities while unarmed. She had been one of the strongest female Republican leaders; in her short life she had been quite active in women's rights. She had been the first woman sentenced in 1976 without special category status (the male equivalent was Ciaran Nugent), led the female dirty protest from February 1980 to January 1981, completed courses from Open University and Queens University, and worked with the Stop Strip Searching campaign. In her own words:

Everybody keeps telling me I'm a feminist. I just know I'm me and I think I'm as good as anyone else and that particularly goes for any man. I'm a socialist, definitely, and I'm a republican. I believe in a united Ireland; a united socialist Ireland, definitely socialist. Capitalism provided no answer at all for our people and I think that's the Brit's main interest in Ireland Once we remove the British that isn't it, that's only the beginning.[6]

Activism abounded when in 1980, at Sinn Féin's annual party convention (Árd Fheis), the woman's platform was introduced and accepted. Creating the Women's Department, founding member Rita O'Hare assisted in the institutionalization of women's issues and ensured a female face at the front of the party's National Executive (Ard Chomharile). O'Hare went on to serve as the director of publicity for Sinn Féin in the 1990s and is currently the Sinn Féin representative to the United States. As she rose through the ranks of the party's leadership, other women were alongside her: Bairbre de Brún, Mary Lou McDonald, Michelle Gildernew, and Caitríona Ruane.

A former member of the Women's Department, former Cultural and then International Department chair, Bairbre de Brún has steered Sinn Féin and the Republicans through the development of the Northern Irish peace process. Working hard on the development of the 1992 "Women in Ireland" policy document, de Brún has long been an advocate for women's health and educational issues. This is one reason for her appointment to be the first Northern Ireland minister of health, social services, and public safety in 1999. Her involvement in the creation of the Belfast Agreement is largely minimized, although she was figured prominently in the negotiation team. Along with Bairbre de Brún, the Sinn Féin negotiation team, headed by Martin McGuinness, also included Gerry Kelly, Conor Murphy, Mary Lou McDonald, Arthur Morgan, Caoimhghín Ó Caoláin, Martin Ferris, and Mitchel McLaughlin. Perennially photographed over the shoulder of Gerry Adams and Martin McGuinness, de Brún's oration and negotiation skills from her teaching experience certainly assisted in crafting an agreement. She was first elected to the European Parliament in 2004, and then again in 2009, for the Six Counties as a Sinn Féin MEP.

Also elected to the European Parliament in 2004 for Dublin was Sinn Féin negotiator Mary Lou McDonald. An advocate for women's issues, McDonald is additionally serving as national party chairman in 2005–2006. She has overseen the implementation of the 2004 "Women in an Ireland of Equals" policy for Sinn Féin. McDonald states that even today "[w]omen continue to suffer discrimination and inequality with Irish society. Women suffer disproportionately in the workplace through unequal pay with their male counterparts, are more likely to fall into the poverty trap, suffer as a result of physical, sexual and psychological abuse and many rural women continue to be disadvantaged resulting from a lack of services and a sense of isolation."[7] In 2009, Mary Lou lost her Dublin seat but became the vice president of Sinn Féin. Coordinating with McDonald's efforts are two more up-and-coming youthful members of the Sinn Féin party—Michelle Gildernew and Caitríona Ruane.

The former organizer of the West Belfast Féile, Caitríona Ruane is a human rights advocate (spokesperson) for the Colombia Three and serves as a Sinn Féin member of the Northern Ireland Assembly for South Down. An avid human rights activist, Ruane is well traveled, well educated and well presented. Committed to international standards of equality, she became a key component of the Sinn Féin delegation to the Saint Andrews Conference in 2006. In 2007, Ruane became the minister of education in the newly constituted Northern Ireland Assembly.

Michelle Gildernew was first elected to the Westminster Parliament in 2001 and then reelected in 2005. Her election saw the return of an articulate Republican female to the British stage. In keeping with Sinn Féin's policy of abstentionism in the House of Commons, she has not taken her seat. In addition to being an MP, Gildernew is Sinn Féin's national spokesperson on equality and housing and is also a member of the Northern Ireland Assembly (MLA) for Fermanagh/South Tyrone. In 2007, she became the minister of agriculture and rural development in the Northern Ireland Assembly. Her career has already been very distinguished, even at a young age, but this might be influenced by the fact that her grandmother was an integral part of the antidiscrimination movement in housing in the

1960s. In the midst of significant developments in the peace process that would ultimately lead to the Good Friday (Belfast) Agreement, Gildernew was appointed to be the Sinn Féin representative in London. During her 1997–1998 tenure in this position, she enacted some of the most delicate and precise negotiations of the peace process, notably the historical arrival of Sinn Féin back to 10 Downing Street in December 1997. She emerged onto the electoral stage in 1998 when she began running for public office.

Since the Northern Ireland Assembly was reconvened in 2007, several other notable women have emerged as frontline activists and elected representatives. Sue Ramsey is the member of legislative assembly (MLA) for West Belfast and has been active in the Women's Department since 1992 and children's movement since she was young. Martina Anderson, former political prisoner, who served to streamline the All-Ireland strand of the Good Friday Agreement is the MLA for Derry and also serves as the director of Unionist Engagement and party spokesperson on human rights. Jennifer McCann, also a former political prisoner, who formerly who worked on the anti-Collusion campaign, is the MLA for West Belfast. Michelle Ó Neill, MLA for Mid Ulster, has served as political advisor in Sinn Féin and was the first female deputy mayor of Dungannon and South Tyrone Borough Council. Carál Ní Chuilín, MLA for North Belfast, has served as the coordinator of the Tar Anall family center for 10 years and is a former political prisoner, and Claire McGill, MLA for West Tyrone, is a hospital and school advocate.

In the wake of the Belfast Agreement, Sinn Féin was thrust onto the international stage. Having engaged in high-level negotiations with internal and external politicians, Sinn Féin was poised to enter elected governance. Transitioning from a conflict society party to a parliamentary party reframes platform issues and implementation proposals. Crafting legislation for governance, as well as complying with the conditions of the agreement, became simultaneous priorities. As the peace process became stagnant over issues of decommissioning of Republican weapons and quid pro quo demilitarization, Sinn Féin continued to reshape its internal structure to reflect the parliamentary shifts for governance. The creation of the Equality Department in 2002, headed initially by former General Secretary Lucilita Bhreatnach, further facilitated a governance objective. Combined with her experience in electoral strategy, Bhreatnach heightened awareness of the plight of social inequalities in Ireland. Farming and training female Republicans has reaped a new crop of Sinn Féin party members. Teetering on the precipice of realized peace, Sinn Féin is not simply a viable electoral choice but the embodiment of a heightened awareness of political strategy as well.

HEREIN LIES THE ROLE

The role of women in Sinn Féin has been consistent yet varied—often in a supportive capacity simply below the surface, but also not just behind the scenes or in the shadows. Republican women have been foot soldiers in the movement, but they have also been generals leading the command for equality. Yet, despite, perhaps even in spite of, having been relegated to traditional support roles at various points, Republican women have made significant contributions to the Republican movement since 1905. From logistical support in 1916 to the ballot box in 2005, Sinn Féin Republican women have been a central part of the armed struggle, hunger strikes, political platform, electoral strategy, and peace strategy. Although history may have overlooked the contributions of Republican women, their stories beg to be told. Each woman, no matter whether she served in the public sector, in the streets, or in the prisons, has shaped the deliberate actions of a century-old party. There is, within the Republican community, disputed areas of continuity, and even the Sinn Féin of Gerry Adams, Dodie McGuinness, and Bairbre de Brún must acknowledge the reincarnations of Sinn Féin. In his book *Sinn Féin: 1905–2005—In the Shadow of Gunmen*, Kevin Rafter expanded upon Maurice Manning's classifications of the Sinn Féin reincarnations. An assistant editor for the *Sunday Tribune*, Rafter identifies five distinct periods in Sinn Féin history: Monarchical Sinn Féin (1905–1917), Separatist Sinn Féin (1917–1922), Republican Sinn Féin (1922–1926), Isolationist Sinn Féin (1926–1969) and Militarist Sinn Féin (1969–2005).[8] The Sinn Féin of today claims to "Céad Bliain Sinn Féin" or 100 years of we ourselves, which has been a movement and a federation of causes for nationalists and Republicans. Tracing the implementation of the political philosophy of Sinn Féin by women over the past century shall be the focus of this book.

BOOK ORGANIZATION

Each chapter shall review a decade in a thematic overview. Within each decade, the chapter details the roles that women played related to the dominant theme. A representative selection of these women's stories from each decade will demonstrate how each role impacted the party. These themes are punctuated by the major historical developments and internal party decisions, such as shifts in strategy and infrastructure reorganization.

Chapter 1 shall identify the "ring of day" for a new, independent Ireland. Set against the backdrop of the successes and failures of the Irish Parliamentary Party (IPP) and the Gaelic revival, the birth of Sinn Féin in 1905 was the cumulative effort of many nationalist actors. Carving out a role for the modern Irish women to play was a difficult task. Embroiled in a seemingly entrenched division between the traditionalist and feminist women, Sinn Féin captured a diversity of many nationalist actors in its struggle to define a party platform. The emergence of a rebirth of de-Anglicized Irish culture and language in the midst of nationalist aspirations led to a strong strain of feminism and equality becoming embedded in Irish republicanism for the ensuing century. As the dawn of the 20th century cut against the Irish horizon, Sinn Féin women took on both leading and supportive roles in the movement.

Supported by a band of Republican brothers, a circle of sisters committed themselves to the acquisition of an independent Ireland through revolutionary means. Having been prevented from joining the ranks of the Irish Republican Brotherhood (IRB) and the Irish Volunteers (IV), Sinn Féin women organized a sisterhood of combatants within the Irish Citizen Army (ICA) and then exclusively under the banner of Cumann na mBan. With a gun in one hand and a party platform of gender equality in the other, the Sinn Féin woman was relegated no longer to the realm of domestic nationalism. The adoption of gender equality, as a Sinn Féin principle in 1917, strengthened such demands for the universal acquisition of suffrage. In 1918, a moderate form was granted for all citizens, regardless of gender, for all over 30 years of age.

Chapter 2 embodies the shift from traditional nation building to state building in the "construction of a new Irish home." The divisive issues dominating the constitutional conundrum in the Anglo-Irish Treaty of 1920 produced schisms in Sinn Féin sisterhood across Ireland. Many women fell on the anti-treaty side of the division, and the metamorphosis of Irish nationalist into Irish Republican prevailed within Sinn Féin. The result was a Civil War (1922–1923) across Ireland and an ideological division of Irish patriots. With a Free State in place and a government to elect, the Sinn Féin policy of abstentionism took root. When Sinn Féiners left to form Fianna Fáil and other political parties, nationalist Irish women across the 32 counties faced a crisis of state and nation building. In the midst of this turmoil, one central figure—Margaret Buckley—rose to the challenge of tending to the party's sustenance as the first, and only, elected female president of Sinn Féin.

Chapter 3 captures the fallen resistance to partition and the internal battles for support of the Republican movement in the imposition of a "partition of the mind." As Sinn Féin entered into a two-decade period of latency, its leadership took on unabashedly brash female dominance under the leadership of Margaret Buckley in 1937. In the evolution of the Irish Free State in 1923 to the declaration of full independence in the republic in 1949, Sinn Féin women conducted hunger strikes to raise awareness of their continued resistance to partition, debated publicly on the impact of Fianna Fáil on a Republican cause, and supported the ensuing border campaign of the 1950s. Battling for the hearts and minds of nationalists, Sinn Féin women offered no apologies for their continued, though dwindling, existence.

Chapter 4 broadcasts the "voice of equality" as the beginning of the Troubles are ushered into Irish contemporary history. With an overtone of sectarian oppression and civil violence, Sinn Féin emerged as the mouthpiece for equality, justice and community defense. Once static, the support for the republic was ignited by the flames of petrol bombs in the Six Counties. And as the imagined community of a united Ireland reemerged onto the national stage, Sinn Féin women found themselves in precarious and powerful positions. Undaunted by the overwhelming task of restructuring and assuming new roles in the party apparatus, the women become agents of change and voices of equality.

Chapter 5 reveals a "hunger for justice" in the 1970s. The call to action in the 1970s spotlighted growing concerns about suspended governance in the North and the conflagration of community violence. As "isms" ignited across Ireland, the women of Sinn Féin engaged in a discourse on radicalism, feminism, socialism, racism, and so on. Plagued with life in a militarized state, women like Máire Drumm became the voice of opposition and social action.

Chapter 6 captures one of the darkest spots in Irish history, the sustained struggle of the "oppressed flowers." As the 1980s unfolded, the hunger strike campaign would bring international human history to Ireland. The world watched as basic human liberties were ignored and the sorrow and rage mixed into a new generation of activism. Sinn Féin women found themselves at the mercy of the end of a gun or corned in a prison strip search, but their voice of opposition shouted clear across prison walls and barricades. Principally committed to the achievement of a 32-county democratic socialist republic, Republican women took action. Unwilling to rule out the use of armed force to achieve these ends, many women joined the ranks of the Provisional Irish Republican Army when they were allowed full membership in 1986. In that same year, Gerry Adams became president of Sinn Féin and the policy of abstentionism was dropped for the Irish Dáil. Moving toward Danny Morrison's "ballot and the armalite" strategy, Sinn Féin women engaged aggressively in many roles that included the hunger strikes, Relatives Action Committee activities, community center training, international solidarity networking, and political lobbying. Reorganizing in 1980 as the Women's Department, a vocal group of women sought to empower Republican women by identifying and discussing issues that impacted women in a conflict torn society.

Chapter 7 presents the efforts of Sinn Féin women to pursue a policy of peace by "tending the lily in an international garden." Integral in the development and the implementation toward a lasting peace strategy, women shaped the negotiation environment and resolution process. In the context of a global network of sisters and friends, Sinn Féin engendered the peace process that led to the Belfast Agreement in 1998. Based on the activities of veteran activists in the 1970s and 1980s, the role of Sinn Féin women was reconfigured in the 1990s to suit the needs for a cross-border, cross-sectarian conflict transformation process.

Chapter 8 provides a glimpse into the "modern Sinn Féin women in the 21st century," who is no longer a footnoted foot soldier but now is a parliamentary presence. Having removed the constitutional question from the official party rhetoric, Republican women utilize an engendered perspective to social, economic, and political issues in concrete governance solutions. As the transition from a conflict society to a peaceful, democratic society continues to evolve in the 21st century, the roles of Sinn Féin women will continue embody an activist, rights-based approach to equality across Ireland and Europe.

REFERENCES

Buckley, Margaret. 1938. *The Jangle of the Keys*. Dublin: James Duffy and Co. Ltd.

Calamiti, Silvia. 2002. *The Trouble We've Seen*. Belfast: Beyond the Pale Publications.

Farrell, Mairéad. 1980s. "Mairéad Farrell." Relatives for Justice. Belfast. http://www.relativesforjustice.com/victims/Mairéad_farrell.htm.

Litton, Helen, ed. 1991. *Kathleen Clarke, Revolutionary Woman*. Dublin: O'Brien Press.

McCoole, Sinéad. 2003. *No Ordinary Women*. Dublin: O'Brien Press.

Mulholland, Marie. 2002. *The Politics and Relationships of Dr. Kathleen Lynn*. Dublin: Woodfield Press.

O Duigneanin, Proinnsios. 1997. *Linda Kearns: A Revolutionary Irish Woman*. Cork: Cork University Press.

Sli na mBan. 2006. http://www.tallgirlshorts.net/thewayofwomen/.

Taillon, Ruth. 1996. *When History Was Made: The Women of 1916*. Belfast: Beyond the Pale Publications.

Ward, Margaret. 1993. *Maud Gonne: A Life*. Ontario: Pandora Press.

Ward, Margaret. 1995. *Unmanageable Revolutionaries: Women and Irish Nationalism*. London: Pluto Press.

Ward, Margaret. 1997. *Hanna Sheehy-Skeffington: A Life*. Cork: Attic Press.

Ward, Margaret. 2001. *In Their Own Voice, Women and Irish Nationalism*. Cork: Attic Press.

Ward, Margaret, and Louise Ryan, eds. 2004. *Irish Women and Nationalism: Soldiers, New Women and Wicked Hags*. Dublin: Irish Academic Press.

Chapter 1

THE RING OF DAY FOR SINN FÉIN, 1905–1919

> She had found her vocation. Ireland was her vocation; she would devote her life for working for the realisation of the Irish ideal.[1]
>
> —Mary Butler

CHAPTER OVERVIEW

As the dawn of a new century stretched out across the Irish political landscape, women across Ireland responded to the call for national reform. Heeding the ring of the day, women assembled in various formations across the nationalist forum. Leadership in the 19th-century land reform movement had groomed the women for revolutionary action. Irish nationalist women played significant roles in the development of the *sinn féin* movement.[2] They were cultural advocates, domestic nationalists, political party founders, revolutionary activists, suffragettes, and social reformers.

Each nationalist woman made a contribution to the *sinn féin* movement. Some women assumed a primary role in one organization, and some assumed roles in several organizations. Every contribution that an Irish woman made in this historical period came with a price—time away from family and children, exhausting travel, risk of clandestine activities, prison time, defiance of social norms, exile, and so on. In recalling each role, one must remember the social expectations of a woman at the dawn of the 20th century and the audacious bravery it must have taken to make women rise to the call of duty.

An Irish nationalist woman could have been an extraordinary cultural advocate. As a patron for the arts or actress on the Abbey Theatre stage, she supported thinly veiled nationalist literature and Gaelic cultural expression. She was often a writer, providing columns to various newspapers, writing allegorical fiction, sharp-witted editorials, and metaphorical poetry. As a domestic nationalist, an Irish woman utilized the "traditional" role in the family to promote nationalist culture by teaching her family Irish language, history, sports, and culture. Since many women did not work outside of the home, the guardianship of cultural socialization was one of the primary roles women fulfilled.

Perhaps unconventional in contrast to some of their contemporaries, the women who founded Sinn Féin were, at times of such allowances, visible social activists and political commentators. Some patrons quietly financed the party or the nationalist newspapers and pamphlets it produced. Others were on the front lines of the nationalist debate by contributing articles to the newspapers, serving as secretaries or assistants for the preeminent men of the day, traveling across the United States, Ireland, and Europe giving speeches and raising monies, and developing the party's organizational infrastructure. As revolutionary activists, nationalist women facilitated gun running, organized demonstrations of agitation, served on the front lines of the Easter rebellion, and traveled around the world to raise support for the Irish nationalist cause.

The suffragettes were deeply committed to political and social equality for Irish women. Universal suffrage and legal recognition for women became intertwined with the nationalist agenda, though women's rights were not wholeheartedly advanced by the *sinn féin* movement. The prioritization of the nationalist agenda led many suffragettes to pursue their goals outside the scope of a Sinn Féin party. The concerns about the status of workers, women, and children in Ireland led to the formation of many organizations for social reform. This chapter explores these roles in the context of the prerevolutionary and revolutionary periods of Ireland from the ring of day for the 20th century until 1920.

Every woman who assembled along the nationalist landscape found a place to step in line with her sisters (and brothers) in the cause for Ireland. No singular manifestation of service should be prioritized, glorified, or denigrated, on account of one's gender. Many women assumed overlapping or intertwined service roles, but each contribution heeded the call of service for Ireland.

Chapter Organization

The chapter is organized into three main sections. Beginning with a general historical review of significant developments in Irish nationalist history, the pertinent events at the turn of the 20th century are recounted to provide sufficient background on the Home Rule movement, the advancement of Irish women, and the birth of Sinn Féin. In the second section, the chapter highlights 10 nationalist women who shaped the course of Irish nationalism leading up to 1916. The author attempts to provide a glimpse of both prominent and not so prominent contributions in the development of Sinn Féin's political foundation and ideological support in other nationalistic organizations. In the third section, the chapter examines the part that women played in the Easter Rising, its aftermath, and the First Dáil (Irish Parliament). Through an examination of historical portraitures of women activated in the revolutionary period, the author recounts the significant elements of female contributions that are often overlooked in Irish history. From military commanders to medical support and weapons procurement, Irish revolutionary women executed these roles with precision and dedication. In the wake of the 1916 Easter Rising and the surge of support for Sinn Féin, these women sacrificed their time and risked their personal freedom for Ireland. This chapter provides an overview of events following 1916, including the selection of a new National Executive (central party organ) for Sinn Féin in 1917 and the establishment of the First Dáil in December 1919. The chapter concludes with another snapshot of the political landscape before Ireland burst into the War for Independence.

HISTORICAL BACKGROUND

- Home Rule Movement
- Women in Ireland circa 1900
- The Birth of Arthur Griffith's Sinn Féin
- Sinn Féin's Infancy

Home Rule Movement

Before one can begin to examine 20th century Irish political history, it is necessary to recognize the development of the sinn féin movement in the 19th century. Built on the foundation of Irish rebellions and resistance throughout the 17th and 18th centuries, Irish nationalism possessed elements of self-reliance and self-sufficiency. These ideas were embodied in the Home Rule Party, championed by Irish statesman Charles Stewart Parnell who was duly elected as a member of Westminster Parliament on the political platform in 1875. Parnell rechristened the Home Rule Party the Irish Parliamentary Party (IPP) upon assuming office.

Charles Stewart Parnell was born into a prominent Protestant family in 1846. His childhood in the idyllic countryside of Wicklow County as

a member of the gentrified landowning class was hardly the conditions
that one might expect to produce a fervent Irish nationalist. In his youth,
he studied at Cambridge University where Parnell developed his noted
eloquence and gained valuable insight into the body of English law. This
knowledge created a deep distaste for the Irish land laws, which placed virtually no limits on a landowner's ability to raise rents or perform evictions.
In 1878, he became a vocal opponent of them and subsequently founded
the Irish National Land League. His position as a member of Westminster
Parliament elevated his personal sentiments concerning land reform a national platform for Irish nationalist hopes. While serving as the president
of the National Land League, Parnell traveled across the United States to
raise awareness, and the necessary financial support for land reform in Ireland. In his absence, while Irish American support for a nationalist Ireland
began washing across the North American continent, his sisters Anna and
Fanny maintained the organizational support back for the Irish Parliamentary Party in Ireland.

As a new member of Westminster Parliament, Parnell initially backed
Prime Minister (PM) William Gladstone's Liberal Party government in
England. Perhaps Parnell believed that the IPP could establish a political
alliance with the Liberal Party to rid Ireland of those land laws? Efforts to
forge a legislative coalition culminated when Gladstone proposed the Irish
Land Act of 1881 in an effort to produce limited land reforms, but Parnell
withdrew his support when the bill failed to deliver on the IPP's expectations. Disturbed by the legislative failure, Charles Stewart Parnell organized a land rent strike in protest. While moderately successful, the 1882
National Land League strike suffered when the de facto leader of Irish national resistance was thrown in Kilmainhaim Jail for his agitation. Parnell's
sisters, Anna and Fanny, assumed control of the National Land League's
finances to facilitate payments to land tenants who participated in the rent
strike. This was particularly difficult work for Anna and Fanny, for those
who refused to pay their rent were in danger of eviction, imprisonment, or
worse. While the Parnell sisters worked expeditiously to convince them to
remain steadfast in the strike, they were rushing to distribute funds that
might defray the cost of participation in the strike.

Thus, as the men in the Land League were arrested across Ireland, Anna
Parnell coordinated the efforts of the Ladies Land League—established
in 1881 in anticipation of such events. Her efficiency may have been her
downfall, as the men became concerned that the women were overly effective in their absence. Later released from jail, Parnell reassumed control of
the Home Rule movement and again supported William Gladstone against
a challenge from Conservatives. Retaining his position as prime minister,
Gladstone introduced the Irish Home Rule Bill of 1886. The bill failed in

the House of Commons, and shortly thereafter, in 1889, Parnell was named as an adulterer in a divorce case. His mistress of many years, Mrs. Kathleen O'Shea, had born three of his children. The personal scandal was too much for Parnell's political career, and the Irish Parliamentary Party, to bear. He died two years later in 1891.

In 1893, a second version of the Home Rule Bill passed the House of Commons. This time, it was stopped by the House of Lords. Eleven years later, the third Home Rule Bill for Ireland (1914) was passed. With each parliamentary proposal, hopes rose and then fell, but the outbreak of World War I delayed the implementation of the (third) Home Rule Bill indefinitely. Thus, as the preeminence of Charles Stewart Parnell faded, so did the parliamentary pursuit he advocated. It would take a revolution to change the course of Irish history in 1916, but there was a very important lesson in the lifespan of the Irish Ladies Land League—women were a valuable resource to the Irish Cause. The women activated in 1882 during a period of crisis had proven to be a powerful network for synergy.

Women in Ireland circa 1900

The path to active resistance was paved with small steps to organizing and empowering women in Ireland. Table 1.1 highlights a few early developments in the organization of Irish nationalist women. Building upon the success of the Irish Ladies Land League, women demonstrated the collective power that could be harnessed by nationalists. When the Gaelic League was founded in 1893, female members were allowed to join. This was in stark contrast to most organizations in Ireland that strictly prohibited female membership. The central mission of the Gaelic League, as banal as it may have seemed to some, may have shaped the advancement of both Irish nationalism and female empowerment in the 21st century.

Table 1.1
Early Gains for Irish Women

1881	Irish Ladies Land League founded
1893	Gaelic League founded
1900	Inghinidhe na hÉireann (Daughters of Ireland) founded
1900	Cumann na nGaedheal founded
1908	Irish Women's Franchise League founded
1908	Bean na hÉireann first published
1909	Fianna Éireann founded
1913/14	Irish Citizen Army founded
1914	Cumann na mBan founded

Formed as an anti-Anglicization movement, the Gaelic League sought to incorporate Irish language into the national school curriculum and to promote the preservation of Irish culture, sport, dress, and history. Therefore, a radical departure in the traditional roles of Irish women was not the targeted mission of the league, since many of the organizational values could be accomplished by women as teachers in the schools and as mothers in the homes. The enlightenment surrounding social equality was certainly not the focus of the Gaelic League, though it did allow a forum for women to become actively engaged in the overarching goals of Irish nationalism and provided a forum for leadership skill development.

Over the course of the next decade, several organizations with female members emerged. One could argue that the situation was ripe for women or perhaps that the force of personalities defied conventions. It might also be overstating the point to assume that women were not still constrained by social forces. However, while it is accurate to recognize that most revolutionary Irish women were largely unrepentant in breaching traditional expectations of their gender, it is more insightful to acknowledge the virulent tradition of women who broke the gender stereotypes before them.

The role of strong women in Irish history was not unfamiliar in periods of crisis and turbulent political change. Women, under the auspices of the United Irishwomen, had procured arms, raised money, and hidden fugitives during the 1798 Rebellion. Though they did not participate in direct combat and were prohibited from joining the United Irishmen, women served as dispatch couriers on the battlefield through the combat engagement.[3] Later, women became involved with the Young Irelanders in 1840s. Marginally more progressive than the United Irishmen had been, Young Irelanders allowed women to become more directly involved as contributors to their publication, *The Nation*.[4] Articulating a voice for change in *The Nation*, women mobilized in 1881 when Anna Parnell founded the Ladies Land League (as recounted earlier). Their efforts to sustain the land reform debate included assuming the leadership of the catering centers, dispersing strike subsidies for those refusing to pay rent, and assuming the publication of *United Ireland*. The impact that the Ladies Land League made was clear in the Kilmainhaim Treaty, in which their disbandment was a condition for Charles Stewart Parnell's release. Encouraged by these small successes and bolstered by the principles of equality embedded in the socialist ideology sweeping across Ireland, many Irish women, though certainly not all, saw an opportunity to become catalysts for change in the 20th century. The flurry of excitement produced several new organizations in 1900, notably Indhinidhe na hÉireann and Cumann na nGaedheal.

Inghinidhe na hÉireann (Daughters of Ireland) was formed in 1900 by a young woman named Maud Gonne. Many in the Dublin literary circles

came to know her as the muse of William Butler Yeats. Her society connections and engaging personality demanded attention, which she accomplished in the boycott of Queen Victoria's visit to Ireland in April 1900.
Her organization handed out sweets to the children who refused to attend
the reception of the queen and hung black flags around Dublin as a form
of demonstration against the royal visit. Beyond the initial boycott, the
Daughters of Ireland developed a five-pronged agenda that is displayed in
Table 1.2.[5]

In addition to its organizational mission, perhaps the strongest advancement for nationalist women was the network of relationships the Daughters of Ireland produced among the members it attracted. The organization
provided a forum for women to explore nationalism through the arts and
through the promotion of local Irish industries. The engendered appeal
exposed women to a foray into politics in a manner that was seemingly
tame. The network connections that the Daughters of Ireland provided,
however, were anything but tame. The cultural agenda encompassed a
powerful political heart, and the recruitment of women to the Daughters
of Ireland introduced strains of militant nationalism to cultural advocates.
By opening the nationalist ideological doors, female support for gun running, safe houses, and recruitment for the Irish Republican Brotherhood
(IRB) increased. Later in this chapter, Maud Gonne and the Daughters of
Ireland will be explored in more detail.

Table 1.2
**The Objects of Inghinidhe na hÉireann from the United Irishman,
1900 (Inghinidhe na hÉireann)**

1. the re-establishment of the complete independence of Ireland.
2. to encourage the study of Gaelic, of Irish literature, History, Music
   and Art, especially among the young, by the organizing and teaching
   of classes for the above objects.
3. to support and popularize Irish manufacture.
4. to discourage the reading and circulation of low English literature,
   the singing of English songs, the attending of vulgar English
   entertainments at the theatres and music hall, and to combat in
   every way English influence, which is doing so much injury to the
   artistic taste and refinement of the Irish people.
5. to form a fund called the National Purposes Found, for the furtherance
   of the above objects.

Another organization formed around the time of the royal visit in 1900 was Cumann na nGaedheal. Founded by a printer for *The Nation* named Arthur Griffith and a poet named William Rooney, Cumann na nGaedheal served as an umbrella organization for the various literary and cultural societies that had popped up across Ireland during a golden era for Irish writers. With overtly nationalist undertones, Cumann na nGaedheal consolidated the literary, society, and political realms. It also established clear links to the elements of revolutionary action and agrarian agitations bubbling beneath the surface within the Irish Republican Brotherhood. Later, the Daughters of Ireland would join with Cumann na nGaedheal to form Sinn Féin in 1905.

In 1898, women had been granted the conditional right to vote in local elections, but it resulted in obstacles to universal suffrage that were tantamount to no suffrage at all. The suffragettes of the early 20th century were largely identified as radical, urban middle-class women. They found a substantial voice and staunch political advocate in Hanna Sheehy-Skeffington. Founding the Irish Women's Franchise League (IWFL) in 1908, Sheehy-Skeffington served as its secretary while overseeing the development of suffrage, cultural, and nationalist activities. Hanna's husband, Francis Sheehy-Skeefington, was an enlightened man who took on his wife's maiden name of Sheehy when they married in 1903. Francis was an early member of the trade unionist groups, including the Irish Citizen Army (ICA). It was through this association that his comrade James Connolly became a frequent speaker at IWFL meetings. Both men would later be killed by the British military, but Francis's part was that of a bystander amidst the siege. The nationalist circles overlapped organizations of various forms, including the Irish Citizen Army and the Irish Volunteers.

Established as a defense force for the trade union activists in 1913, the Irish Citizen Army initially provided security for union activists in demonstrations. In addition to James Connolly and Francis Sheehy-Skeffington, the ICA housed some of the greatest activists in Irish history including Séan O'Casey, James Larkin, and Countess Markievicz. Shortly after the strike lockout in Dublin in 1913, the Irish Citizen Army was reorganized with a more pointed nationalist agenda. It embraced the armed element of the Irish Republican Brotherhood (IRB). O'Casey and Sheehy-Skeffington departed the ICA over the move, while Larkin immigrated to the United States. Left in charge of the ICA, Connolly infused a healthy dose of revolutionary socialism into its ranks and led the ICA's participation in the Easter Rising.

More ideologically neutral than the ICA, the Irish Volunteers were founded in November 1913 after the armament of the Ulster Volunteer Force (UVF) by Sir Edward Carson. The Volunteers were committed to armed defense, not revolutionary socialism. Among the founding members of the Volunteers were Patrick Pearse, Éamonn Ceannt, and Eoin MacNeill. In 1914, the women founded an auxiliary force called Cumann na mBan (often translated as League of Women or Council of Women). The women were immortalized in the song written by Brian O'Higgins entitled "The Soldiers of Cumann na mBan" in which the chorus refrain is:

They stand for the honour of Ireland . . .
The Soldiers of Cumann na mBan.

Cumann na mBan was an independent women's organization, much as the Daughters of Ireland and the Ladies Land League had been before it. The Ladies Land League had, in the prevalence of discontent with land rights, developed of a female network of rural women and landed aristocratic women—two societies that did not intersect before. The Daughters of Ireland connected the literary societies and the activists, and Cumann na mBan reintroduced women into the clandestine, military activities of their 1798 predecessors and their Irish Volunteer and IRB brothers. Though gender equality in the Volunteers might have advanced women more substantively, the development of an all-female force was significant. Cumann na mBan assumed the drudgery of dispatching couriers among the network of Republican and nationalist circles and performing logistical support for the Volunteers. They stood arm in arm with the male nationalist forces in the Easter Rising and constituted a bulk of the women in the First Dáil of 1919.

When Arthur Griffith founded Cumann na nGaedheal with William Rooney in 1900, he combined forces with the literary and society nationalists in Dublin. At this point, his vision for an independent Ireland was still a little cloudy. Within the network of patrons, writers, educators, and culturalists, he found a consensus for political and social change. Though the political ideology included a range of radical socialism, trade unionism, feminist suffragettes, and domestic nationalists, Griffith saw agreement in a "sinn féin" movement in 1905. Activating women and men whose organizational memberships frequently overlapped (in the Gaelic League, Inghinidhe na hÉireann, Cumann na nGaedheal, Irish Women's Franchise League, Cumann na mBan, and Irish Citizen Army) allowed Griffith to harness the most powerful and influential nationalists for his Sinn Féin party. The petition for Sinn Féin support was not received equally among nationalist women; many felt it did not advance the position of women onto the top tier of party concerns. Others remained unconvinced by Arthur Griffith's ideas. However, the diversity of opinions that defined the various groups, and indeed often divided them over means and ends, would bind them together in the wake of the Easter Rising.

The Birth of Arthur Griffith's Sinn Féin

"Sinn féin" is often translated "ourselves alone," but the direct meaning in Irish is "we ourselves." Originally adopted as a motto for the Gaelic League, "sinn féin sinn féin amháin" would, over the next 100 years, be adopted by various groups and purposes, but its meaning in Irish remained the same: empowerment and self-sufficiency. When Douglas Hyde and Eoin MacNeill founded the Gaelic League in 1893, the men had hoped to arouse interest in Irish language. Stigmatized as stagnate in contrast to English modernization, Irish language and culture had been virtually eliminated from all educational curricula and branded as a form of radical defiance to the English Crown. While the Gaelic League aimed to be a cultural organization, it quickly garnered a political affiliation, as had the Gaelic Athletic Association before it. The Gaelic Athletic Association (GAA) was founded in 1884 with the intent of promoting the advancement of indigenous Gaelic athleticism and Irish culture, including sports like hurling; however, it soon became apparent that the GAA served as a network for those with a more progressively political agenda. Thus, the revival of a Gaelic Ireland conjured up support for Irish nationalism on the eve of the 20th century. As both a political theory and a cultural dictum, "sinn féin" emerged as a virulent form of Irish nationalism based on self-sufficiency.

The birth of Sinn Féin, the political party, was the product of a tumultuous labor.[6] Conceived in a changing political landscape of Land Reform and Home Rule debates, 19th-century Irish activists bore a family of like-minded 20th century children. Like siblings do, the nationalist organizations often quarreled among themselves and yet there was a collective support for the efforts of each individual mind.

Irish nationalism has a complicated family genealogy. As many anti-colonial movements worldwide experienced in the first half of the 20th century, the principles of national determination appealed to many organizations seeking to throw off the yoke of social, political, and economic repression. In Ireland, the result was that Sinn Féin the political party became a home of sorts for the disaffected. The creation of Sinn Féin may have been understated at the time. Sinn Féin members often belonged to a number of different groups that all needed financial and organizational support. Each organization prioritized a particular issue while lending support to the overarching goal of national, and sometimes personal, liberation. Those championing the issues of Catholic land rights, the revival of Irish language and culture, the rise of feminist liberation, the manifestation of universal suffrage, and the realization of national determination were interwoven into a sinn féin movement. Sinn Féin was one of many groups seeking similar goals, but at least for those present at the first convention in November 1905, the birth of Sinn Féin—recounted here through Mary Butler's eyes, changed the course of history.

> As I write these lines, there lies before me a crumpled little linen badge bearing the words "SINN FÉIN, 1905" [from the first party conference]. Here is a relic indeed—one to be viewed by the Irish woman with much the same sentiment that might grip her as she surveyed a lock of bright hair from the brow of an infant who, in later years, became a looming giant in the nation's affairs.[7]

Arthur Griffith was the founder and the first president of Sinn Féin. He was an often disheveled and unassuming man born in 1872 to a Catholic Dublin family. His father was a newspaper printer, and the younger Griffith apprenticed in the trade and then worked at *The Nation* and the *Irish Independent*. In 1893, he cofounded the Celtic Literary Society with poet William Rooney. The Celtic Literary Society and the Gaelic League both sought to protect Irish literature and culture, though the Gaelic League was more intolerant of the Anglicization movement. As young adult, Griffith spent a couple of years in South Africa working in the gold mines, where he became increasingly intolerant of British colonialism. When he returned to Ireland, he turned to a career in newspapers and founded his own paper called the *United Irishman* in 1899. His close connection with Irish nationalists led to his brief membership in the Irish Republican Brotherhood until 1910 when he reportedly renounced the physical force tradition.

Although Griffith was a printer by trade, he mastered the task of nationalistic propaganda. Initially a supporter of Charles Stewart Parnell's Irish Parliamentary Party (IPP), Griffith's support had waned as the IPP fell into disarray in the late 1880s. With the publication of a weekly newspaper, Arthur Griffith had a mouthpiece for his political ideas. During its seven-year publication, the *United Irishman* published contributing articles from many prominent Irish nationalists including William Butler Yeats, Patrick Pearse, Roger Casement, and Maud Gonne.[8] When the *United Irishman* ceased publication, Griffith reorganized and published under the title *Sinn Féin* until 1914. His literary network raised his awareness of the need to protect Irish culture. Therefore, in 1900, a year after the *United Irishman* went to press, Griffith helped to found Cumann na nGaedheal. With Maud Gonne, the founder of the Daughters of Ireland, serving as vice president, Cumann na nGaedheal often used the *United Irishman* to publicize their agenda.

As a member of the Celtic Literary Society, the Gaelic League and the Irish Republican Brotherhood (IRB), Griffith's overlapping memberships solidified his network of prominent nationalists and united them in a cause

Table 1.3
Five Initial Sinn Féin Proposals (1904)

1. Home Rule
2. Dual monarchy
3. Economic nationalism
4. Abstentionism
5. Social equality

of an independent Ireland. This network would bring him into contact with many prominent figures in Irish history, including Michael Collins, Countess Markievicz, James Connolly, and others. He would regularly entertain visitors in his home to discuss the politics of the day, and it was in this manner that Mary Butler and her sister became regular guests. Mary is also known by her Irish name, Máire de Buitléir. Mary's articles were featured in his *United Irishmen* in 1901, along with various contributions from Maud Gonne concerning the early years of the Daughters of Ireland. In 1903, the National Council, also founded by Griffith, was established to coordinate the protest to King Edward VII's royal visit. Not surprisingly, Maud Gonne was also an active participant in the National Council.

In 1904, Arthur Griffith began to develop what would become the initial platform issues of Sinn Féin. Over the course of six months, in a series of articles, Griffith laid out ideas for a nationalist Ireland. *The Resurrection of Hungary: A Parallel for Ireland* pamphlet suggested a five-point political agenda contained in Table 1.3.[9]

Proposal 1—Home Rule

Pragmatically, the platform proposed a variant form of home rule. Home rule itself was a tainted idea. Affiliated with the defunct Irish Parliamentary Party, home rule seemed an improbable achievement and unstable foundation to achieving a nationalist agenda. Griffith's proposals went even further than the Home Rule Bills had gone toward a national, independent Ireland, but the Home Rule movement had been quite unsuccessful. As previously discussed, both the Home Rule Bill of 1886 and of 1893 had failed to pass in Westminster. The initial Irish Government Bill (1886) failed in the House of Commons, despite pleas from Prime Minister William Gladstone. Gladstone's second draft (1893) passed the House of Commons but was blocked in the House of Lords due to its controversial nature. The expanded version of Home Rule in 1893, radically proposed allowing a bicameral Irish parliament for domestic affairs, a Lord Lieutenant of Ireland as the chief executive power, and an elected Irish parliamentary delegation empowered to vote in Westminster on issues affecting Ireland. Such proposals seemed radical in 1893, so Griffith's proposals in 1904 must have seemed even more radical. In a climate of failure, 12 years later, Sinn Féin proposed another version of home rule, parliamentary abstentionism and economic nationalism. Arthur Griffith articulated a new stance on the home rule government that reinvigorated the idea. A national governance, he argued, could be achieved through legitimate political means, if the Irish played by the English rules of democratic participation.

Proposal 2—Dual Monarchy

In the second platform item, Griffith went on to explain that nationalists should pursue achieving a dual monarchy based on the Austro-Hungarian Empire in the 1860s. The idea proved too problematic for many nationalists, and dual monarchy was quickly dismissed by Griffith's critics. Many felt that Griffith's idea allowed for a risk of recognizing English legitimacy, and this risk was too high. It quickly became clear that any form of monarchist rule was simply too much for many Irish people to accept. The idea was discarded as quickly as possible, much like the American patriot Alexander Hamilton's proposal for an American president elected for life at the Constitutional Convention in 1787. The dual monarchy proposal was a selective read of history, at best, and under enormous criticism, Arthur Griffith later renounced the idea.

Proposal 3—Economic Nationalism

The third component of the Sinn Féin platform was economic nationalism. By promoting the consumption of Irish goods alone, the Irish would return to self-reliance. Rejecting both the system of English taxation and English goods and services—including the military security service, the Irish economy would be promoted, nurtured, and harvested by the Irish people. In a world economy that predated economic interdependence, it may have been more economically feasible, but the principle driving this agenda was simple nationalism not economic theory.

Proposal 4—Parliamentary Abstentionism

The fourth component was the idea of parliamentary abstentionism, which unlike dual monarchy, took deep root in the nationalist mind. Abstentionism meant that elected members of Sinn Féin would not take their seats in Westminster government as a protest to the status quo of Anglo-Irish relations. Rather, the elected Irish members of Parliament (MPs) would reconstitute as an Irish government in Dublin and swear allegiance to the king of Ireland, not the king of England. Although the idea of a king of Ireland was not embraced, it referenced the premise that Irish people should be governed by Irish government. "Ourselves alone" was becoming the lynchpin of the Sinn Féin platform.

Proposal 5—Social Equality

The platform was not without further controversy. In the last agenda item, Arthur Griffith addressed the idea of social equality. Surrounded by economic exploitation and squalor in Dublin, Griffith felt compelled to speak out against it. However, the extent to which he called for progressive equality for women was not clear. Griffith surrounded himself with strong Irish women, but these ladies were mainly cast in traditional social roles of patron, secretary, and socialite. One could point to the uneven level of support given to the Sinn Féin platform by members of the Daughters of Ireland and deduce that the lack of redress to gender concerns might have cost Sinn Féin support from more radical suffragettes and feminists.

Although the 1906 National Council of Sinn Féin included a strong base of women such as Jennie Wyse-Power and Mary Murphy, both Mary Mac-Swiney and Helena Molony refused to join a movement that had, in their opinion, deteriorated the nationalist agenda. Griffith could not please all of the women in his dual role as both editor of the *United Irishman* and the founder of Sinn Féin. He seemed, for many of the women, to have provided nothing that addressed the plight of the Irish woman. Helena Molony expressed the militant feminist reaction to Sinn Féin's initial platform as disappointment with the *United Irishman*. She wrote in *Bean na hÉireann* that "[t]he *United Irishman*, starting as a physical force, separatist journal, had gradually changed its policy to one of reactionary social and dual kingdom ideas. . . . We wanted a paper to counter-act this. We wanted it [*Bean na hÉireann*] to be a women's paper, advocating militancy, separatism and feminism."[10]

In 1905, Sinn Féin was composed of moderate nationalists. This became clear when the serious opposition facing the political party emerged. Vocal critics of the Sinn Féin platform included "radicals" like the Irish Women's Franchise League (IWFL) and the Irish Republican Brotherhood (IRB). In the pursuit of the fire of freedom, Sinn Féin displayed some lukewarm ideas to an impatient nationalist audience. It supported equality but did not place female suffrage at the top of its priorities. It supported self-governance but did not initially dare to advocate full republicanism. It called for a serious reawakening of Gaelic culture but did not actively support the use of physical force to achieve an independent, de-Anglicized Ireland. On the one hand, Sinn Féin was a party with modest proposals embodying tepid Irish nationalism, but on the other, it was Griffith's genius to be the genesis of chaste Republican ambitions. "Sinn Féin" cast a wide net for membership and would find itself rising above the turbulent personalities and approaches. It was also easily infiltrated by them.

Sinn Féin's Infancy

In November 1905, Arthur Griffith had announced the arrival of the Sinn Féin political party. The domestic nationalists and the radical feminists stood in unequal support of Sinn Féin, as did the female supporters of the Gaelic League, the Daughters of Ireland, and the Celtic Literary Society. In later years, the IRB financed Griffith's *Sinn Féin* newspaper until it was banned by the British government in 1914. It did, after all, advance each organization's own agendas, so their support, however limited, could be viewed as self-preservation or mutual advancement. Conceived in an illegitimate state to a long lineage of controversial and conflicting relatives, Sinn Féin aspired to be a force of Irish nationalism. Mary Butler, one of the early female members of Sinn Féin, knew she was a part of a movement that could change the course of Irish history. In her memoir of the November day on which Sinn Féin was born, she wrote:

When I look on the little linen badge that lies before me, I remember I wore it the first time as a delegate to the first Convention of the National Council of Sinn Féin, on Tuesday November 28th, 1905. And this is the scene that rises before me: A shabby room in the old Rotunda of Dublin, with less than a hundred men and a handful of women and girls seated in rapt attention.

They are listening to an earnest young man who faces them with a sheaf of papers in his hand. He is very tranquil, very modest, quite unaggressive—yet also full of suppressed flame and ardour. Some of us present do not even know the speaker's name; and presently I catch "Arthur Griffith" passing from mouth to mouth with eager zeal. I am glad to know that I, at least, was not aware of the new apostle's identity, nor of his revolutionary evangel. Had I not often called upon him in that untidy den at 6, Harcourt Street? And had I not also dropped in again and again at Arthur Griffith's still earlier office at 17, Fownes Street, to converse of things which were near and dear to his great heart? And was it not I—I say it with a thrill of pride—who first proposed to him the title of SINN FÉIN for his new vision of self-help to among the Irish people?[11]

Arthur Griffith was an interesting man with facets that often compromised his positions. He was married in 1910 and had two children, a son and a daughter, yet little is known about them. His position in Irish history after 1905 seems to be obscured by his contribution of the foundation of Sinn Féin. A man at the nexus of Irish nationalism in the 20th century, Griffith's chosen path impacted the cause of republicanism and equality across Ireland. The women who supported him, and even those who did not, were directly challenged by his party to heed the call to action. To remedy a frequent oversight of Griffith's personal contributions, a brief overview of the later years of his life is recounted below.

In addition to his newspapers, Arthur Griffith was committed to protecting the rights of workers and advancing the cause of Irish nationalism, so he joined the Irish Volunteers in 1913. In July 1914, he assisted in offloading the Volunteers' guns smuggled into the Howth harbor. However, even though he had been in the IRB, Griffith did not have a taste for violence. So, although he offered to serve at the General Post Office (GPO), he was advised to not take an active role in the Easter Rising. Regardless of his lack of personal armament in the Easter Rising, Griffith was jailed. In the aftermath of the executions, Griffith's Sinn Féin emerged stronger than it ever had hoped. Many nationalists, and British intelligence sources, falsely attributed the Easter Rising to Sinn Féin's plan. The wave of anti-English sentiment solidified Sinn Féin's position going into the War for Independence.

In 1917, Arthur Griffith was replaced by Eamon de Valera as the president of Sinn Féin, and a new constitution for Sinn Féin was written. The Sinn Féin of 1917 was more radical and more Republican, and it should most certainly be interpreted in the context of the public reaction to the executions of the men of Easter 1916. Of particular heartache was the execution of James Connolly, who was suffering from a gangrenous leg wound received in combat. Since he could not stand, he was strapped to a chair and then shot in Kilmainhaim Jail. Despite Connolly's conviction of "treason" in an expedited martial process, his execution was widely viewed as inhumane, and Sinn Féin reaped the electoral benefit of the public outrage over his death in 1918. Arthur Griffith was among the Sinn Féin delegation elected in the winter of 1918 to the British House of Commons. As articulated in his initial Sinn Féin platform, the elected Sinn Féin MPs refused to assume their seats and formed an assembly in Dublin known as the First Dáil Éireann. Griffith then served as the acting president of Sinn Féin in de Valera's absence for a speaking tour in the United States from 1919 to

1921. In the fall of 1921, at the request of the man who had deposed him as the president of the party that he founded, Arthur Griffith accompanied Michael Collins to London for the Anglo-Irish negotiations. Griffith, like Collins, supported the resulting Anglo-Irish Treaty of 1921. When Eamon de Valera resigned in protest of the treaty that he sent Griffith and Collins to negotiate, Griffith assumed the position of president of the Second Dáil Éireann. The stress of the negotiations and the allegations of betrayal deeply impacted Griffith. Eight months later in August 1922, he died suddenly of a brain hemorrhage in the midst of the Civil War.

Griffith's little "sinn féin" movement had provided a unique opportunity for Irish nationalists to unite in the wake of his death; sadly, this opportunity disintegrated into quarrels, civil conflict, and partition. However, the disorganized offices of Griffith's press center had provided an interesting nerve locus for the movement, and in its disorganization, perhaps concealed the empowerment of women in the Irish resistance.

THE STORY OF INDIVIDUAL NATIONALIST WOMEN LEADING UP TO 1916

- Jennie Wyse-Power
- Mary Butler (Máire de Buitléir)
- Maud Gonne MacBride
- Constance Gore-Booth (The Countess Markievicz)
- Helena Molony
- Kathleen Lynn
- Elizabeth O'Farrell
- Alice Milligan
- Hanna Sheehy-Skeffington
- Kathleen Clarke

On April 24, 1916, as many as 200 (sources differ in the exact numbers) women deployed with their male comrades to Dublin. Prepared to die for Ireland, these revolutionary women were armed with guns and spirits filled with Irish insurrection. With each step that they took toward their assigned posts, the women followed the path that their predecessors had paved in the advancement of women at the turn of the 20th century. Their knowledge and training had come at a price. Irish nationalist women had been sacrificing their time and freedom in the development of gender roles for their sisters. They embraced political and social roles in new and innovative ways. Seizing the light of the Irish cultural renaissance in the theatres and literature of the day, they became actresses, Irish linguists, writers, orators, and teachers. Drawn to the alluring romanticism of Irish nationalism, they instilled a social consciousness and progressive activism in the development of political parties. They were effective fundraisers and event organizers. They raged against the unromantic social ills stifling the Irish people—the labor conditions, the health crises, and the lack of gender rights. They became the voice of change for a nation and a call to arms to achieve that change. They were unconventionally conventional women who acknowledged that their gender was not a hindrance to their capabilities.

The women of 1916 stood on the shoulders of the 10 women selected below. Each woman demonstrated a call to service, the recognition of the ring of day for Ireland. It is, however, important to note that there were many Irish nationalist women before them and still more of these ladies' contemporaries whose stories are not recounted here. The women selected by the author demonstrate a representative sample of figures in Irish political history who directly impacted the establishment and development of Sinn Féin. Some were never even members of Sinn Féin, but their actions so clearly defined the shape that Sinn Féin would take, or the issues debated within the party at the time, that they must be included. These women embodied the spirit of "sinn féin." Others, like Countess Markievicz and Jennie Wyse-Power, would leave Sinn Féin in the 1920s, but their contributions to Sinn Féin long lingered after their departure. Still others, like Mary Butler, literally defined what Sinn Féin would become and justify their inclusion independently. Each one of these women embodies the spirit of sinn féin and the heart of Irish nationalism.[12]

Jennie Wyse-Power

Within the context of the Home Rule debate and demands made by the Irish Parliamentary Party (IPP), the 1881 Coercion Act had opened the curtains on the Republican stage. With IPP leader Charles Stewart Parnell in jail, his sister Anna assumed the national helm of the Land League under the auspices of the Ladies Land League. Although historians seem to dispute the degree to which the ladies were effective, there seems to be consensus that the incarcerations allowed the women to be in positions of power with which they had previously been unacquainted.

Among the early members of the Ladies Land League was Jennie Wyse-Power. A regular visitor to Mr. Parnell's cell at Kilmainham Jail, she assisted in the compilation of the *Book of Kells,* which was a record of the land evictions occurring during the 1881–1882 Parnell imprisonment. The aptly named compilation interestingly bore the name of a more famous Book of

Kells, which is the illuminated manuscript of the New Testament illustrated by Celtic monks. In the wake of the Parnell scandal, Jennie Wyse-Power remained one of the only Ladies Land League's former executive council members who vehemently defended Parnell in public editorials and even personally attended to his grave after his death.

Jane O'Toole (the future Jennie Wyse-Power) was born in 1858 in Baltinglass, County Wicklow, to a nationalist family. The family household was a safe house for the Fenians, and in 1883, she married a member of the Irish Republican Brotherhood (IRB) who founded the Gaelic Athletic Association (GAA) named John Wyse-Power. She had four children, one of whom died in childhood, while she balanced her increasing involvement in the suffrage movement. A founding member of Hanna Sheehy-Skeffington's Irish Women's Franchise League (IWFL) and Maud Gonne's Daughters of Ireland, Jennie Wyse-Power raised three young ones in the midst of revolutionary social activism.

She was even a small business owner. Her Irish Farm Produce Company, founded in 1899, became a Dublin hot spot for political activists and cultural advocates. She later opened multiple locations around the city. She was committed to a number of organizations, but her ardent focus was political action by any means. When Sinn Féin emerged onto the scene, she saw an opportunity for women to become more directly involved in the movement. She joined Sinn Féin as a founding member.

As she detailed in "The Political Influence of Women in Modern Ireland," the role of nationalist women from 1893 to 1905 was often ill defined. In the following text, she details the importance of national organizations that admitted and empowered women—notably, the Gaelic League and Sinn Féin. Explaining the gap in history, she offers a succinct answer— they could not belong to a group that publicly advocated politics. Female nationalists, she asserts, were emancipated by the emergence of the Gaelic League and Sinn Féin.

> The echoes of the Parnell affair [with Kathleen O'Shea] had not yet died when a new movement was inaugurated by the founding of the Gaelic League. This novel, cultural body rejected the false sex and class distinction which were the result of English influence. And to the Gaelic League is due the credit of having established the first Irish national society which accepted women as members on the same terms as men.
>
> From the beginning, women sat on its Branch Committees and Executives, and helped to carry out the programme. The work was of such a nature that women's help was essential. The study of the Irish language was for all; the social side was wholly in the hands

of the women members, who by absorbing the Irish tradition, and themselves giving expression to the Gaelic ideals and culture, influenced in no small degree the growing effort to wean the people from the Anglicisation which had gone all too far. In 1905 the Sinn Féin movement was formally launched at a public meeting in the Dublin Rotunda.[13]

From its birth, Sinn Féin would be committed, on paper, to equal membership for women and strove to represent women on its National Executive since its inception. Although its early membership would be a dedicated (often characterized as radical) few, it was a group that welcomed women, unlike so many of its contemporaries. When Hanna Sheehy-Skeffington, Mary MacSwiney, and the Countess would later become aggravated by the circumstantial support, rather than primary support, of Sinn Féin for the feminist agenda, Jennie Wyse-Power would remain steadfast in her Sinn Féin convictions.

Jennie and John Wyse-Power were the vortex of Fenian secrecy and revolutionary action. Her children embraced the ideology, and the family often participated in activities together. Her strong commitment to Irish nationalism led her to assume many leadership roles prior to 1916. In 1911, she became the vice president of Sinn Féin. This was quite early in the party's evolution, when most nationalist women had not found a political voice. She assisted in the formation of Cumann na mBan in 1914, and the Easter Proclamation was written in her home. On the eve of the rebellion, Jennie Wyse-Power, operating as a personal courier, was sent by Patrick Pearse to deliver a message to the Volunteers in County Wexford that the Rising would take place. The fact that she was trusted with such covert dispatches reflects the position she maintained within Cumann na mBan and the IRB.

During the Easter Rising, Mrs. Wyse-Power provided the food rations to the insurgent companies until her Henry Street shop was destroyed. Many of the diaries and personal documents of the Wyse-Power household were destroyed as well, but this did not dissuade her from assisting her revolutionary sisters. Over 70 of the Cumann na mBan comrades were arrested after the throws of the rebellion, a sampling of the 43 branches now spread across Ireland in 1916.

In the aftermath of the Rising, Jennie Wyse-Power remained a vocal proponent for Irish nationalism. Deeply troubled by the effect of the Rising of the rebels' families, she and daughter Nancy worked tirelessly for the prisoners' dependents. She was actively engaged in Sinn Féin meetings at the same time, often chairing meetings and raising awareness of public health policy. By 1917, she was on Cumann na mBan's national executive and, in 1920, she was elected to the Dublin Corporation. Unlike many of her female contemporaries, especially those in Cumann na mBan, Mrs. Wyse-Power embraced a pro-Treaty position during the Civil War.

Jennie Wyse-Power then entered politics. In 1922, she was one of the first women appointed to the Free State Seanad (Irish Senate). She retained this position until 1936 when the government was dissolved. She briefly joined the pro-Treaty Cumann na nGaedheal Party but broke with them over the treatment of political prisoners in 1925. Widowed the year after, Mrs. Wyse-Power eventually closed her food shops in 1929. In 1936, she retired from public life. Though she often disagreed with her Sinn Féin colleagues, Wyse-Power was a vocal advocate of their cause. Jennie Wyse-Power died five years later at the age of 78 in 1941.

Mary Butler (Máire De Buitléir)

Mary Butler was, like so many Irish women, cast as an "antihero" in the play for Irish independence.[14] She is footnoted in every historical piece on Sinn Féin for having gifted the name of "sinn féin" to Arthur Griffith, but little else concerning Mary Butler beyond this factoid is usually recorded. Removing her from the footnotes of Irish history, one finds that her background does not explain her significance in Irish Republican history. In fact, it defies the conventional logic that Republican resistance to English rule is simply a familial, generational tradition. It does, however, explain how so many of the most zealous Republicans have been drawn to commit their lives to an adopted cause.

Mary was born in 1872 in County Clare to Peter Lambert Butler, son of William Butler. She was from a landowning Catholic family with Protestant relatives, including Mary's notable cousin Sir Edward Carson. Sir Edward Carson led the fight against the Third Home Rule Bill and founded the Ulster Volunteer Force (UVF) in 1913. In recalling this earlier in the chapter, it was noted that the Irish Volunteers, whose membership included Arthur Griffith, were founded in response to the Protestant militarization (the UVF). The irony lies in the fact that the mutual armament of the UVF and the Volunteers, who merge with their IRB comrades and evolve into the Irish Republican Army, occurs within a microcosm of Mary Butler's family.

Mary Butler was not from a Fenian family, nor had she been taught Irish language or culture in her childhood. She happened upon the nationalist revival, like many of her contemporaries, through literature. Mary's deep love of Gaelic culture led to a literary career in the *United Irishman*, the newspaper founded by William Rooney and Arthur Griffith in 1899. Butler's weekly contribution to the paper included articles such as "Womanhood and Nationhood" where she asserted that Irish women were nation builders in the sphere of the home while "gifted women may sometimes do useful public work."[15] Her unassuming domiciliation is often overlooked in favor of more aggressive female agitators or suffragettes, but it is more likely the portrait of conservative popular female opinion at the time.

In an article entitled "Women's Role in Sustaining Gaelic Culture," Butler suggested that the domestic realm would serve to de-Anglicize Irish culture through the preservation of Irish language. She "countenanced many of the worst stereotypes held by a fundamentally patriarchal culture about strong-minded women."[16] For many, it was utilizing an existing network to maximize effectiveness. In the domestic realm, women were seen as natural, capable leaders. Through the traditional roles as wife and mother, an Irish woman could invigorate the nationalist cause by infusing Irish language, dance, singing, and history. In many regards, it was practical, but in others it was reinforcing oppressive stereotypes of a British imperial conquest. Controversial in nature, the expansion of "domestic nationalism," as it became known, began to spread through the mobilization of Gaelic League members. Recalling that the Gaelic League was a society that defied contemporary social roles in Ireland by allowing female members, it cast Mary Butler in many circles as "radical" for assuming a role of equal membership in an organization of both genders.

Although her critics point out that Mary Butler's domestic nationalism seemingly advocated the self-imposed perpetuation of gender oppression, her views should be held in the context of her upbringing, social expectations, and familial pressures. With a cousin who was committed to the use of violence to defend the union with Britain, Mary Butler must have seemed quite radical to her family. Her devotion to a nationalist Ireland is clear in her 1906 semiautobiographical book *The Ring of Day*; in it, a young woman awakens to the cause of Irish nationalism and finds her cultural soul.

In 1905, Mary Butler was one of seven women selected to serve on the 45-person Gaelic League Executive, making it comprised of 15.6 percent female membership. While on the executive, she would enjoy the company of many prominent figures in Irish history, including Patrick Pearse who served as the editor of the league's newspaper *An Claidheamh Soluis*.

As a domestic nationalist, Mary Butler may have been typical of women in her day. She maintained conservative views of the role of women in society, and, perhaps, she is unfairly judged for her modest aspirations by contemporary standards of equality. She did, however, carry a fire of Irish freedom in her heart and saw a part, however small, for women of her ilk to play. Based on the contextual revival of Gaelic language and culture ongoing by the Gaelic League, the principles of domestic nationalism were consistent with harkening to the role of women's rights in Ireland under Brehon law. Although women were clearly not equal partners in a patri-archal, pre-Victorian Ireland, there were limited concessions to women's rights that might have seemed radical to the Victorian Briton. Even so, domestic nationalism was not what would fuel the drive for equality. It was infuriating to many Irish nationalist women who viewed the idea of the domestic realm as tantamount to substantiating the repression of women. For the early feminists and aspiring suffragettes, returning to a pre-Victo-rian Brehon law was nothing more than a patriarchal concession. Believing sincerely in a liberal, cultural revival meant pragmatically that truly radi-cal action was necessary. Dedicated to the cause that will forever bear her inspiration, Mary Butler died in 1921.

Maud Gonne MacBride

Perhaps one of the best-known Irish nationalists of the time was Maud Gonne, celebrated in history by the unrequited yearnings of William Butler Yeats. Maud Gonne was born in Tongham, near Aldershot, England, in 1866 to a captain in the British Army.[17] Her mother died while Maud was still a child, so she joined her father when he was posted to Ireland in 1882. Shortly thereafter, her father passed. Thus, as a young adult, she was finan-cially and socially independent. She ventured back to continental Europe to embark on a new life. Spending time in France while recuperating from an illness, she became the mistress of a French journalist named Lucian Millevoye and bore him two children. Her son George was born in 1891 but died in infancy. Her daughter Iseult was born in 1895. The affair ebbed, and Maud left France to return back to Ireland.

When Maud Gonne arrived back into Dublin literary society in the late 1890s, women were far from welcome. Her position as an unwed mistress would have been somewhat scandalous, and little is written of her daughter Iseult, who would later marry a writer named Francis Stuart. Iseult was apparently concealed as Maud's niece around Dublin social circles. Years later, William Butler Yeats would propose marriage to Iseult, who rejected him just as her mother had. Meanwhile, Maud's attempted foray into the National League, Contemporary Club, and the Celtic Literary Society, were brief. Although the Celtic Literary Society, unlike the Contemporary Club and National League, would eventually permit female membership, this conciliatory gesture was unsatisfactory to Miss Gonne. Decisively, she decided to found a female organization that would suck the membership marrow of Ireland's patriarchic bones. This would become her beloved "Daughters of Ireland."

From their first meeting, Gonne had been warmly received by Arthur Griffith and William Rooney, who secured her financing for the *United Irishman*. She later recounted an immediate bond with the fellows:

Arthur Griffith and Willie Rooney both disapproved of the exclusion of women and, when I did actually start Inghinidhe na hÉireann in 1900, gave me all the help they could, and the Celtic Literary Society generously lent us their rooms for our meetings and classes, till we were big enough to have a house of our own, and run lectures on History and Irish, dancing, singing, and drilling classes for children in three halls in Dublin.[18]

She published the organization's missions in *United Irishman,* which served as a propaganda advertisement and recruitment opportunity for her cause.

Her activities brought her both respect and attention befitting an agitator. In 1900, she famously dubbed Queen Victoria the "Famine Queen" and, in a scathing revue of her anticipated visit, wrote: "Queen, return to your own land; you will find no more Irishmen ready to wear the red shame of your livery. In the past they have done so from ignorance, and because it is hard to die from hunger when one is young and strong and the sun shines, but they shall do so no longer; see!"[19] Chapters of the Daughters of Ireland began to spring up across Ireland in support of Gonne's distain for the queen. But membership was more than a wave of pop culture—the Daughters of Ireland required a strong commitment from their members. All women had to be of Irish birth or descent, and each adopted a Gaelic version of her name to conceal her identity for protection. Members had to be formally nominated and approved by a ballot.

Each branch of the Daughters of Ireland developed at a different pace due to the nature of nationalist concentration in the area. The Cork branch was extraordinarily organized and effective. Coordinating over 100 children in Irish language and history classes and giving concerts for the community was masterfully facilitated by the branch president, Margaret Goulding Buckley.[20] Buckley would later become the first female president of Sinn Féin. The early enthusiasm of its membership set Inghinidhe na hÉireann in motion and became a mechanism for social change.

Maud Gonne also became the focus of William Butler Yeats. He penned plays and poems celebrating her beauty. Lovesick, he pursued Gonne tirelessly. In 1902, she relented by agreeing to portray the title lead in his play *Cathleen ní Houlihan.* She did, however, continue to refuse his marriage proposals, opting to marry Irish Republican Brotherhood (IRB) member Major John MacBride in 1903. Although the marriage failed, Maud gave birth to a son whom she named Séan.[21] Major MacBride was executed in 1916 for his part in the Easter Rising.

Eventually, Maud Gonne MacBride, with her two young children in tow, fled to Paris to avoid an arrest warrant. For the rest of her life, Maud split her time between Ireland and France. In her intermittent absence from Ireland, the literary society ignited. Dublin became alive with nationalist allegorical plays and essays written by her colleagues and friends—including William Butler Yeats, James Joyce, and Séan O'Casey.

While back in France, Maud continued her passionate involvement with the Women's Prisoners' Defence League. She cofounded the League with Charlotte Despard during the Civil War to advocate on behalf of the Republican prisoners. Maud was no stranger to the plight of the prisoners, as she had served time in Kilmainhaim Jail and even participated in a hunger strike to earn her release. She remained active in Irish politics, often writing handwritten letters to Irish politicians, until her death in 1953.

Constance Gore-Booth (The Countess Markievicz)

Countess Markievicz, born Constance Gore-Booth, serves a narrative link in the nationalistic tale, as she was a member of Maud Gonne's Daughters of Ireland and James Connolly's Irish Citizen Army.[22] The Countess, as she is known, was a woman with many hats in the nationalist movement. She was a patron by virtue of her financial status. She was an active revolutionary, an elected politician, a clever writer, and a tireless party activist. She remains one of the most recognizable figures in Irish history, alongside her male counterparts.

Like Maud Gonne, Constance Gore-Booth was from a well respected family. Born in 1868, Constance was the daughter of an Artic explorer and English gentrified Lady Georgina from York. She was educated by a governess in Lissadell, County Sligo, and she was an accomplished horsewoman. William Butler Yeats was a frequent visitor in her family home, and his touch of Irish nationalism influenced her greatly. In her social debut around London, she had been presented to Queen Victoria in 1887. Given the nature of her later life, this moment serves as a stark contrast to her gun-toting revolutionary activities. She later studied art in London and in Paris. In 1900, she married a penniless Polish aristocrat named Casimir de Markievicz. The count was a widower with a son, and Constance moved to their home in the Ukraine until shortly after the birth of their daughter Maeve in 1901. They arrived in Ireland in 1903, and the marriage began to falter. The couple soon separated, and Maeve was sent to be raised by Lady Gore-Booth, Constance's mother, at Lissadell House in Sligo. The Countess remained in Dublin alone, where she filled her time with nationalist activities.

The escalation of the Countess's involvement in nationalist groups was quite rapid. In 1908, she joined Maud Gonne's Daughters of Ireland and Arthur Griffith's Sinn Féin. She had been inspired by a Sinn Féin pamphlet left by a previous tenant in a cottage she had rented several years before. She became a regular contributor to both *Bean na hÉireann* and the *United Irishman*. Still a regular on the Dublin society circuit, she attended her last ball at Dublin Castle in 1908. She later recalled that she preferred to blow the seat of English government up rather than attend a society ball in it. In 1909, she founded Na Fianna Éireann, an organization that trained young boys how to use guns in the fight for Irish nationalism. Many of the Na Fianna Éireann joined the Irish Volunteers as men, and many served under her command during the Easter Rising.

On the surface, she was a curious nationalist, but she soon joined or founded most of the subversive organizations in Ireland. It is clear that the Countess became bored with the trappings her affluence could afford. Her appearance, specifically her attire, reflected the militaristic style she was assuming. Her portraits in 1908 and 1915 document the evolution of a socialite in a ball gown to a revolutionary with a gun. Irish nationalism intrigued her so much that it became the focus of her life hereafter.

The Countess believed that women should play a part in the fight for Irish independence and wholly embraced the use of force for them to achieve it. Her position was summarized in a *United Irishman* editorial reviewing her speech to a Cumann na mBan convention in 1915: "What distinguished Ireland chiefly of old was the number of fighting women who held their own against the world, who owed no allegiance to men, who were the super-women—the Maeves, the Macas, the warrior-queens."[23] The Countess urged all women to buy a revolver and learn to use it in Ireland's name. Since women were not granted positions in the Irish Volunteers nor the Irish Republican Brotherhood, she assisted in the foundation of Cumann na mBan in 1914. The Countess even designed the signature metal badge worn by Cumann na mBan members.

Shortly after the Dublin lockout of 1913, she also joined James Connolly's Irish Citizen Army (ICA). As an ICA officer, the Countess served as the second in command at St. Stephen's Green and the College of Surgeons during the Easter Rising in April 1916. Her skills as a marksman and passion for the cause made her a strong presence on the battlefield. At her surrender, she reportedly kissed her gun before handing the revolver over to her captors. She received a death sentence for her role in the Easter Rising. It was later suspended on account of her gender; the condition of the pardon often made the Countess scoff. She and Eamon de Valera had been spared; the seven signatories to the Easter Proclamation were not.

Her political career was brief but significant, marked by waves of popular support and empty office seats. In 1918, she became the first woman elected to Westminster Parliament, but she never assumed her seat since she was an abstentionist Sinn Féin candidate. Serving in the First Dáil Éireann, however, was a source of pride for the Countess, and she was selected as the first female minister in the cabinet. As the minister for labor, she participated in a nonsanctioned legislative assembly from the British point of view. In Irish history, however, serving in the First Dáil Éireann was revolutionary. The Countess became an advocate for independent Ireland, and her prominence carved out avenues for women in the nationalist circles. She defied the conventions of her birth and, in doing so, opened the door for women of all backgrounds. Her evolution from Countess to revolutionary would inspire future generations of women to embrace their talents and skills for Ireland.

She opposed the Anglo-Irish Treaty and argued against it in the Dáil debates. Along with the other female members of the First Dáil, she followed Eamon de Valera out in protest when the Treaty was accepted. During the Civil War, the Countess traveled extensively on a series of speaking tours across the United States. In 1923, she was arrested for anti-Treaty activities and served time in the North Dublin Union. Elected again to the Dáil in 1923, she refused to take her seat due to an Oath of Allegiance to the English Crown in Ireland. In 1926, she left Sinn Féin to form Fianna Fáil with Eamon de Valera. Once again elected to the Dáil in 1927, she died before she could assume her seat as a Fianna Fáil TD (member of the Irish Parliament).

Helena Molony

With Maud Gonne MacBride living in France, the Daughters of Ireland required an in-residence leader. Helena Molony took control of the organization from 1902 until its collapse. Born in 1884 in Dublin, Helena was drawn to the nationalist community of women early on in her life. Assuming the pseudonym of "Emer," she became increasing active in the Gaelic revival and nationalist organizations. Helena was an actress with the Abbey Theatre, but she possessed both a sharp eye for the spoken word and the sniper's scope.

Molony was still a teenager when she joined the Daughter's of Ireland (Inghinidhe na hÉireann) in 1903, a result of a speech by Maud Gonne herself. Her zealous conversion impressed Countess Markievicz, whom Molony recruited in 1907. Tirelessly committed to the cause, Molony became the editor of *Bean na hÉireann*, the first female paper in Ireland, established in 1908. The newspaper published clever, intelligent debates concerning the role of women in Irish nationalism, notably including the Countess's column entitled "Woman with a Garden" that offered advice to Irish women on how to tend the allegorical, national garden. Under the auspices of a gardening expert, the Countess penned that the lily, symbolizing Eire in nationalist coloring of white pedal, orange pistil, and green stem, should be allowed to bloom in the open, free air. Other frequent columnists included Kathleen Lynn, Sydney Gifford, and Mary MacSwiney. Though its tenure in Irish history was short, *Bean na hÉireann* produced close to four glorious years of feminist nationalist reviews that even the men would read.

In 1911, Helena was arrested for throwing stones on Grafton Street to protest King George V's visit. She became the first female political prisoner since the Ladies Land League members had been detained in the 1880s. To further connect Helena to her nationalist sisters before her, it is interesting to note that Anna Parnell—who was surprised to find Helena mad at her for doing so—paid her bail! In 1913, she joined the Irish Citizen Army and was one of the dedicated ICA women who participated during the Easter Rising.

Carrying her personal revolver, she was deployed to the City Hall garrison on April 24, 1916. Séan Connolly, her close friend from the Abbey Theatre acting guild, served as Helena's commander. When Séan was killed by a sniper while trying to hoist the tricolor, Helena responded by shooting the policeman blocking the ICA's escape. She received one of the longest sentences of all of the women involved in the Easter Rising. Upon her surrender, the ICA women were taken to the barracks before being transferred to Kilmainhaim Jail. In a 1966 radio interview, Helena described the female prisoners' awareness of what was happening to their male comrades:

> But every morning we heard shots in the yard below and there was something sinister about them, we knew the men were being shot. Which the truth was, they were. So that was a terrible experience, and that went on . . . a week or so, maybe more. We were then removed to Mountjoy prison.[24]

Helena was released in December 1916, and within a year, she had risen to a national position in Sinn Féin. She, along with the Countess and Dr. Kathleen Lynn, became a force of Republican reckoning. The three ladies developed a deep network of trust based on their shared militant involvement built on her City Hall garrison experience in the Easter Rising earlier that year. During the War for Independence, she served as a courier for Michael Collins, and later, she assisted the Countess in her role as the minister of labor in the First Dáil. She also was a Republican court judge in Rathmines and a passionate member of the Irish Women's Workers' Union

(IWWU). Throughout the 1930s, she dabbled in various splinter movements, including Saor Éire and Mna na hÉireann. In 1936, she became the second woman president of the Irish Trade Union Congress. Helena Molony assumed many roles in the nationalist struggle, and she is often quoted as having said that "there can be no free women in an enslaved nation." Helena Molony passed away in 1967.

Kathleen Lynn

Born in 1874 to an Anglican family in County Mayo, Kathleen Lynn is remembered as a passionate advocate for women and children. Her politics caused a great strain on her relationship with her family, especially her father who was a Protestant preacher. After receiving her medical degree in 1899, she set up a practice in Rathmines in 1904. The focus of her medical career became treating those who had no one to speak for them—the children and the poor. Her commitment to the labor movement brought her into contact with the Countess, with whom she remained lifelong friends, and James Connolly, who enticed her into the ICA.

Shortly after the Dublin lockout in 1913, she joined the Irish Citizen Army as its chief medical officer. Captain Kathleen Lynn served in the City Hall garrison with 16 men and 8 other women (including Helena Molony). When the ICA commanding officer Séan Connolly was killed, she assumed the command of the garrison. As the highest ranking officer, Dr. Lynn tendered the ICA's surrender of the City Hall.

After her capture, Dr. Lynn was held in the Ship Street barracks before being transferred to Kilmainhaim Jail. In her diary accounts of the Rising, Dr. Lynn described the conditions of her imprisonment as gross negligence for health concerns. Given blankets full of lice, the women slept by the stench of open garbage at the Ship Street barracks. In Kilmainhaim, they had no heat and no light, but Kathleen was kept in a cell with Helena Molony (and her beloved Madeleine ffrench-Mullen) until May 1916 when Dr. Lynn was moved to the Mountjoy Jail. Shortly after the transfer from Kilmainhaim, Kathleen was briefly exiled to England that June. Through her family's status and persuasion, she was placed in care of a family friend rather than being remanded to an English prison.

In 1917, shortly after her return, Dr. Kathleen Lynn was elected to the Sinn Féin National Executive (Ard Chomhairle). Her activities in the Easter Rising frustrated her medical employment, so she turned to politics to remedy the conditions challenging Ireland. As a clever, educated nationalist woman, her home was frequently raided. She often traveled in disguise to avoid capture. In 1918, she was arrested and detained for subversive activities. Dr. Lynn was released by the Lord Mayor of Dublin to

assist the medical community in combating a flu epidemic. In 1919, she
and Madeleine ffrench-Mullen established St. Ultan's Hospital, the first in-
fant hospital in Ireland, where they implemented an aggressive program of
immunizations during an influenza crisis. The hospital staff was initially
all female, a reflection of Dr. Lynn's feminist ideologies and ties to the suffrage movement. She frequently served as a consulting doctor when the
suffragettes went on hunger strike.

Kathleen's political career briefly spanned the 1920s. She was elected to
the First Dáil as an anti-Treatyite. She lost her seat in the 1927 election and
returned to her medical career and work as a humanitarian activist, for
which she is more prominently remembered.

Her close friendship with her comrades was a lifelong devotion. In 1927,
she cut short a holiday to return to Countess Markievicz's bedside. She had
been notified by her Irish Women's Franchise League (IWFL) colleague
Hanna Sheehy-Skeffington that the Countess's health had declined. During
the election campaign that June, the Countess had broken her arm while
cranking her motorcar. Her health continued to deteriorate. Kathleen had
recommended her for hospitalization, and she underwent an appendec-
tomy as well as follow-up surgery. Shortly after Dr. Lynn's return from holiday, she joined Helena Molony and other ICA veterans in a prayer vigil on
the eve of the Countess's death.

Resigned from national politics, Dr. Lynn expanded her medical practice and participated in local politics on the Rathmines City Council. Her
excitement for revolutionary action resurfaced as dynamic social activism.
In 1934, she implemented a Montessori ward in St. Ultan's shortly after
Maria Montessori visited the hospital. In the late 1930s, she was the vice
president of the Save the Children campaign that found Irish homes for
German children orphaned by the war. She remained active at St. Ultan's
until her death in 1955.

Elizabeth O'Farrell

Miss Elizabeth O'Farrell represents the intersection of revolutionary
women. Born in 1883 in the heart of Dublin, Elizabeth was constrained
by the social conditions of working class Ireland. Her father was a Dublin
dock worker who died when she was still in school. Her mother ran a small
shop but was unable to provide for the children alone. Once dreaming of
becoming a nurse, Elizabeth left school to work in a printing company to
help provide for her family.

Politics found her at the tender age of 16. Elizabeth joined the Daughters
of Ireland in 1906 and, shortly after, Cumann na mBan and the Irish Citizen Army. O'Farrell received first aid training from Dr. Kathleen Lynn and

ballistics training from Countess Markievicz. In the months preceding the Easter Rising, she served as a courier to arrange the details of the Rising in Galway. Her training and her bravery made Elizabeth an indispensable asset for Patrick Pearse during the Easter Rising. As a Cumann na mBan nurse attached to the ICA at the General Post Office, Elizabeth was one of the three women left with the Easter Rising leaders when Commandant Pearse dismissed volunteers from their duties that Friday. The other two women were James Connolly's personal secretary Winifred Carney and a dispatch courier named Julia Grenan.

On Saturday morning, April 29, 1916, Elizabeth O'Farrell walked out onto Moore Street with a makeshift white flag displaying a red cross. She had witnessed the summary discussions of Patrick Pearse and James Connolly, who lay injured on a stretcher inside. Having been given the task of personally delivering Pearse's surrender papers, she announced their intent to the British commanding officer. After a thorough search of her person, she was allowed to return back into the rebel headquarters to convey the acceptance of the surrender. When Commandant Pearse surrendered his sword to General Lowe, Elizabeth O'Farrell remained at his side. Interestingly, her image is brushed out of the photos of the surrender; only her boots can be seen standing next to Pearse's. The following morning after the surrender, she was sent to circulate the surrender order to the remaining Volunteer outposts.

Following the surrender, Elizabeth was held in the Ship Street barracks with Dr. Kathleen Lynn and Helena Molony. Like her comrades, she was transferred to Kilmainham Jail where she was later released. Her commitment to Sinn Féin was so deep that she refused to join Fianna Fáil in 1926, even after her mentors departed from Sinn Féin. She eventually completed a course in midwifery, fulfilling her dreams of becoming a nurse. An ardent hard-line Republican, Miss O'Farrell canceled her engagement when her fiancé insisted that she would need to leave Ireland for his business in Chile. In 1957, unmarried and in poor health, she spoke at a Republican rally in Phoenix Park protesting the proscription of Sinn Féin. She died just days later.

Alice Milligan

In Ulster, the Gaelic League began to take a new form under the direction of Alice Milligan. Born into a wealthy Protestant family in 1866, Alice Milligan's radical republican sympathies must have provided many divisive discussions in her family. In 1878, the Milligan family moved from outside Omagh to Belfast. Alice was educated at the Methodist College, where she developed a passion for literature. In 1888, while in Dublin studying

Irish, Alice made the acquaintance of Yeats and IRB founder Michael Davitt. Among her close friends were O'Donovan Rossa, Douglas Hyde, and Roger Casement. Her eclectic association with Fenians, Gaelicists, and literary giants makes Alice Milligan's story of particular interest.

Alice was a very talented writer, celebrated by her contemporaries. She published under a number of pseudonyms including "Irish Olkyrn," or I.O., and the Gaelicized version of her name, Eilis Ní Maeleagain. Though she directed a number of the Daughter of Ireland's *tableaux vivants*, contributed to various newspapers, and wrote novels, Alice was best known for her poems. George Russell, known by his nom de plume AE, celebrated her work for her poetic brilliance. As a member of the Gaelic League, Alice Milligan drew attention to the Irish Renaissance occurring across Ireland with her novels and poetry. Alice was not a fluent Irish speaker, but she often gave lectures to members of the Gaelic League and celebrated the nationalist cause in the publication of *Life of Theobald Wolfe Tone*.

Along with Anna Johnston, Milligan published the Belfast-based paper *Shan Van Vocht* from 1896 to 1899. Roughly translated as "the poor old Irish women," the Gaelic phrase was chosen to conjure up a symbolic image of Ireland. In a September 1897 editorial, Milligan references the role Irish women should be playing:

> It may be urged that to form a committee solely of women is narrow, but in our opinion, as far, at any rate, as Ulster is concerned, you will best revive interest in the cause of Ireland by some such union amongst women for the purpose. Our aim will be not to exclude men from our sphere of national work. But to revive their interest in it, and to give them safe guidance out of the hurly-burly of the political faction fight into which they have wandered from the straight path.[25]

Seizing on an early opportunity to foster a network of supporters, Milligan recommended that the Irish Women's Centenary Committee facilitate exhibitions of rebellion artifacts and tending of rebel graves to showcase their sacrifice for visitors coming to the centennial celebrations of the 1798 United Irishmen uprising. It was a modest call for action, but one that nationalist women in the North were intent to follow.

After the Easter Rising, Milligan visited the prisons where her friends were held. She attended Roger Casement's trial and saw him hanged outside the prison. Her politics were in stark contrast with that of her family, and in 1919, she and her brother William, a British Army officer, found themselves without a safe place to live in Ireland. They moved to Bath, England, to find refuge.

Over the course of several decades, the siblings (Alice and William) engaged in a wild exchange of family and homeland. Alice and her brother searched for a home that would accept them both. Back and forth between Ireland and England, either she or her brother remained a virtual prisoner of their political surroundings. Ireland did not want William, and England did not want Alice. Together, the siblings found themselves ostracized. Though she had been celebrated by literary giants and political figures, Alice Milligan, a lifelong cultural advocate, died nearly destitute in her family home in 1953.

Hanna Sheehy-Skeffington

Whether in Belfast or in Dublin, the role that women would play across all of Ireland was as defenders of the disenfranchised. Although inequality was spoken of and nationalistic revivals were undertaken, the national voice of women was still muted under heaps of social limitations and political reality. There was no national vote. Many women had been "allowed" to participate in limited capacities in local political theatres, but the cornerstone of citizenship—voting—was still not a comprehensive right. The issue of female suffrage was a complicated one, invoking images of irrational, radical feminists who would then abandon their domesticity and that of a rebellious agitator who was a threat to domination.

The debate centered around the order of nationalist focus. Would the demands for universal suffrage be a pebble in the nationalist shoe or the rock upon which it stumbled? Many felt that the national question must be the primary focus, and that female suffrage would complicate things. But Hanna Sheehy-Skeffington did not.[26]

Convinced that the Gaelic League remained unwilling or unable to depart with a domestic approach to nationalism, Hanna Sheehy-Skeffington set out to engage the national question in the electoral realm. In 1909, she founded the Irish Women's Franchise League (IWFL) in order to refocus the principles of "sinn féin" into an examination of citizenship rights. In doing so, the IWFL brought national suffrage to the forefront on the nationalist agenda.

Although Hanna Sheehy-Skeffington may have been atypical of many awakening nationalists, her insistence that women emerge as prominent players in the drive for independence may have been typical for her background. Born in County Cork to a nationalist family, Hanna Sheehy was a dedicated student who received an advanced education. When she married in 1903, her husband took her name (Sheehy), and the couple became the Sheehy-Skeffingtons. She was militant in her beliefs and actions, which often landed her in the public eye. An unrepentant feminist, she saw a nationalist Ireland as an opportunity to reform Irish society and to undo the chronic injustices perpetuated upon women. It was her passion, and her fury, that pushed the issue of suffrage into nationalist debate.

At the turn of the century, the public arena of female activists, led by Gonne and the Countess, was in dire need of a practical method to concentrate the drive for equality in Irish society. The overwhelming inequality in social, economic, and political realms loomed in a dominant cloud over the nationalist question. If Home Rule, daresay even independence, was to be won, what would a modern Ireland look like? The answer seemed to point to the need for enfranchisement for all Irish, not just men. Simply, "we ourselves" would apply to women as well. Whether this was hopeful revisionism or not, a nationalist Ireland claimed to be throwing off the yoke of Victorian oppression. It need not, in this argument, be stopped short of a complete commitment to social equality. Centering on the question of political participation, Sheehy-Skeffington offered a feminist approach to nationalism.

Reconciling the expectations of traditional, social conservatism and radical feminism, she redefined participatory democracy—where an Irish woman could be in the traditional roles of wife, mother, and daughter as well as active, engaged citizen. By forming a separate, distinctly female organization, Hanna ensured that the IWFL could complement the goals of the Gaelic League, the Daughters of Ireland, and Sinn Féin. Most certainly, she must have thought, a nationalist solution should not be crafted in the absence of women. It was a calculated risk to increase the mobilization of Irish women in the nationalist community. In the ebb of Inghinidhe na hÉireann's prominence, the IWFL provided a solid female voice for those who perceived the marginalization of women in nationalist causes. Whether or not Sheehy-Skeffington's perception of Sinn Féin's commitment to theoretical equality was a fair assessment of the burgeoning movement, the creation of the IWFL launched a new vigor into the nationalist debate concerning the issues of suffrage and equality. However, as an editorial from *Bean na hÉireann* articulated, Hanna pointed out that this discussion did not have to place a wedge between sisters: "We hold in the first place that principle cannot be too high, and that uncompromising people, who are prepared to stick to their principles, cannot do either Sinn Féin or any movement any harm."[27]

Opposed to the use of violence, Hanna's husband Francis did not directly participate in the Easter Rising. The Sheehy-Skeffingtons did, however, provide food and messages to those who did. While overseeing a citizen militia he formed to prevent looting during the Rebellion, Francis was arrested and shot. In an inquiry into his death, it was revealed that the British captain who ordered the execution was operating out of line with his mission. Hanna refused the compensation offered by the British government for the officer's actions. Instead, she embarked on a speaking tour across the United States and raised $40,000 for the Irish nationalist movement. Hanna then deposited the money into the hands of Michael Collins.

Hanna joined Sinn Féin in 1918, after serving in prison with Countess Markievicz and Maud Gonne MacBride. She was eager to advance the position of women in the nationalist movement, and there was quite a bit of support emerging for Sinn Féin. Winning her release after a hunger strike, Hanna was quickly appointed to Sinn Féin's National Executive. As she rapidly advanced in Sinn Féin, it became clear that her strength as a party activist was in propaganda. In 1919, she became the party's secretary and served as a republican court judge during the War for Independence. During the Civil War, Hanna's distaste for violence resurfaced, and she left for the United States on a speaking tour. When she returned, she was disillusioned with Sinn Féin's lack of action on women's rights.

She left Sinn Féin with Eamon de Valera in 1926 and was appointed to serve in Fianna Fáil's executive, but Hanna's loyalty was to the advancement of women not to a political party. She resigned when she felt Fianna Fáil was compromising her beliefs. Seeing elements of gender equality in the radical socialism in the USSR, Hanna traveled to Russia to learn more. As the assistant editor of *An Phoblacht* and the secretary of the Friends of Soviet Russia, her politics seemed to be further radicalizing. She was banned from the North of Ireland, which did not impact her intent to travel there, and she was imprisoned in the Armagh Jail for defying the ban.

Her work for women's liberation continued throughout the 1930s and 1940s. She protested the 1937 Irish Constitution and the legislation the Dáil passed that restricted the rights of women. In protest, she formed a Women's Party and unsuccessfully stood for election. Until the day that Hanna Sheehy-Skeffington died in 1946, she remained a radical, uncompromising spokeswoman for gender equality.

Kathleen Clarke

In 1878, Kathleen Daly was born in Limerick to a nationalist family. Her father worked in the timber yard, and her mother owned a small dressmaking shop in town. Both Kathleen's father Edward and his brother John had been imprisoned for Fenian activities, which cost the family's business and livelihood. When Edward died in 1890, relatives supported Kathleen and her siblings financially until 1901 when Kathleen immigrated to the United States.

She was a bright, talented woman who had a love of music and was a capable baker and dressmaker. Now in New York, Kathleen married Tom Clarke, a Fenian who had served in prison with her uncle, John Daly. Kathleen and Tom Clarke had three children. Their first son, John Daly Clarke, was born in Brooklyn in 1902, but both Tom Junior and Emmet were born back in Ireland in 1908 and 1910. With the Clarke family back in Dublin, they opened a tobacco shop that became a communication point for the Irish Republican Brotherhood (IRB).

Kathleen shared her husband's deep commitment to an independent Ireland. While her husband remained a leading force in the IRB, Kathleen supported his efforts. Her brother Ned Daly and her husband were among the principal organizers of the Easter Rising. Tom's signature appeared first on the Easter Proclamation, and he was the second to be executed after Commandant Patrick Pearse. Kathleen's dedication to her husband and the cause of Irish independence was embodied in her insistence to be addressed as Mrs. Tom Clarke throughout her life.

Kathleen was a mother of three small boys and a small business owner when she became a founding member of Cumann na mBan. Her position as the wife of Tom Clarke placed her in a unique position during the Easter Rising. She was entrusted by the IRB to maintain the network of IRB men throughout Ireland and serve as the funnel of communication for all Supreme Council decisions related to the IRB. Accordingly, she did not participate directly in the Easter Rising. She planned to coordinate the distribution of assistance to the families of the Volunteers throughout the rebellion. However, the summary surrender and execution of the Easter Rising redirected Kathleen's duties to coordinate aid to the prisoners' dependents. Kathleen, pregnant at the time, had a miscarriage and faced the loss of the family shop, which had been destroyed during the Rebellion.

She returned to Limerick to recuperate, but Kathleen Clarke found herself facing a challenging life. She was the widow of a twice-convicted Fenian with no means to support her three young children. Even so, she was not dissuaded from politics. Her sister was the president of the local Cumann na mBan chapter, and Kathleen began to assist her in the chapter's efforts. Reinvigorated by her activities, Kathleen returned to Dublin in 1918. Shortly thereafter, she, along with Maud Gonne and the Countess, was arrested in the "German plot" in which the British government alleged that Republicans were seeking weapons from the Germans. She served eight months in an English prison before her release in February 1919. During the War for Independence, Kathleen provided a safe house for IRA men and Cumann na mBan women, conducted fundraising, and served as a Republican court judge in Dublin's north city district. In 1920, like so many of her Republican sisters, she became an active member of the White Cross.

During the Civil War, Kathleen was a vocal opponent of the Treaty. She initially tried to lead a committee to reconcile the conflict, but her efforts were unsuccessful. With the Treaty approved, she sided with the Anti-Treatyites. She volunteered at a first aid station outside the Gresham Hotel before being arrested in February 1923. Her detainment in Kilmainhaim Jail was brief, but her home was frequently under siege by Free State Forces throughout the Civil War. Throughout the remainder of the decade, Kathleen continued to serve as a fundraising orator for Republicans as she traveled across the United States. She often drew large audiences due to her husband's earlier work with Clan na Gael and her affinity for her adopted residence at the turn of the century.

Though she had been co-opted into the Sinn Féin Ard Chomhairle in 1917, Kathleen's republicanism was hardly contained in a political party. It came as no surprise to most that she backed Eamon de Valera in the 1926 split with Sinn Féin. As a founding member of Fianna Fáil, Mrs. Tom Clarke served from 1928 to 1936 as a senator. In 1937, she opposed the Fianna-backed constitution, though she did not resign her position on the Fianna Fáil National Executive. In 1939, she became Dublin's first female Lord Mayor. Her involvement in politics faded in the 1940s, and she moved to Liverpool in 1965 to live with her youngest son Emmet. She died in Liverpool in 1972. Nineteen years later, her grandniece Helen Litton edited her autobiography, *Revolutionary Women*.[28]

WOMEN IN THE EASTER RISING AND THE FIRST DÁIL

- Revolutionary Women
- Margaret Skinnider
- Winifred (Winnie) Carney
- Linda Kearns
- The Gifford Sisters: Grace, Nellie, Sidney, Muriel, and Katie
- Julia Grenan
- Leslie Price
- Áine Ceannt
- The First Dáil and War for Independence

The celebration of Easter took on an ominous tone in 1916. An ill-fated rebellion seized government buildings in Dublin, and an Irish Republic was proclaimed.[29] By the close of Easter Week, some of Ireland's greatest nationalists surrendered to British forces. They solemnly accepted their fate. The seven signatories to the Easter Proclamation were quickly tried for treason and executed. Their female comrades lay wait in jail, unsure of their own future. The confusion of the Easter Rising's planning and implementation is the source of much historical debate, but the bravery of those who led the rebellion against insurmountable odds is not. In their lives, the Irish rebels inspired pockets of resistance into action. In their death, they inspired a nation to war.

By April 1916, Irish nationalist men and women had grown impatient with the failure of the Irish Parliamentary Party and constitutional politics. The waves of Home Rule Bills had failed to pass the Westminster Parliament, and the cultural enlightenment of the Irish Renaissance embodied the rising support for nationalistic change. The cultural activism of Maud Gonne, Mary Butler, Alice Milligan, and Helena Molony was being harnessed for more radical action. The establishment of Cumann na mBan and the admission of women into the Irish Citizen Army secured the armament of the women for a revolutionary charge. Among those on the front lines of battle were the Countess, Helena Molony, Elizabeth O'Farrell, and Kathleen Lynn. Deeply committed to the cause of social revolution, the female activists supported the cause of Irish nationalism through the logistical support for their armed sisters and brothers. Doing their part for Ireland, Hanna Sheehy-Skeffington, Jennie Wyse-Power, and Kathleen Clarke were there to pick up the pieces and fight for an Ireland with equality. Using their voices, their guns and their minds, these ladies stood up for the call to duty when they heard the ring of day for Ireland, and they were joined by their sisters on the battlefield and in the political games that followed.

Revolutionary Women

On Easter Sunday 1916, a group of rebels met in Liberty Hall to implement the final stages of Joseph Plunkett's countrywide mobilization plans. There was great concern about the timing of the Rising. A shipment of arms from Germany aboard the *Aud* had been intercepted by the British the day before. The crew had sunk the boat off the coast of Cork and surrendered. The president of the Cork branch of Cumann na mBan, Mary MacSwiney, spent the week leading up to the rebellion organizing food rations and housing Volunteers. It was a job that her comrades in Dublin, Galway, and Belfast had also been performing, but now, especially in Cork, there was confusion about mobilization orders. The discovery of the *Aud* and the arrest of Roger Casement meant that the British intelligence was aware of an effort to organize. Responding to the crisis on Saturday morning, orders were sent from Dublin for all Volunteers to stand down. Then, on Sunday afternoon, new couriers were sent with remobilization orders for Monday, April 24.

In Dublin, Áine Ceannt helped her husband Éamonn write the dispatch orders while her sister Lily O'Brennan assembled first aid kits for the Dublin Fourth Brigade. The Countess, Helena Molony, and Dr. Kathleen Lynn prepared to fight. Female couriers set out across Ireland. Elizabeth O'Farrell was sent to Galway, and Nora Connolly was sent to Belfast. Not all of the dispatches arrived. The Cork Volunteers did not receive final orders to commence their rebellion. Based on the demobilization order on Saturday, the Cumann na mBan women and Irish Volunteers had been sent home by Terence MacSwiney and Tomas MacCurtain. The disarray led to an isolated mobilization of rebels in Dublin on Monday, April 24, 1916 at noon.

That Monday morning, a group of rebels from the Irish Citizen Army, Irish Volunteers, Fianna Éireann, and Cumann na mBan began the rebellion. A battalion seized the General Post Office (GPO) in Dublin and read the proclamation that declared an Irish Republic. By the close of day, there were 34 women attached to the GPO unit. Under the command of Patrick Pearse, the rebels continued to seize various outposts around the city, including St. Stephen's Green, the College of Surgeons, Boland's Mills, Jacob's Biscuit Factory, Marrowbone Lane, and City Hall. Winifred Carney, James Connolly's faithful secretary, typed out the first dispatch to the four battalions poised around the city—they were now all a part of the Irish Republican Army. Over the next six days, the women played important parts in the Rising. They were soldiers, serving as snipers, cooks, and commanders. They facilitated operations through typing dispatches, delivering food, and relaying courier messages. They gathered intelligence, replenished ammunition, and tended to the wounded. In the final hours of the rebellion, it was a woman who carried the white flag of surrender and delivered the final orders to stand down. These women were active revolutionaries who joined their sisters, brothers, husbands, and friends on the front line of a rebellion.

A May 3, 1916, article in the *London Times* recounts the surprise of the British Army when they encountered the surrendering insurgents. Not only were there women among them, they were executing operations based on excellent training. The superior qualifications of Countess Markievicz's marksmanship earned her a unique nickname.

Countess "Markovitch", who was one of the insurgents who held houses by St. Stephen's Green, and was the last to surrender, wore man's clothes, and that among the prisoners are several other women and one or two young girls who also dressed themselves as men. They showed themselves particularly aggressive as snipers.[30]

The women of the Irish Citizen Army and Cumann na mBan were actively engaged in a number of activities during the Easter Rising. Many of them served as snipers, scouts, spies, and couriers. Their ICA uniforms allowed them to blend in with the Fianna boys and the Irish Volunteers. Other women served as on-site secretaries, food suppliers, cooks, medical support, and weapons suppliers. Assuming a logistical support capacity was not inherently engendered. Supporting the front lines was not simply "women's work." Women participated in each garrison across the city, with the exception of the Boland Mills factory. The Cumann na mBan women who assembled for the task were dismissed by Eamon de Valera, who was uncomfortable with the idea of women engaging in direct combat in his Second Battalion. Other women simply missed the rebellion due to a lag in communication, such as the unit brought by Nora Connolly O'Brien, James Connolly's daughter, from Belfast via train. By the time they arrived, a surrender order had already been given.

There were many costs to the five-day-long siege, and the women were prepared to play a vital role in the sacrifices. Only one woman, Margaret Skinnider, was shot in the line of duty. Her injury was sustained while dressed as a man. The women had risked their lives willingly, but many were surprised when the Easter Rising organizers were executed. Just days after the surrender, beginning on May 3, 1916, Kathleen Clarke, Áine Ceannt, and Grace Plunkett became widows. Kathleen also lost her brother.

In the wake of such personal and national loss, many women were converted to Irish nationalism. Their call to arms and revolutionary action advanced the force of Irish nationalists in Cumann na mBan and Sinn Féin. The women who joined their revolutionary comrades on the battlefield brought a fresh energy and inspired generations of Irish women.

Margaret Skinnider

Margaret Skinnider was a pragmatically stubborn and hard-nosed woman. She was born in 1893 in Glasgow, Scotland, and often used her Scottish heritage to conceal her operations. She found politics quickly and became an early member of Cumann na mBan. Though she was a mathematics teacher by profession, her political activities took up the better part of her life. In 1915, she smuggled in bomb materials to Dublin from Scotland at the request of Countess Markievicz. She was reportedly so nervous that she remained on the deck of the ship the entire cruise. Arriving undetected, the wee Scottish girl made her way to the appointed drop point. Her loyalty to the Countess was unwavering, and so a week before the rebellion, Margaret made her way to the Countess's home where she stayed until the Irish Citizen Army deployed to St. Stephen's Green.

During the Easter Rising, she served as a dispatch courier, scout, and sniper. While at her post with Countess Markievicz, she wore an ICA uniform commissioned by the Countess herself. When she was called to deliver a message, she would change into a gray dress and bicycle across Dublin to deliver it. As she covertly bicycled along the streets, she was collecting intelligence for her comrades. She proudly darted across enemy fire until her luck failed. In an excerpt from her autobiography *Doing My Bit for Ireland*, she described her injuries and the ensuing surrender:

> They laid me on a large table and cut away the coat of my fine, new uniform. I cried over that. Then they found I had been shot in three places, my right side under the arm, my right arm, and in the back on my right side. Had I not turned as I went through that shop-door to call to the others, I would have got all three bullets in my back and lungs and surely been done for.
>
> They had to probe several times to get the bullets, and all the while Madam [Countess Markievicz] held my hand. But the probing did not hurt as much as she expected it would. My disappointment at not being able to bomb the Hotel Shelbourne was what made me unhappy. They wanted to send me to the hospital across the Green, but I absolutely refused to go. So the men brought in a cot, and the first-aid girls bandaged me, as there was no getting a doctor that night. What really did distress me was my cough and the pain in my chest. When I tried to keep from coughing, I made a queer noise in my throat and noticed everyone around me look frightened . . .
>
> . . . Soon after I was brought in, the Countess and Councillor Partridge disappeared. When she returned to me, she said very quietly:
>
> "You are avenged, my dear."[31]

The Countess was referring to two soldiers who had tried to interfere with the ICA's collection of the body of 18-year-old Fred Ryan. The Countess shot and killed the two soldiers on the spot. Shortly thereafter, with the surrender imminent, Margaret was released to be sent to the hospital as a condition of surrender. Before she left, the Countess slipped a copy of her personal will into Margaret's coat with the instructions to pass it onto her family.

Declared unfit for imprisonment, Margaret Skinnider was released from custody and mistakenly received a travel permit to go to Scotland. She briefly returned to Ireland in August 1916 after the executions had taken place. In 1917, she fled to the United States to avoid internment. She returned to Ireland during the War for Independence, and during the Civil

War, she served as the Paymaster General for the Irish Republican Army (IRA). For the rest of Margaret's life, she was a committed Republican volunteer. She died in 1971.

Winifred (Winnie) Carney

On April 29, 1916, Winnie Carney tended to her close friend James Connolly as he lay injured on a stretcher in the General Post Office (GPO). Refusing his requests to flee, she continued to type up his dispatches for the couriers to deliver. She was armed with her typewriter, a revolver, and a deep commitment to Connolly's ideologies.

Maria Winifred Carney was born in Bangor, County Down, to a Catholic mother and a Protestant father. Early in her childhood, her father Alfred returned to London, and her mother was left to raise her six children by running a treats shop on the Falls Road in Belfast. Drawn to Irish nationalism through the Gaelic League, Winnie used her training as a typist to serve as a secretary for the movement. She was eager to create social change, so she also joined the suffrage movement and Irish Textile Workers' Union (ITWU). Through her work with the ITWU, she befriended James Connolly, who was then living in Belfast. Winnie began to assist him directly in his efforts by utilizing her fundraising and secretarial skills. In 1914, she joined Cumann na mBan.

Days before the Easter Rising, James Connolly sent for her via telegram to come to Dublin. There, she remained at Connolly's side, even after Commandant Patrick Pearse discharged people from the GPO in a retreat to a safe home on Moore Street. The evening of the surrender, Winnie lay on the grass outside the Rotunda with the other prisoners. James Connolly gave her his coat for the cold, but seeing Joseph Plunkett shiver, she draped it over Plunkett. She was held as a prisoner until December of that year. Her male comrades were not as fortunate.

Winnie Carney was a deeply committed socialist, and her radical positions often placed her left of her comrades. After the Easter Rising, she briefly entered politics. She unsuccessfully stood as a Sinn Féin candidate in the 1918 general elections and served as the Belfast delegate for Cumann na mBan. During the War for Independence, she provided a safe house in the North for men on the run. Winnie did not support the Treaty and was targeted by security forces in the North as a seditious element. She was arrested and served a couple of weeks in the Armagh Jail. In 1928, she married a Protestant unionist named George MacBride, a former member of the Ulster Volunteer Force. After years of work with the labor movements in the North, Winnie Carney died in 1943.

Linda Kearns

Linda Kearns was born in County Sligo in 1889. She was a brilliant student with a sharp attention to detail that made for an excellent nurse and a spy.[32] Linda received her nursing training in Belgium and traveled across France and Switzerland. She had planned on moving to France at the outbreak of World War I in 1914, but a chance meeting altered her future. Thomas MacDonagh, one of the seven signatories of the Easter Proclamation, convinced her to remain in Dublin and assist in the Easter Rising.

During the rebellion, she set up a Red Cross field hospital for the wounded. It operated until the British soldiers shut it down for treating the republicans. According to personal accounts, Kearns had female patients at her clinic. Undeterred by the threats and danger, Linda began to treat the rebels directly. Shut down by the British, she referred her patients to local hospitals and served as a dispatch courier for the remainder of the Rising. Her secretive nature allowed her to avoid capture after the Rising and to operate a safe house under the auspices of a Dublin nursing home. Kathleen Clarke was briefly a patient during this time. During the War for Independence, she became a spy for Michael Collins and transported personal communications and documents for him. The British authorities alleged that she was transporting more than documents when she was caught in 1920 with a large cache of weapons (a reported 10 rifles and 500 rounds of ammunition).[33] She was arrested in Sligo and sent to a series of prisons.

Her evolution from continental European nurse to gunrunner was smooth and frank. After a hunger strike won Linda a transfer to Mountjoy Prison, from which she escaped in 1921, she returned to clandestine activities as an "OTR" (on the run) with the IRA until the Treaty was passed by the Dáil. Though she was never a member of Sinn Féin, Linda Kearns's direct involvement with the IRA demonstrates the willingness of the Republican men to utilize female resources.

During the Civil War, she visited garrisons around Dublin treating the wounded. She provided medical treatment for Irish hero Cathal Brugha as he died. Her talents on the battlefield were matched by particularly keen oration skills. Shortly after the establishment of the Free State, Eamon de Valera sent her on a speaking tour across the United States. Raising significant sums of money for de Valera, she was then dispatched to Australia to do the same. She married an IRA veteran named Wilson MacWhinney in 1929 and had a daughter named Ann. Balancing family, politics, and nursing seemed to be effortless for Linda. She was a founding member of Fianna Fáil and remained an active member of the party executive and the nursing profession until her death in 1951.

The Gifford Sisters: Grace, Nellie, Sidney, Muriel, and Katie

The Gifford sisters demonstrate the extent that Irish nationalism captured the hearts of families during the revolutionary period in Irish history.[34] The family seemed unremarkable at first glance, but the Gifford sisters each embraced a radical vision. Their mother was Protestant, and their father was Catholic. The Gifford parents made a family agreement to raise the girls Protestant and their brothers Catholic, but the girls soon became interested in Countess Markievicz's activities. This was wholly disagreeable to their mother, but the girls' involvement only deepened. They were also keenly involved in the Abbey Theatre through Helena Molony and the suffragette movement through Hanna Sheehy-Skeffington.

Each Gifford sister found her own way to serve the goal of Irish independence. Katie, the eldest, was living in Wales at the time of the Rising and returned to Ireland after her husband died of the flu in 1918. Sidney was a journalist who served on the Sinn Féin Executive and was a regular contributor to *Bean na hÉireann* and *Sinn Féin*. Most of Sidney's writing was conducted under the pen name of John Brennan. Grace was a cartoon artist who was engaged to Joseph Plunkett, one of the signatories of the Easter Proclamation. They were married by candlelight in the prison chapel on the eve of his execution. Muriel also became a widow in May 1916 when her husband Tom MacDonagh, a signatory who had persuaded Linda Kearns to stay in Ireland, was executed. Nellie Gifford Donnelly was the lone Gifford sister directly participating in the Easter Rising.

Nellie had been a founding member of the Irish Citizen Army. Like her sisters, she had become politically active in the Irish Women's Franchise League and the Daughters of Ireland. The sisters participated in a school lunch program for city school kids that was organized by James Connolly and supported by Maud Gonne. Nellie's sister Grace was among those arrested with Helena Molony at the 1911 protest of the King's royal visit. In 1913, Nellie, who was particularly active in the labor movement, posed as Jim Larkin's niece to sneak him into the Imperial Hotel to deliver the speech that set off the Dublin lockout. Using her talents as a domestic economy teacher, she taught the ICA lessons in camp cooking that were used in the Easter Rising. Nellie was attached to the garrison at St. Stephen's Green with Countess Markievicz, and she turned the College of Surgeons into a mess camp for the rebels. She also assisted in the distribution of food stock to the outposts. She was captured upon the surrender and served in the same cell with Winnie Carney in Kilmainhaim Jail.

With both Muriel and Grace widowed by early May, the sisters rallied around them. Muriel later drowned in 1917, leaving two small children behind. That same year, Grace served on the Sinn Féin Executive. Grace turned to her art, which she had studied at the Dublin Metropolitan School of Art with Willie Pearse, the commandant's younger brother. In 1919, she published a book of political cartoons titled *To Hold as Twere*. Of the sisters, Grace was quite vocal concerning her displeasure over the Treaty. In a March 1922 editorial she wrote:

> That is the point—the price to be paid. Ireland must pause and think before she pays it. The woman, who in desperate circumstances, accepts comfortable conditions at the price of her honour, has many good material arguments to back up her decision. Having more money, she can then assist others in their distress, give employment, perhaps, and get, for the first time, "the right to live her own life."[35]

The sisters' political involvement did not end during the Civil War. Both Grace and Katie were jailed for seditious activities in 1923, though it was thought that Katie had been initially mistaken for Grace. Later, both Katie and Sidney became regular contributors to 2RN as radio journalists, until Katie was fired for her politics. The sisters continued their political involvement throughout the rest of their lives and collectively serve as an example of the impact of Countess Markievicz on young women in Ireland.

Julia Grenan

Julia Grenan was a school friend of Elizabeth O'Farrell's who joined the Daughters of Ireland in 1906 around the age of 16. She quickly joined Cumann na mBan as well. She was a self-sufficient woman who supported herself working in a Dublin dress shop. In the weeks before the Easter Rising, Julia served as a courier bringing mobilization dispatches to Dundalk. On the eve of the rebellion, the Countess summoned them to Liberty Hall where she presented both Grenan and O'Farrell to James Connolly as prized, trustworthy couriers. Connolly asked Julia and Elizabeth to assemble with the Irish Citizen Army at the GPO garrison during the Easter Rising. The women delivered messages across the city from GPO headquarters and were responsible for bringing the sole copy of *War News* to the printers.

Julia carried several important messages that week. Among them was an order to blow up the Linen Hall Barracks and a personal message from Commandant Pearse to the British concerning the Red Cross stations. She showed no fear, and Connolly was quite impressed with her bravery. Julia and Elizabeth also purchased food for the battalion at the College of Surgeons with money provided to them by James Connolly. As Julia navigated the streets of Dublin, she was concealed by her gender and lack of concern for danger. She passed in and out of battalions without notice, even transporting munitions concealed in her undergarments. She was warmly greeted by the second lieutenant Countess Markievicz and the other women of the Second Battalion stationed at St. Stephen's Green.

Julia Grenan was among the last three women left in the General Post Office before the evacuation to Moore Lane. Julia, along with Winnie Carney and Elizabeth O'Farrell, tended to Connolly and the other wounded until the surrender. She served a short time in Kilmainhaim Jail before her release on May 9, 1916. Perhaps if her actions had been more documented, she would have been held longer. Throughout her life, Julia remained a committed Republican. Though she initially backed Eamon de Valera, she became a vocal opponent of the Fianna Fáil when it advocated the 1937 constitution. She lived with her friend Elizabeth O'Farrell until Elizabeth's death in 1957. Julia remained an active volunteer until her death in 1972.

Leslie Price

The confusion about the Easter Rising mobilization orders impacted the members of the Irish Volunteers and Cumann na mBan more than the Irish Citizen Army. Cumann na mBan activist Leslie Price recalled the disarray: "We had no knowledge of the imminence of the situation."[36] The morning of the rebellion, Leslie remained at her home awaiting orders. She had been a recent addition to the movement due to her age, but her family was well known in nationalist circles.

Leslie Price joined Cumann na mBan in 1915 after attending O'Donovan Rossa's funeral. She was from a strong nationalist family and had studied to be a teacher at the Dominican Training College in Belfast. Leslie's mother may have influenced her daughter's politics early on, as Mrs. Price was a Parnellite and member of Sinn Féin. As a child, she had participated in Maud Gonne's Patriotic Children's Treat in protest of King Edward's visit to Phoenix Park. Leslie was also a young member of the Gaelic League. The political socialization must have affected her brothers as well; they joined the Irish Volunteers in 1913 and served during Easter Week.

Leslie wore a number of hats during the Easter Rising, but she primarily served as a courier, delivering ammunition and messages to the various battalions. She was initially attached to Edward Daly's unit bound for the Four Courts, but she grew impatient waiting for final mobilization orders. By midday, she walked into the General Post Office and asked to help. She remained as a dispatch courier for the battalion. As part of her duties, she funneled in more ammunition for the Volunteers every evening and even made tea for the men. She assisted the wounded in the field by fetching Father Flanagan for a dying Volunteer in the GPO and delivering the injured to Jervis Street hospital just before the surrender.

After the Rising, Leslie was an active volunteer with the prisoners and was quickly elevated to the Cumann na mBan Executive. In 1917, the constant security surveillance forced her to give up her teaching position. Traveling across Ireland, she became an active recruiter for Cumann na mBan. Her friendship with Michael Collins brought her into the fold of the IRA Flying Columns during the War for Independence. She later married Tom Barry, head of the Cork column, and adopted the Irish version of her name—Leslie Bean de Barra.

Her life with Tom was challenging. He was often on the run from the authorities, and she was the subject of constant surveillance. As the former director of organization for Cumann na mBan, she was a person of interest for the British authorities. As a wife, she endured many years with her husband in prison for IRA activities. This gave her a special link to the plight of the Republican prisoners' families, which, interestingly, she understood from her post-Rising fundraising support for the Prisoners' Dependents' Fund. Tom Barry was a leading figure in the IRA. During the War for Independence, his IRA column killed almost an entire "Auxies" platoon in Kilmichael, County Cork. With her husband in jail or on the run, Leslie filled her time with humanitarian causes, including orphan and antipoverty campaigns in the third world. She died in 1984, after a long battle with stroke-induced paralysis.

Áine Ceannt

Áine Ceannt was not present at the Easter Rising, though her husband assisted in the planning and implementation of it. She was at home with a young (10-year-old) child that week, peering out of her home as Grace Plunkett and Muriel MacDonagh had been. She was, like Grace and Muriel, thrust onto the world stage in May 1916 and publicly assumed the role for which her husband had died.

Áine Ceannt was born Fanny O'Brennan in 1880 in Dublin. She joined the Gaelic League at its inception and adopted a Gaelic name, Áine. She married fellow Gaelic Leaguer Éamonn Ceannt in 1905. Áine came from a strong Fenian family, and her siblings were also involved in the movement. Both Áine and her sister Lily joined Cumann na mBan in 1914, and Lily, who lived with the Ceannts, was arrested for taking part in the Rising.

On the evening before the Rising, Áine and Lily attended an evening Easter mass. When the sisters returned home, they found bicycles littering the street outside their home. The Dublin Brigade that Áine's husband Éamonn was in charge of was in a state of confusion. They spent the evening preparing the Volunteers for their deployment to South Dublin.

During the Rising, Áine's sister Lily joined Éamonn Ceannt's Fourth Battalion at Marrowbone Lane. The ladies busied themselves by assembling grenades out of milk tins. Of the 70 odd members under Ceannt's command, 26 were women. Later that week, Lily was captured and imprisoned. Shortly after the surrender, Áine's husband Éamonn was executed.

Áine, however, had not assumed an active role in the Rising. It was not uncommon since the principal organizers were prepared to die during the fighting. To involve the spouses would have orphaned many children. Like most of the Easter Rising widows, she became involved with Cumann na mBan in 1917. From 1917 to 1925, she served as the vice president while raising her son Ronan. During 1917, Áine went to Tralee to participate in an undertaking by Cumann na mBan to raise recruitment and solidify a woman's voice in the revolution. She also served on Sinn Féin's standing committee during this time, and her house became a safe house during the War for Independence. With no training other than Sinn Féin support and good sense, she served as a judge in the Republican courts for Clare. In the 1930s and 1940s, the O'Brennan sisters served in the White Cross. Áine herself served as the White Cross's chief administrator for a number of years. She died in 1954.

The First Dáil and the War for Independence

In the chaotic aftermath of the Easter Rising, public support for Sinn Féin rose. Although the rebellion had been enacted by the more militant elements of the nationalist movement, Sinn Féin became the political beneficiary. During the Easter Rising, the members of the Irish Citizen Army and the Irish Volunteers had adopted the name of the Irish Republican Army (IRA), established in the Easter Proclamation by the seven signatories. Among the new IRA leadership was General Michael Collins.

In 1917, Sinn Féin reorganized under a new executive. Building on his electoral success in the local East Clare elections in the spring of 1917, Eamon de Valera made a bold move to assert a more Republican tone to Sinn Féin. A republic by definition is a form of government that does not have a monarch. The Sinn Féin Executive seemed ready to abandon Griffith's dual monarchy proposal in favor of a republic. The platform revision followed in the ideological footsteps of the Proclamation signatories who had declared an Irish Republic on April 24, 1916. At the Ard Fheis conference in the fall of 1917, de Valera made another bold move. He was unanimously selected to replace Arthur Griffith as the president of Sinn Féin. De Valera quickly set about involving the Republican women who surrounded him. A new party constitution was written, and two women were selected to be Sinn Féin candidates in the upcoming election for Westminster Parliament.

The 1918 Westminster elections coincided with the increasing number of Irish men being conscripted into the British Army. Sinn Féin seized on the moment. Combining support for Irish neutrality in the world war, anti-conscription fears, and outrage over the 1916 executions, Sinn Féin hoped to reap a solid electoral benefit. Keenly aware of the oratory and fundraising skills that the women possessed, Eamon de Valera deployed several women to the United States to gather support for Irish nationalism. Later, in June 1919, as the Anglo-Irish tensions heated, he would join them.

Thus, in the fall of 1918, Sinn Féin organized a slate of candidates. The party fielded two female candidates to the Westminster Parliament. Sinn Féin put forward Countess Markievicz in Dublin and Winnie Carney in Belfast. Although Winnie Carney solicited a poor electoral turnout, Countess Markievicz won. She became the first female member of Westminster Parliament. Their male comrades did quite well. Sinn Féin won 73 of the 105 Irish seats.

According to the Sinn Féin platform of abstention, the party's members of Parliament (MPs) did not take their seats. Instead, they formed an illegal legislative assembly in Dublin called Dáil Éireann. The 1919 Dáil is referred to as the Revolutionary Dáil or First Dáil. Countess Markievicz was the only woman of this Dáil. She was assigned the portfolio of minister of labor. Other prominent members included Eamon de Valera, Michael Collins, Arthur Griffith, Terence MacSwiney, W. T. Cosgrave, and Austin Stack. Approximately 40 of the members of the Revolutionary Dáil were unable to attend session since they were on the run from the British government or in prison. It was a product of the political situation; in the 1918 election, there had only been one Sinn Féin candidate who had never been in prison.

With a legislative council in place and the militant elements of the Irish Republican Army strategically placed in the Sinn Féin Executive, the War for Independence commenced in January 1919. That June, having been sprung that spring from jail by Michael Collins, Eamon de Valera departed for the United States. This left Collins in charge of the war. The Royal Irish Constabulary (RIC) targeted Sinn Féin activists and supporters, while Collins implemented an elaborate network of IRA flying columns across Ireland. Cumann na mBan, under the direction of ladies like Áine Ceannt, Jennie Wyse-Power, and Lily O'Brennan, supported the war by developing a network of safe houses, gathering intelligence, procuring weapons, and providing combat training. The ladies were not content to be handmaidens to the male soldiers. Sinn Féin was the voice of a moderate nationalist people, and the women of Cumann na mBan were prepared to take military action alongside their male comrades in order to achieve an Irish republic.

Developing politically during the War for Independence was difficult, and often the issues that nationalist women were fighting for fell into the background. There were, however, two developments that allowed for women to become more politically involved. First, Sinn Féin solicited a slate of women for local elections in early 1920. However, the recruitment of candidates proved to be less than feminists were hoping for and the overture may have been making its practical intent. Fewer of the women were known to the authorities at the time, making it easier for them to run for local office and operate politically. Secondly, in February 1919, the Sinn Féin Executive recommended to Dáil Éireann that a system of Republican courts be established to create an Irish system of justice for Irish people, in place of the English system. The recommendation was supported by the Dáil, and the courts were organized in early 1920. Many of the arbitrators and judges of these courts were women, including Áine Ceannt, Hanna Sheehy-Skeffington, Terence MacSwiney's sister Mary, and Margaret Buckley. Serving as Sinn Féin's party secretary in 1919, Hanna Sheehy-Skeffington was still concerned about one thing—universal suffrage.

The position of women in the 1917 Sinn Féin Executive was real, but their power may not have been. Although Kathleen Clarke, Dr. Kathleen Lynn, Countess Markievicz, and Grace Gifford Plunkett had been elected to the National Executive, the issue of universal suffrage and gender equality was not foremost on the party's agenda. When Hanna Sheehy-Skeffington arrived back in Ireland, she was concerned with what she saw. Immediately detained upon her arrival to Dublin, Hanna joined the Countess, Maud Gonne, and Kathleen Clarke at Holloway jail. The three had been imprisoned on grounds of the "German Plot." Their reacquaintance allowed the women to talk about Hanna's experiences in America and the status of Irish nationalism since 1916. Hanna began a hunger strike and was quickly released. Her reception was carefully organized. She was greeted by Winnie Carney who came down from Belfast for the IWFL annual conference that September and was warmly received by Margaret Pearse.

As a member of the Sinn Féin Executive, Hanna attempted to bring women's rights to the national political debate. Suffrage was a ripe issue in 1918, as the Representation of the People Act had been passed that February. It granted all British and Irish women over 30 the right to vote. The upcoming election in December 1918 would be a whole new opportunity for Hanna, but her excitement was soon dampened by the announcement of the Sinn Féin slate. Though two of her colleagues would appear as candidates, Hanna Sheehy-Skeffington was not selected. Though many speculated that Hanna's feminism was too radical for Sinn Féin, Irish historian Margaret Ward recounts a letter from the Countess to her sister Eva Gore-Booth. To address her sister's concern that Hanna did not appear on the

Sinn Féin ballot, she replied: "Hanna S. could have been an M.P. *if she had wanted to.* A seat was offered her. She is not altogether an S.F. I think, and I *know* prefers to work from the Women's platform."[37] Perhaps her work was more suited for social action rather than electoral politics. In truth, Hanna was very skeptical of the formation of the First Dáil Éireann, and her public criticism may have pushed more reforms. In 1919, when Sinn Féin's organizing secretary went to the United States to prepare the way for Eamon de Valera's trip, Hanna assumed his position. She was now in a position to correct the disorganization that she saw during the 1918 election campaign and to ensure more female candidates for the Second Dáil.

As the decade came to a close, the War for Independence was in full swing. Collins's IRA, supported by Cumann na mBan, was on the attack, and the Royal Irish Constabulary was increasingly unable to match the strategic threat. The British government, seeing the tide close on World War I, could now prioritize a security concern in Ireland. Internally, the Republicans were facing challenges too. By the close of 1920, IRA armament and money were dwindling. De Valera was back in prison, as was Arthur Griffith. In turn, the nationalist women were demanding more involvement in Sinn Féin and the prioritization of women's issues. The 1920s would be a new military and political game altogether.

CONCLUSIONS

Revolution is the process of bringing about complete social, economic, and political change. In each of these women's lives, they were revolutionaries. Born into a society that strictly defined what a woman could and could not do, the Irish nationalists of the early 20th century were fighting the conventions of their time. In the climate of stifling reality, these ladies felt called to change the status quo. Battling the demands of family and social responsibilities, Republican women struggled to not just maintain their dreams of a united Ireland but to redefine the society in which they lived.

At the dawn of a century, Irish nationalist women became cultural advocates, domestic nationalists, political party founders, revolutionary activists, suffragettes, and social reformers. Each woman profiled in this chapter embraced her role or roles. Many of them sacrificed personally. They lost loved ones and friends to death or disapproval. They risked death, imprisonment, and economic livelihood to pursue nationalist ambitions. They sought to create an Ireland that was self-sufficient and that afforded them the opportunity to be self-sufficient.

In the call to duty at the Easter Rising, nationalist women became Republicans. They armed themselves with guns, words, and hope to achieve an independent government without a monarch. The Irish Republic was declared in the Easter Proclamation. Although their immediate aims were not realized in 1916, their actions would indeed bring about a revolution.

The Irish nationalist woman became a valuable tool of revolution. The cultural revolution of Gaelic revivalism allowed female actresses, poets, and writers to embrace Irish language. They brought stories of Irish heroes to the stage and to literary circles. In the home, nationalist women taught Irish language and culture to their families. As teachers, the women were able to spark the interest of Irish children. By founding the Daughters of Ireland and the Fianna Eireann, the women cultivated young Ireland into revolutionary action. They coordinated protests and held training sessions in marksmanship. By empowering the youth with a nationalist vision of society, the women became agents of a cultural revolution. The celebration of Irish literature, language, art, and sport promoted pride in Irish identity, but it also facilitated the development of nationalist networks with a specific political agenda.

After reading the nationalist literature of the Irish Renaissance, many women took action themselves. Picking up the mighty pen, the women wrote articles for nationalist newspapers and journals. Using skills acquired as secretaries, store workers, and assistants, nationalist women became the organizational mainstay of revolutionary Ireland. They served as bookkeepers, fundraisers, personal assistants, and couriers. Their gender often allowed them to circumvent the security forces undetected. In other cases, their position in society cleverly veiled their revolutionary intentions. Their gender often enabled the women to promote defiance openly, since women were not viewed as influential agents of change.

The misdiagnosis of engendered impotence permitted nationalist women to serve in many subversive capacities. The nationalist women were political revolutionaries that assisted in the armament for their cause. They offered safe houses for the IRB and Irish Volunteers. They collected intelligence as spies for the movement. They held training sessions for the Easter Rising and maintained membership records. They ran guns and ammunitions across Ireland. Nationalist women founded Cumann na mBan as an auxiliary force for the Irish Volunteers and began to join the Irish Citizen Army. As members of armed militias, the women trained in marksmanship and operational support. The women were soldiers and commanders as well as nurses, cooks, and ammunition support. They assumed roles based on their skills not their gender.

Though revolution is often achieved through force, true revolution must embody political ideas of change. As ideological revolutionaries, nationalist women aided in the development of Arthur Griffith's political proposals. Griffith's concept of Irish independence was based on political equality and self-sufficiency. These ideas were appealing to many women who were not content with the status quo. For many revolutionary women, equality also meant universal suffrage. The redefinition of a citizen and a citizen's rights was clearly a revolutionary goal. When the initial political vision of Sinn Féin was reshaped in 1917, many women joined the movement to build out the party infrastructure, coordinate speaking tours across the world, and promote the cause of Irish independence wholeheartedly.

Many nationalist women were initially called to duty in the Irish Citizen Army. Women seemed to join James Connolly's Irish Citizen Army for two reasons. First, it allowed women to be full members. The prospect of equal standing in an organization was, at the time, quite new, and some of the more radical elements of nationalist women were attracted to Connolly's socialism. Secondly, Connolly's commitment to eradicating the oppression of people was very desirable for women. Many of them worked in factories or shops without decent working conditions or sufficient pay. Others had been mobilized by the Dublin workers' lockout in 1913. The disequilibrium of capitalist power held by managers over laborers had a direct impact on the struggling working class. The women were quick to heed the call for social and economic change, and through Connolly's army, they saw a way to accomplish that goal.

In April 1916, the forces of economic, social, and political revolution came together in a disorganized display of insurrection. In this moment, Irish revolutionary women shaped history. In three of the four battalions mobilized that day, women took up guns, gauze, and dispatches. Their bravery on the front lines of battle evidenced the women's capabilities. Although there was only one female injured, several of the female rebels were imprisoned. Other women remained undetected and evaded capture. There was a significant public outcry against the executions of male leaders of the Easter Rising. The array of sympathies for the widows and outrage over the martyrs ignited support for Sinn Féin in 1918 and consolidated resistance for the War for Independence in January 1919. Revolutionary Ireland reflected the goals and efforts of the nationalist women who devoted their lives to cultural, social, economic, and political change.

Chapter 2

CONSTRUCTION OF A NEW IRISH HOME, 1920s–1930s

It could be that when we have won and are putting our Republican house in order, Mrs Buckley and those who like her have seen the degrading and degraded conditions of those . . . will be given the task of devising a more humane and Christian method of dealing with them . . . we are not fighting for a Republic which will continue or tolerate such a system.

—Mary MacSwiney[1]

CHAPTER OVERVIEW

Walking by the General Post Office in Dublin, one cannot help but see the Easter Proclamation through the glass window and the chunks torn from the mountain granite Ionic columns by bullets. Though its facade shares the stories of many Republican martyrs and veterans, tragic and inspiring as they were, it is what the GPO symbolizes that can be of utmost inspiration: the birth of a new Irish home. Built on the foundation of Republicans before them, such as 18th-century nationalist Daniel O'Connell for which the GPO street was renamed in 1924, the women and men of the Easter Rising had inspired a nation to action. The birth of the modern Irish nation promulgated the War of Independence, often recorded in history as the Anglo-Irish War, in an anticolonial revolution.

Like many families, the Irish nation bickered amongst itself, sibling against sibling, in the struggle to establish the Irish state. The bitter division resulting from suspicions, jealousies, and betrayals tore chunks from the columns supporting the establishment of an Irish nation-state, scars that are still visible today. But the foundation of the Irish home, the desire for a republican government without a British monarch, was unshaken. As with many epic moments in history, shared goals often come from divergent paths, and Irish history is no different. What constituted a Republican home differed depending on who the architect was.

The 1920s opened with solid momentum against British imperialism, was sprinkled with moments of victory, and then disintegrated into civil war and partition. At the conclusion of the 1920s, Unionism had swallowed the Six Counties, and the Free State was enveloped by disagreement. In the midst of the peaks and valleys of the development of an Irish Republic, the debate of universal suffrage—specifically that of Irish women—pulled latent discussions about gender equality from the Easter Proclamation onto the national platforms of Sinn Féin and Fianna Fáil. The bitter division over the Treaty transcended gender, religion, and citizenship rights, and this delayed discussions of female suffrage, once again, in favor of the national question. Every Republican had a part to play in the establishment of a new Irish home, though Irish Republican women intended to fulfill the metaphorical duties of architect, general contractor, and laborer while simultaneously tending to the chores of the cultural nation.

Serving as founders of activist organizations and leaders within Sinn Féin, Republican women supported the foundation of the Irish political consciousness by taking on the roles of revolutionary, activist, political prisoner, party leader, and feminist. Throughout the 1920s and 1930s, Sinn Féin was confronted with serious challenges concerning Irish independence; in the end, many of the Republican women left Sinn Féin, including Jennie Wyse-Power, Countess Markievicz, and Kathleen Clarke. But five of the women who remained—Mary MacSwiney,[2] Margaret Buckley, Máire Comerford, Lily O'Brennan, and Kate O'Callaghan—shaped the course of Sinn Féin history. These women were among the most committed Republicans, and often times, they found their "home" in Sinn Féin.

Chapter Organization

The 1920s and 1930s were a turbulent time in Irish history. The War for Independence led to a disastrous civil war. The disagreement over the 1921 Treaty would change Ireland forever. Having just lost the sons of the rebellion, Ireland lost some of her most promising leaders. The turmoil troubled the movement for a free Ireland, and Sinn Féin struggled to remain intact with the departures of the Fianna Fáil founders, the partition of the North, and the intermittent roundups of its members. Table 2.1 identifies the key dates during this time period. The complex nature of the Irish Free State governance is also diagramed in Figure 2.1.

Table 2.1
Key Dates in Irish History 1920–1940

The Anglo-Irish War 1919–1921

The Irish rebels challenge English authority in Ireland in the War for Independence.

The Anglo-Irish Agreement 1921

The treaty partitioned Ireland into North/South and created the Irish Free State.

Irish Civil War 1922–1923

The civil conflict divided the new Irish Free State into the Treatyites (who supported the Anglo-Irish Agreement of 1921) and the Anti-Treatyites (who did not).

Fianna Fáil 1926

Éamon de Valera founded the "Soldiers of Destiny" party.

Constitution 1937

The country of Ireland establishes a controversial constitution.

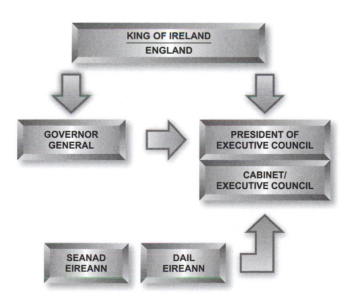

Figure 2.1. Irish Free State Government Executive Power

In the midst of it all stood several legendary women—Mary Mac-Swiney, Margaret Buckley, Máire Comerford, Lily O'Brennan, and Kitty O'Callaghan. This is a "twilight" period in Republican history, with little written on the small group that remained in Sinn Féin. History has paid Ms. MacSwiney a partial due. Several biographies of her courage exist. But there is no definitive work on Mrs. Buckley, the sole female president of Sinn Féin to date, or her contemporaries.

With the creation of the Irish Free State came the creation of a new constitution. The challenge of dominion status forced many compromises and brought up many issues, including the status of women in the new society. Nearing the conclusion of the 1930s, a woman—Margaret Buckley—was at the helm of a fledgling Sinn Féin as it struggled to find its way out of the Irish Free State and into a 32-county Irish Republic.

HISTORICAL OVERVIEW

- The Anglo-Irish War 1919–1921
- The Anglo-Irish Agreement 1921
- Irish Civil War 1922–1923
- Post–Civil War Politics

The Anglo-Irish War 1919–1921

As Eamon de Valera toured the United States drumming up support for an Irish Republic, his comrades in the IRA and Cumann na mBan had been leading the fight against the Black and Tans. An elite British military deployed to Ireland in early 1920, the Black and Tans' operational mission was to eradicate the IRA. The IRA had been targeting the Royal Irish Constabulary (RIC) in assassination plots across the counties, with much success. The threat lingered in the air for any agent of the British government in Ireland. Thus, a highly specialized British unit, comprised of men with questionable tactical efforts, arrived to root out the Republican leadership and stifle rank and file recruitment. Facing rising unemployment and carrying residual battlefield experiences from World War I, many of the former British soldiers were eager to stamp out yet another threat to the British Empire. Lacking the organization of a traditional military unit, the Black and Tan activities commenced around June 1920. They terrorized the Irish community, offering indiscriminate application of their tactics to civilians. Their activities did succeed, but not in accomplishing their primary mission; rather, the draconian terror of the Black and Tans fostered resurgence in the support for the IRA. In a classic miscalculation of the Irish public will, the Black and the Tans' oppressive manipulations manifested Irish solidarity against them.

The most egregious display of this misapplication of objectives came in November 1920 when the Black and Tans infiltrated a football match in Croke Park in Dublin. Twelve civilians were killed, including one of the football players. Outraged, the IRA targeted 18 members of the Auxiliaries ("Auxies"), a unit of the Black and Tans, in Kilmichael, County Cork. The IRA tactics, under the command of Michael Collins, included attacking the British forces with guerrilla tactics in "flying columns," the nickname by which they came to be known. The retaliation was swift as the Auxies responded by burning the city of Cork.

Cork was a rebel city. Many of the most solidly Republican families in Ireland called Cork home. The values of resistance served both Mary Mac-Swiney and Margaret Buckley for a lifetime. To burn Cork was a miscalculation by the Auxies; for it did not quell the resistance . . . it fueled it.

The Anglo-Irish Agreement 1921

On July 11, 1921, a truce was signed between the Irish revolutionaries and the British government. The negotiations that ensued are the source of much debate and political discourse in Irish history. But, absent the politics of what did or did not occur in London that fall, there were concrete consequences. IRA commander Michael Collins and Sinn Féin president Arthur Griffith had been the principal negotiators of the agreement. When they returned in December 1921 with the Anglo-Irish Treaty authorized by British prime minister David Lloyd George, the Treaty spawned first a national debate and then a civil war. The Treaty had three controversial components, discussed in Table 2.2.

The subsequent Constitution of the Irish Free State Act created a convoluted set of political institutions under the framework of a constitutional monarchy in 26-county Ireland. The Treaty additionally called for the partition of the northern Six Counties, which would remain a part of the United Kingdom of Great Britain and Northern Ireland. The 26-county Irish government would be called the Irish Free State.

The Free State government consisted of a bicameral Oireachtas (Irish Parliament) with an Irish Dáil Éireann and Seanad Éireann. Executive power was vested in the king of Ireland, who would—by default arrangement of title—be the king of England.

The president of the Executive Council (the Cabinet) would serve as head of government for Ireland. The president of the Executive Council was nominated by Dáil Éireann (lower house of Irish Parliament and only elected chamber), under the appointment of the governor-general who himself served at the discretion of the king of Ireland, and served with the confidence of the Dáil. Presidential powers were limited by the collective

Table 2.2
Elements of the Anglo-Irish Treaty of 1921

1. The Irish Free State would hold dominion status, not Republic independence. This amounted to more autonomy than the Irish Home Rule movement had striven for, but less than the 1916 Proclamation had declared. The Crown was represented in the Free State by a governor-general who would be appointed by the king of England but accepted on the consent of the Irish government.
2. The Free State would only consist of the southern 26 counties. The northern 6 counties could remain a formalized part of the United Kingdom. For Republicans, this partition is still unresolved close to a century later.
3. An oath of allegiance to the Irish Free State with a fidelity clause to the king of England in Ireland. The fidelity clause outraged Republicans across Ireland who felt that the abolishment of the monarchy over Ireland was a central element for which they had fought.

approval of the Executive Council, and the office was interpreted to hold minimal executive authority.

Only two men served as the president of the Executive Council until the demise of the office: William (W. T.) Cosgrave (1922–1932) and Eamon de Valera (1932–1937). In 1936, Amendment 27 eliminated the position of governor-general and transferred those powers to the president of the Executive Council. In December 1937, the presidency itself was reconstituted when the 1937 constitution redefined executive powers under the office of the newly created Taoiseach (Prime Minister).

Meanwhile, back in 1921, the Republican women and men who had banded together in 1916 through the ICA, the Volunteers, Cumann na mBan, Sinn Féin, and the IRB were split through and through. The coalition for independence dissolved under the weight of the Treaty. Those who opposed the Treaty, including all of the female TDs (Countess Markievicz, Mary MacSwiney, Kathleen Clarke, Ada English, Margaret Pearse, and Kate O'Callaghan) alongside Eamon de Valera, became known as the Anti-Treatyites. Those who supported it, led by Arthur Griffith and Michael Collins, became known as Treatyites. The Treaty was then presented on behalf of the Irish public to the Revolutionary Dáil for a vote in January 1922. With the tally of 64 in favor and 57 against, the Treaty was accepted, thereby creating the Free State. The Anti-Treatyites walked out of the Dublin Mansion House in disgust.

Irish Civil War 1922–1923

In 1922, the island of Ireland had been literally torn in two by the provisions of the Anglo-Irish Treaty—two geographic territories (north and south of the partition border) and two dominant sentiments on the Treaty. The Irish Civil War broke out in April 1922 and lasted until May 1923. Acting as the president of the Free State, Arthur Griffith set about institutionalizing the new provisions of governance while Michael Collins assumed command of the Irish National Army. Their tenures in office would be brief, however, as the pace of the war escalated and the violence claimed many Irish patriots. One of earliest tragedies was the loss of Cathal Brugha at the outbreak of the Civil War on O'Connell Street in Dublin. Brugha refused to surrender to the Free State forces that July day in 1922 and was shot dead. Brugha died refusing to acknowledge the Treaty that he had refused to negotiate in 1920. By the end of 1922, both Griffith and Collins themselves were dead, and civil war ravaged the Irish countryside.

During the Irish Civil War, the Anti-Treatyites used the IRA cover and were known as the Irregulars in many areas. Meanwhile, the former IRA Regulars, the Pro-Treatyite component, had transitioned into the National Army under Michael Collins's command. Although history is somewhat cloudy concerning the circumstances of several significant deaths in the Civil War, it is perfectly clear that some of Ireland's greatest heroes were lost. Among them was the August 22, 1922, death of Michael Collins outside Bandon, County Cork, and 10 days before him, Arthur Griffith lost his life to a sudden hemorrhage. Many speculate that the Irregulars were behind Collins's assassination and that the stress of the November/December 1921 negotiations killed Griffith.

The Civil War was not contained to the Free State; in fact, many of the Irregulars initiated activities in the northern counties. Sectarian acts on Catholics accused of supporting the Irregulars led to bloodshed across the Six Counties. The Special Powers Act of 1922 and the Offences against the State Act of 1924 reinforced an increasing level of intimidation for Catholics and Nationalists in particular. The creation of the B Specials in 1920, an elite police force, trained in counterinsurgency methods, served as a Unionist-led effort to eradicate the IRA from the border. The tactics of the B Specials represented the Unionist resistance to the perceived threat of Republicanism. During 50 years of service, the B Specials battled the border infiltrations and perpetrated heinous activities in the name of this "mission." In 1970, they were disbanded upon the recommendation of the Hunt Report and reconstituted as the Royal Ulster Constabulary (RUC) police.

With the B Specials in the North and the National Army in the South, security forces across Ireland were hunting Sinn Féin and IRA Irregulars members. Sweeping rounds of internment captured many of the key leaders, while still others were simply killed. The impact was devastating to the political structure of Sinn Féin and to the infrastructure of the IRA.

Past (Provisional and Republican) Sinn Féin president Ruairí Ó Brádaigh was born in 1932 into a strong Republican family. His father, Matt Brady, was an IRA man who had been active in the War for Independence, and his mother May (Caffrey) was a Cumman na mBan affiliate. He lived among the Republican corps in his early childhood, and he recalls from them the impact of the security sweeps. Today, he is a fixture at Republican funerals, protests, and the small party headquarters on Parnell Street in Dublin. As he talks about the dark times for Republicans in the 1920s, he says that it

Ruairí Ó Brádaigh, past president of Sinn Féin. (Courtesy Kelly Morris)

was not that women were promoted in the movement during this time but that they ascended to a natural level of leadership on their merits as committed Republicans. "To say that women were the same as men just doesn't say it. It didn't arise, so there were no particular arrangements, you see, they were automatically in their place."[3] Thus, as internment of the men increased, the movement relied heavily on the women; Cumman na mBan asserted themselves and "to a certain extent, the genie had been let out of the bottle."[4]

Post–Civil War Politics

The politics that had once unified Irish Republicans, regardless of gender, turned divisive with the Civil War. The rubble of the Free State politics was a vacuum of political direction, until Eamon de Valera led a contingency of followers into a new era of Free State politics. The resulting factionalization and marginalization of hard-line Republicans was a catalyst for the debate of a new society, one in which the Irregulars became somewhat regular and the Irreconcilables became outlaws.

The Fianna Fáil Ireland

A Free State Ireland opened some doors for women, though not all; most of the women who left with Eamon de Valera had been developed as leaders with Sinn Féin and Cumman na mBan. De Valera was a force of history, and his charismatic appeal pulled many Revolutionary women into his Fianna Fáil fold.

Twenty-two women were elected to the Irish Dáil between 1918 and 1969; of those, 8 women had Sinn Féin experience. Of the 14 elected before 1950, 8 were first elected as Sinn Féin candidates: Countess Markievicz, Kathleen Clarke, Ada English, Mary MacSwiney, Katherine O'Callaghan, Margaret Pearse, Caitlin Brugha, and Kathleen Lynn.[5] When the *Irish Times* published the IRA's October 28, 1922, statement concerning the organization of its leadership going into the Civil War, female TDs Kitty O'Callaghan and Mary MacSwiney were listed as Eamon de Valera's Council of State.[6] Although many of the initial Sinn Féin women had remained together during the Civil War, 1926 would split them wide open. Though the Countess walked out with de Valera that fateful day, she, despite her election as a Fianna Fáil TD in the 1927 Dáil Éireann elections, would not take her seat, for she died shortly before the opening session. Many others left Sinn Féin in 1926; among the women in the first Fianna Fáil Executive were Linda Kearns, Margaret Pearse, Hanna Sheehy-Skeffington, and Kathleen Clarke.

Interestingly, despite the high profile of the women who left with Eamon de Valera, the women who remained in Sinn Féin advanced quickly to the front lines of Republican leadership. The number of women on the 1926 Sinn Féin Executive increased, with Mary MacSwiney leading the way. The provincial delegations included Margaret Buckley representing Dublin, Máire Comerford representing Leinster, and Kate O'Callaghan representing Munster.[7] Amidst the restructuring within Sinn Féin, the IRA decided to initiate its own political wing, with little success. The subsequent formation of Saor Éire in 1931 and the Republican Congress in 1933 further subdivided Republicans. The normalization of Irish politics would eventually result in the coercion of virulent Irreconcilables in the 1930s.

The 1930s were a decade of economic depression and political upheaval. Although the IRA and Cumann na mBan had briefly been normalized, it was clear that when Eamon de Valera became the president of the Executive Council in 1932, that militant Republicans needed to be wary of the consequences of their politics. By 1935, most of the IRA had dispersed into the countryside. Sporadic violence dotted the historical landscape until the de Valera government declared the IRA illegal again in 1936. Fianna Fáil wanted a new constitution, and considerable debate and revisions went forth into the 1937 constitution.

Margaret Buckley, the first and only elected female president of Sinn Féin, had no interest in the institutionalization of a Free State that her IWWU colleague Louie Bennett had called "most indefensible."[8] On the day that the constitution was rendered, she flew a black flag outside the Dublin Sinn Féin office. As historian Margaret Ward recounts in *Unmanageable Revolutionaries*, Buckley's message to the dedicated Sinn Féin followers was to stand aloof of the constitutional debate, as de Valera's constitution was not for a republic and did not embody principled equality.[9] The decision to not engage the constitutionalists was controversial within Sinn Féin, and, ultimately, the final version of the 1937 Irish Constitution reflected a sexist domesticity for women. The point that Fianna Fáil seemed to be departing from the gender equality embodied in the Easter Proclamation was not lost on Margaret Buckley's Sinn Féin, though the stated calculation to disengage from the process did not exaggerate the revelation.

With a new constitution inked for posterity, Taoiseach Eamon de Valera seemed to be unraveling many of the original terms of the Anglo-Irish Treaty of 1921. Involved in the principal negotiations in 1921 on behalf of the Lloyd George government, Prime Minister Neville Chamberlain was quite agitated at de Valera's accomplishments. In 1938, when Anglo-Irish negotiations commenced on the return of three key ports to Irish control, both the British prime minister and hard-line Irish Republicans seemed equally dissatisfied with the Fianna Fáil government. The IRA initiated a campaign targeting the British ports, which proved quite embarrassing for de Valera in the negotiations. In the wake of the turmoil, Dáil Éireann passed the Offences against the State Act in June 1939 and established the death penalty for such actions in the Treason Act of 1939. For Dáil Éireann, the negotiations seemed to be leading to an independent Ireland, and this necessitated, in the de Valera agenda, saving Ireland from the political embarrassment of principled Republicans, as many men and women discovered first hand in the Curragh camp outside Dublin in the early 1940s.

Feminism and Society

Universal suffrage and the rights of women were contemporary social-policy topics across the world at the turn of the 20th century. Written in 1792, Mary Wollstonecraft's *A Vindication on the Rights of Women* sparked a discourse on women's rights that had proven enlightening and controversial but perhaps not resulting in concrete gender policies. Prompting debate across Europe, the initial sense of feminism became closely affiliated with Irish republicanism quite early on. Attached to the radical left arm of republicanism, Irish feminists seemed to transcend organizational constriction; they simply sought out justice and equality through whatever parties advanced their principles. Though some possessed more social finesse than others, none of these women were meek by any stretch of the imagination. They roared against the patriarchal chains on Irish society; they raged against social injustices; and they refused to accept the status quo on any account.

Engaged and energized, Irish feminists in the 20th century were encouraged by advances in feminism in continental Europe. In 1906, the Grand Duchy of Finland had given women the right to vote and stand as candidates. The Soviet Union, Austria, Germany, and the United Kingdom followed suit in 1918. In the UK, this "universal" suffrage had been qualified by age (30 years old) and ownership (of property). In turn, though the principles of gender equality were enshrined in the Republican values of Easter 1916, their association with Irish insurrection prevented the acquisition of female suffrage until 1922. Since married women in Ireland could not hold property in their name, this further restricted the limited practice of female voting. Hanna Sheehy-Skeffington, a prominent feminist of her generation, called attention to the trap in which women found themselves: "If women in Ireland are not yet sufficiently educated politically to vote for women the blame rests largely with the various political machines that disregard them save as mere voting conveniences. Certain blame, too, of course, attaches to the women themselves, those smug ones especially, who declare that they have 'no interest in politics.'"[10] But there were at least some women interested in politics, and their stories are recounted below.

THE STORY OF INDIVIDUAL REPUBLICAN WOMEN IN THE 1920S AND 1930S

- Mary MacSwiney
- Margaret Goulding Buckley
- Máire Comerford
- Lily O'Brennan
- Katherine Murphy O'Callaghan

In the fall of 1920, an Irish patriot named Terence MacSwiney was on hunger strike in the Brixton prison. Born in 1879 in Cork, Terence MacSwiney was a mirror contemporary of Mrs. Margaret Buckley and the brother of famous Mary MacSwiney, whose fiery letters regularly crossed the desk of W. T. Cosgrave and Eamon de Valera well after the Civil War. Terence had founded the Irish Volunteer branch in Cork and served as president of the Cork branch of Sinn Féin. He later served as the Cork representative in the first Dáil and as the Lord Mayor of Cork after his good friend Tomas Mac-Curtain was killed by the Royal Irish Constabulary (RIC). He was interned from April 1916 until June 1917, and then rearrested in November 1917 for wearing an IRA uniform. He was released after a three-day hunger strike. He was subsequently arrested yet again in 1918 and then again in 1920 for seditious speech, and it was during this later incarceration that Terence MacSwiney endured the longest hunger strike in Irish history—74 days. He succumbed to the fight on October 25, 1920, leaving his daughter Máire Óg at the tender age of two. His sister Mary carried on in his passionate commitment to an independent Ireland, becoming the voice of Republicans both at home and abroad.

Terence's daughter Máire Óg would become known as Máire MacSwiney Brugha after she married Cathal Brugha's only son Ruairí. Máire recalls in "*History's Daughter: A Memoir of the Only Child of Terence MacSwiney*" that her earliest childhood memory was standing on the beach at Oysterhaven near Cork during this time period.[11] She had been introduced to her dad at the age of three months old while he was serving a sentence in the Crumlin Jail in Belfast in 1918. Such was the sacrifice of a Republican family—numerous years apart, extended intermittent stays in prison punctuated with occasional visits and solitary journal reflections. It was all for Sinn Féin, and although the price was high, the choice was for Ireland. The women of Sinn Féin knew this life well, and their sacrifices have been largely unrecognized until now. Those familiar with the sacrifice often re-call Mary MacSwiney first.

Mary MacSwiney

Mary MacSwiney was seven years senior to her brother Terence, an Eas-ter Rising veteran and 1920 martyr, and in many ways, she seems to have set the pace for family activities. Born in Surrey before the MacSwiney family moved to Ireland, Mary—like the Countess—spoke with an English accent despite her deep understanding of the Irish cause. The MacSwiney family protested together, was often in jail at the same time, and went on hunger strike simultaneously on a couple of occasions. A teacher by profession, like her parents, Mary's educational philosophy often included persuad-ing her female pupils to join the Republican movement, that is, until her dismissal after her Easter 1916 internment. Undeterred, she and her sister Annie went on to found the St. Ita's Girls School in Cork in 1917. Mary ini-tially refused to join Arthur Griffith's Sinn Féin; she had an intense dislike for his initial monarchical policies, but she relented in 1917, once she ad-mitted Sinn Féin to be more decidedly Republican. She founded the Cork branch of Cumann na mBan, even serving as the national vice president of Cumann na mBan, and helped Terence recruit his Irish Volunteers. Like her brother, she was elected to represent Cork in the Dáil Éireann in its sec-ond incarnation. In 1920, while Terence was on hunger strike in Brixton, she and her sister Annie were refused admittance to see him; the sisters remained at the gate on hunger strike—one of many Mary undertook—for the remaining three days of his life. The loss of her brother was deep, but Mary would not remain still for long.

In December 1920, Mary MacSwiney embarked on her first speaking tour across the United States. Her initial visit was to testify concerning the Black and Tans before the American Commission on Inquiry on Con-ditions in Ireland (ACCI). She testified before the ACCI Commission in Washington, D.C. that December on various issues, including the history of the Republican movement.[12] Accompanied by her sister-in-law Muriel, Mary explained: "I have seen in the American papers, for instance, 'the Sinn Féin', as if Sinn Féin were a noun. Now, Sinn Féin is a policy, as you have the Democratic policy and the Republican policy . . . Sinn Féin is a policy, but the Irish Republic Government is the authorized recognized government of the Irish people, their chosen government. As so we do not call ourselves Sinn Féiners. We call ourselves Irish Republicans, just as you call yourselves Americans."[13]

It was during this 1920–21 visit that Mary found her voice for the Re-publican movement. Shortly after the ACCI testimony, Muriel returned to

Ireland to care for her daughter. Over the next nine months, Mary visited 58 cities across the United States.[14] Her stirring speeches were clever and insightful. Her niece Máire Óg, of whom she later was awarded custody in a dispute with Máire Óg's mother Muriel, describes a lecture where an audience member protested the tactics of an IRA ambush. To clarify the policy, Mary offered to define an ambush and gave an example of one. When the listener appeared satisfied at the definition but reasserted her disapproval of ambushes, Mary revealed that she had given the example of the American Patriots' ambush at Concord Bridge in 1775![15]

Mary MacSwiney wrote in the preface to Buckley's *The Jangle of the Keys* that though they often met on the outside, she did not cross paths with Mrs. Buckley in the prisons. Released shortly before Margaret's internment in Mountjoy and Kilmainhaim in 1922, the revolutionary Mary MacSwiney experienced many of the similar consequences and sacrifices for her politics. Although MacSwiney's open antagonism for Eamon de Valera may have come to define her among her contemporaries, she shared the same passion for a republic echoed in the hearts of many Sinn Féin women. In the darkest hours of the Civil War, women like Mary MacSwiney, Margaret Buckley, Máire Comerford, and Lily O'Brennan took swift action as Republican activists and set forth the parameters of the code of political prisoner behavior.

MacSwiney's appeal as a vessel of strength was a combination of experience, passion, and skill. She had personal knowledge of the prison plight and a personal connection to hunger strikes. When combined with her passionate oratory skills, Mary MacSwiney was a very powerful woman. Her passionate zeal was apparent even to Eamon de Valera who had, despite their tiffs, persuaded her to extend her stay in the States for a speaking tour. She regularly spoke about the atrocities her people suffered at the hands of the Black and Tans, and her speeches were echoed by Countess Markievicz and Father Michael O'Flanagan in their 1922 speaking tour of the States—the need for Americans to support an Irish Republic.

Mary MacSwiney returned to Ireland in the midst of the Treaty ratification discussions and was outraged at the idea of compromise. Although many of her colleagues in the Dáil relented to the Treaty, Mary did not. Delivering one of the longest speeches at the Treaty debate, nearly three hours long, she rose with de Valera and walked out after the Treaty ratification vote. Publicly and unabashedly calling the Treaty the greatest crime in Ireland made her a target in the ensuing months. She was interned twice, once in November 1922 and again in April 1923, during the Irish Civil War for breeching Free State policies. On two separate occasions, she initiated hunger strikes while interned. And Annie, her devoted sister, joined her on strike in 1922 outside Mountjoy Jail. Upon Mary's release, she returned to Sinn Féin politics, but she refused to take the Oath of Allegiance under the Irish Free State, even after the 1926 split that formed Fianna Fáil. She remained committed to Cumann na mBan and Sinn Féin, for whom she served as a publicity director. At the 1923 Árd Fheis, Mary presided in de Valera's absence, since he was in prison. Close to 1,200 Republicans attended the convention, where Miss MacSwiney argued that a party-wide abstinence from alcohol and tobacco should be a measure of passive resistance against the Free State.

In 1923, Mary MacSwiney wrote an article on hunger striking for the *Daily Sheet* published by Sinn Féin headquarters of Suffolk Street. She describes three classes of hunger strikes: the absolute refusal of English imprisonment as an authority, the call of attention to mistreatment or criminal status when a POW, and an ineffective sympathetic one. She classifies her brother's hunger strike as the first and the 1923 strike as the second form, but claims that attempts to dissuade the hunger strikers, in the third vein, have actually reinforced the rage against injustice embodied in the first. Of the 338 Republican prisoners on the strike, 8 held in the North Dublin Union were women now being held close to two weeks after their unconditional release was promised. Among those expecting release were Maeve Phelan, Eileen Barry, Miss O'Railly, Lily Dunne, Sighle Humphries, Miss Bohan, K. O'Brien, and Miss Haybourne. The women had called off their initial hunger strike after news of their release reached them, but returned to the strike when the "trick" was revealed. In an update of these women on November 22, it is noted that Republican POW Maeve Phelan had been the first to arrive at North Dublin Union on May 6 "[a]nd now she is on her 29th day of hunger strike. Her slight form is attenuated and frail beyond description. The bed has ceased to rest her, and only chafes the weary body with bed stores. Warrior and maid are needed as victims before the Free State appetite for Irish blood is sated."[16]

MacSwiney's outrage at the Free State handling of their plight was personal. Her sacrifice, both of her brother's life and the many days she herself was on strike, carries a sharp shrill in her words: "Will the deaths of these noble men and women ensure lasting peace and stability in the country? Were such an evil deed even contemplated in any country [in] the world there would be an outcry against it. Will you calmly allow Ireland to be disgraced by such a tragedy?"[17] In Mountjoy, the prison conditions seemed to be securing the POWs' compliance. Although fresh linens were refused them, vermin and filth abounded, and the guards had tried to trick them into breaking the strike, the hunger strikers were not taking criminal status.

Mary returned to the United States to raise financial and political support for a republic in January 1925. An American audience did not turn out in the same numbers as they had just four years before. A six-month tour produced little consequence, and when she returned, Eamon de Valera led the Fianna Fáil split, for which she often would call him unloyal to the men and women of 1916. Although she lost her seat in the 1927 Dáil elections, she remained loyal to Sinn Féin until 1934 when she resigned in protest that Sinn Féin members were taking government jobs.[18] Exclusively "Republican" in her ideals, Mary MacSwiney was an omnipresent force in Irish politics until her death in 1942.

Margaret Goulding Buckley

It was in this environment that a young woman from Cork, as she sat in Dublin's Mountjoy Jail with memories of comrades like Mary MacSwiney and others, found her destiny in Sinn Féin—she was in Sinn Féin in the 1920s, '30s and '40s. She was a revolutionary, an activist, a political prisoner, a party leader, and a feminist, though she may not have defined her equality in that term. Born in 1879 outside Mallow, County Cork, Margaret Goulding was the daughter of a Parnellyte who had been deeply impacted by the hotbed politics surrounding her. At the turn of the century, Cork was a nexus of hostile Anglo-Irish relations, and it is not by coincidence that Mary MacSwiney, Michael Collins, and Mary MacCurtain all hailed from the county of Cork. It undoubtedly produced some of Ireland's most passionate Republicans. Growing up in the west of Ireland, the future Mrs. Buckley would have been privy to the plight of land rent and evictions. Margaret's family was involved in the land reform movement and supported Parnell's vision of Irish Home Rule. She was a young teenager, involved in the local arts community, when Charles Stewart Parnell died in 1891. As a young woman in her twenties, Margaret Goulding joined Maud Gonne's Inghinidhe na hÉireann in 1901 and founded the Cork branch of Countess Markievicz's Fianna Éireann. Her dynamic political activism, including her participation in anti-British royal visits in 1903 and 1907, was a curious match for her selection of a husband, however, as she married a British civil servant named Patrick Buckley in 1906. According to limited accounts from her nephew Seamus Goulding, Patrick was a typical civil servant who enjoyed playing rugby.[19]

Throughout her time in Cork, she was active in militant anti-British activities, as she recounted under the pen name of Margaret Lee in *The United Irishmen* in the 1950s, which included but were not limited to pelting the British Army band with rotten fruit. Shortly after her husband's death, Margaret, now an active member of Cumann na mBan and working as an organizer for the Irish Women Worker's Union (IWWU), moved to Dublin. Although she briefly returned to Cork to care for her ill father,

her Dublin residence served as the heart of Sinn Féin throughout the late 1930s and 1940s. When her brother Patrick Goulding's wife died in 1925, she became the primary caregiver for her 10-year-old nephew Seamus. In *The IRA in the Twilight Years 1923–1948*, author Uinseann MacEoin interviewed Seamus Goulding, himself a Republican internee in the 1940s, and he recalled that his aunt's home was comfortable and book-lined. The interview remains one of the rare personal accounts of Margaret Buckley in Irish history to date.

Buckley's Dublin activities were decidedly Republican. Kevin Rafter, in his book *Sinn Féin 1905–2005*, recalled that her Republican passions had led her to participate in the Easter Rising in 1916, for which she was imprisoned until general amnesty was granted in 1917.[20] Well read and highly motivated, Buckley had been appointed to be a Sinn Féin judge in north city circuit of Dublin for the Republican Courts in 1920. Convened under the authority of the 1919 Dáil, the courts established a body of Irish law, based on Brehon laws, where judges arbitrated cases and IRA Volunteers often enforced decisions. A woman in her forties at the time, Buckley assisted in translating the authority of revolutionary force into the implementation of (perceived) impending independent Irish law as the IRA swore allegiance to the Dáil in August 1920. The oath, and her freedom, was short-lived.

Margaret Buckley, like many Republican women who did not support the Treaty, became a target of the Free State government during the Civil War. Rounded up in December 1920 at the same time as Sinn Féin president Arthur Griffith, she was released in July 1921 having served a six-month sentence for being a judge in the Republican Courts. Despite a relatively recent return to freedom, her position on the Treaty was clear: no. As an Anti-Treatyite whose unabashed activities demonstrated her opposition to anything less than a Republic, Buckley landed back in prison. She was interned in Mountjoy Prison, North Dublin Union, and Kilmainham Jail until October 1923.

Margaret was a woman of opinion who was motivated to act on it, regardless of the consequence. Republican Sinn Féin president Ruairi Ó Brádaigh remembers Mrs. Buckley as a spiritual woman, but not in a devotional way: "she took her religion for granted in that it was a part of her make-up and so on."[21] Her transcendent reflections of her imprisonment are captured in *The Jangle of the Keys*, her autobiographical account of her internment during this period. Describing a hunger strike that the Mountjoy women undertook to protest the prison conditions, Mrs. Buckley said that "[i]n the awful days that followed, our religion was our bulwark, our food and our stay. We never confused the Creator with His Creatures."[22] That Easter morning, she suffered from heart palpitations as a condition of the strike but her resolve was complete. "The hunger strike was the only weapon we could wield, and we felt justified in using it, We were twelve Irishwomen of good character, accused of no criminal intent, and we were being deprived of the common necessities which are accorded to the most depraved criminal prisoners."[23] Having won 12 new beds for the women, the strike was called off. That is, until Buckley, as the prisoners' principal negotiator, decided to further the demands with a second, three-day long, hunger strike for letter and parcel mail. Mrs. Buckley, Ruairí Ó Brádaigh recalls, "was a Cork woman, through and through, strong willed and independent minded she was." She would settle for no less than what those women deserved. This privilege intact, Madam Buckley pushed further:

> Shortly after the first hunger strike I asked Paudeen [deputy governor of the prison] if I might have in a typewriter. "A what?" he roared.
>   "Oh, you heard what I said, a typewriter."
>   "Lord God, the next thing you'll want is a machine gun," and he hummed his little song, out of tune, and went his way.[24]

Her humor intact and her demands implicit, Buckley defined the spirit of defiance and Republican solidarity. Although her resolve was complete, she was unprepared for what she would experience next.

It was at the North Dublin Union that Buckley, and other Republican women, experienced the most horrific tactics. Describing it as a concentration camp, Buckley penned the memories that were seared into the prisoners' minds: "The full force of our housing conditions was borne in on us as soon as daylight came. The place was filthy. It had been occupied by the British emergency troops during the Black-and-Tan war, and was now as they had left it. The boards were old and rotten, and caked with mud, and though the beds were now clean, they could not remain so in that venue."[25] Upon their arrival, she recalls that the women were beaten, their clothes torn, with visible evidence of beatings from drunken soldiers. Her towering frame and intimidating manner dissuaded the prison guard from conducting a search of her body, though Buckley admits to being ashamed of what she called the "unladylike" nature of her encounter with the officer. Even in the darkest of nights, Margaret Buckley was a force of reckoning.

Outraged at the circumstances that political prisoners faced, the Women's Prisoner's Defence League was established by Maud Gonne MacBride and Charlotte Despard in August 1922. The need for the organization, according to Ruairí Ó Brádaigh, "[g]rew out of the repression in the 1920s when burying the Republican dead was grounds for internment. It was a campaigning body to highlight the needs of the prisoners. Up to 15,000 internees and about 400 of them were women, and the women were eventually moved to the North Dublin Union. The Union was a work house where the women were put to work; among them was Margaret Buckley. Hunger strikes were on and off."[26] When the public executions of Anti-Treatyites began, Cumann na mBan took on the dangerous responsibility of burying the dead.

Still on the inside of a Civil War prison, Margaret Buckley served as much more than and O.C. (commanding officer) or Q.M. (quartermaster) to her fellow Republicans in prison. Mrs. Buckley's leadership demonstrated a razor-sharp mind, holding debates on women versus men and capitalism versus socialism, and propagating defiance in even the smallest of ways, such as the historical pageant of St. Patrick, St. Brigid, Queen Maeve, and the like in Kilmainhaim Jail. Adorned as St. Patrick with a chalk dust beard, a prison sheet gown with crayon drawing adornment, Buckley led the procession of Caithlin Ní Houlihan, Anne Devlin, Cuchulain, and Mary McCracken characters into the A wing of the prison for a delightful two-play production with musical accompaniment.[27] The imaginative "escape" of spirit stood in stark contrast to the reality of their imprisonment: "We tried not to think of what lay before us and brought all our fortitude to bear on our immediate present: it must have been terrible for the young ones, but then, youth has its compensations and a resurgence all its own, which kept them facing whatever the day brought with equanimity, not to say cheerfulness."[28] The female Sinn Féin Anti-Treatyites interned in the 1920s suffered magnanimously in the prisons while their comrades on the outside fought in perilous valiance. Buckley would become vice president of Sinn Féin in 1935, and in 1937, she became the first female president of a political party in Ireland.

Máire Comerford

In *The Jangle of the Keys*, Margaret Buckley depicts a moment of horror upon her arrival to the North Dublin Union Camp in 1923. Surrounded by women beaten by the soldiers serving as guards, she laid eyes on her comrade Máire Comerford. In the care of the prison doctor, Máire's head was shaven in order for the doctor to sew three stitches for a wound she had received.[29] Born in County Wicklow in 1893, Máire spent part of her youth in London and became a Republican shortly after the Easter Rising. A Cumann na mBan member, she served as an unrepentant gun runner and dispatch carrier for Michael Collins. During the War for Independence, Máire facilitated intelligence across the country. Vehemently opposed to the Treaty, Miss Comerford utilized her position on the Cumann na mBan executive to continue to raise money for Irregular weapons. She was a fearless sort, who was as determined in her mission as she was resolute in Republican principles, and this often landed her behind bars in jail.

It was 1922 when Máire Comerford first arrived in Mountjoy. She was arrested for possession of a revolver, apparently bound for an attempted assassination of the president of the Free State, William (W. T.) Cosgrave.[30] Like Buckley, she was transferred to the North Dublin Union Camp, from which she duly escaped. Fleeting as it was, her escape inspired the women still interned, that is, until her return a few months later. Back in jail, Máire participated in a 27-day hunger strike over prison conditions and political status. That fall, the first executions of Irregulars took place, including the November 24 killing of Erskine Childers, who was found in possession of an illegal weapon—a gift of the recently deceased Big Fellow, Michael Collins, himself. Upon her release from Kilmainham, Máire traveled under an assumed name to the United States. A member of the Sinn Féin National Executive in 1926, she refused to side with de Valera in the split and quickly found herself back in Mountjoy by the end of the year. As the decade came to a close, Máire Comerford was living in poverty, the stinging serendipity of the squalor for which the White Cross volunteer had once identified the destitute recipient of funds in 1920. Although unmarried and childless, she described their impoverishment, and in an ironic twist perhaps foreshadowed her own, with the passionate empathy of a true Republican activist in her autobiography:

> It was in their blood and tradition to suffer in the causes of national, religious and personal freedom. In many a home where children stood around silently, the issues at stake were clear enough. Mothers would face anything if only we could win our present battle. They thought they were rearing the first generation of children who would live out their lives in a free country was enough to support us.[31]

In her post–Civil War activism, Comerford served as the women's editor for the *Irish Press* from 1935–1965.[32] She was arrested once again in 1974, at the age of 81, when she broke the ban on a Sinn Féin march. Thirty years after her passing, her nephew Joe fulfilled his aunt's legacy when he stood for election as a Sinn Féin candidate in Glencullen.

Lily O'Brennan

Elizabeth (Lily) O'Brennan shared some of the same unrepentant qualities of Republican activists in the revolutionary period. She was a member of Cumann na mBan, having joined in 1914 and participated in the Easter Rising. Lily was held, like the Countess, in Kilmainham Jail. She joined Sinn Féin in 1917 and served as a secretary for Arthur Griffith, the 1921 Treaty delegation, and Erskine Childers. A member of the White Cross and active in the Prisoners' Dependents' Fund, she often traveled to raise money. Perhaps one of the most interesting dimensions of Lily's activism was that it was the norm in her family. Known as the "revolutionary sisters," Lily, Kathleen (Kit), and Fanny (better known by widowed name Áine Ceannt) O'Brennan supported the expanding network of Cumann na mBan and Sinn Féin. While Áine remained at home with her 10-year-old son on Easter morning 1916, Lily took her position under her brother-in-law Éamonn Ceannt's command with his Irish Volunteers. Although Kit had immigrated to the United States, she utilized her journalist background to travel extensively around the world on behalf of Republicans. An active Easter widow, Áine Ceannt emerged herself in Republican politics and in 1920 became the chief administrator of the White Cross funds, which Máire Comerford helped to distribute. During the Civil War, Áine served as the vice president of Cumann na mBan and a member of the Sinn Féin Executive. Lily, having taken an Anti-Treaty position, left her work with Griffith to become Erskine Childers's private secretary until her November 1922 arrest in the Sinn Féin offices. Her internment overlapped with that of Margaret Buckley and Máire Comerford.

Lily O'Brennan shared a love of writing with her sister Kit (Kathleen). Although Kathleen seemed to be more allusive than her siblings during this period, perhaps this was, in part, due to her alleged clandestine activities. In a recently unsealed intelligence communiqué, dated January 19, 1923, in the National Archives, the Office of the Minister of External Affairs in the Free State reveals that the authorities tracked a Kathleen O'Brennan to Lausanne, Switzerland, where the woman, accompanied by Dr. Kathleen Lynn, delivered a petition, reportedly from the Irregulars, to the International Red Cross.[33] It is possible that this woman might have been Lily O'Brennan's sister. Both Lily and Áine were very involved in the White Cross, and the three would have shared circles with Kathleen Lynn. However, the report does not provide any confirmation of the woman's identity, other than a circumstantial conversation with hotel management concerning the hotel guest registry of a Miss Kathleen O'Brennan. Nor does the document establish that this Kathleen O'Brennan was definitely Lily and Áine's sister. Thus, while the prospects that it was Kit lodged there are likely, it is not certain since there is no collaborating evidence. If, however, the secret police report authentically portrayed the Kit of the O'Brennan clan, then it is validates many suspicions about the Free State government.

It was suspected that the Irregulars were further soliciting cooperation from the Soviets to further their cause during the Irish Civil War, and the Free State secret policeman trailing this Miss O'Brennan felt that she was the courier, operating out of Paris, to this end. Having delivered communications from de Valera to the Bolshevik commissary in Chicherin, the mysterious Kathleen O'Brennan seems to have provided evidence that the Irregulars sought arms, delivered as one dispatch suggested to a western Irish seaport, from the Soviets to eliminate the capitalist Free State. The Soviet link was not imaginary. The Bolsheviks had been the only country to recognize the Revolutionary Dáil of 1919, and gunrunning from continental Europe was a role with which Republican women were not unfamiliar.

With her sisters actively engaged in Republican goals, Lily O'Brennan joined Mary MacSwiney, along with over 20 Cumann na mBan members, in the February 1923 hunger strike. The O'Brennan sisters were not unlike many Republican families at the time; each committed to a republic, opposed to the Treaty, and forced to accept the fate of Free State politics.

Katherine Murphy O'Callaghan

One such woman who most certainly did have an interest in politics was Mrs. Katherine O'Callaghan. Kate (or Kitty) was born Katherine Murphy in 1885 in County Cork. Educated in the Ursuline Convent like Mary MacSwiney and so many other famous Republican women, O'Callaghan was an active young woman who joined the Gaelic League with her sister. During her time as a student in Eccles Street, Kitty Murphy was a student of the legendary Hanna Sheehy-Skeffington, founder of the Irish Women's Franchise League (IWFL) in 1908. Mrs. Sheehy-Skeffington's influence must have been profound, for in addition to joining the IWFL, Kitty became a lifelong feminist and invited her to speak to her branch of Cumann na mBan in Limerick.

Also active in the Irish Volunteers, Kate met and married Michael O'Callaghan in 1914.[34] Widowed in 1921 when her husband, then the Lord Mayor of Limerick, was assassinated by the Black and Tans, Kate went on to become an outspoken Republican feminist and became the first woman TD in Republican Dáil. A member of the Second Dáil's Council of State, Kate was true to her franchise values and Sinn Féin republicanism. During the 1922 debate on suffrage, many suspected that Hanna Sheehy-Skeffington was the push behind Kate's parliamentary overtures on franchise. As Margaret Ward points out in the seminal work on Hanna, "Now, with the cooperation of her old pupil and friend, she was frantically busy in preparing for this stand on behalf of the women of Ireland."[35] Mrs. O'Callaghan TD put forth a motion on March 2, 1922, that would enfranchise Irishwomen between the ages of 21 and 30. In her speech, Kate argued that the women of Ireland had earned the right to their vote, through their efforts and their sacrifices. However, the opposition, surprisingly including Arthur Griffith, was too strong, and the motion failed. The Pro-Treatyites viewed the expansion of suffrage as a threat to the ratification of the Anglo-Irish Treaty, as many of the younger women in Ireland were likely to not support it. Caught in yet another layer of national debate, the franchise movement and, in many regards, Irish feminism was set back decades.

The ensuing Civil War was not kind to Kate O'Callaghan. Having emerged a strong Anti-Treatyite, she was arrested in April 1923 with Mary Mac-Swiney, and participated in the hunger strikes that Margaret Buckley wrote of in *The Jangle of the Keys*. When the Free State was established, she lost her seat in the 1923 elections. Though de Valera's ladies tried hard to recruit her, she refused to join Fianna Fáil in 1926. Kate O'Callaghan had been deeply committed to women's issues, and perhaps more importantly, she knew that being an outspoken advocate could carry a high price. Even after having lost her husband for his outgoing opposition, Mrs. O'Callaghan carried on throughout the Treaty debates in 1921 and dangerous times of the Civil War with "outrageously" unconventional ideas of equality, universal suffrage, and social rights for women.

In Maud Gonne MacBride's journal *Prison Bars*, Mrs. Kate O'Callaghan wrote of her vehement objection to the burgeoning discussion of a new constitution in 1937: "My main objection to the Constitution is based on its acceptance of the British Crown and membership of the British Group of Nations, an acceptance veiled by the untrue declaration in Article 5 that 'Eire is a sovereign, independent, and democratic State.' This fundamental objection is strengthened by other features in the document, none more than by the articles dealing with women. These articles I regard as a betrayal of the 1916 promise of 'Equal Rights and Equal Opportunities guaranteed to all citizens.' "[36] The perceived abandonment of the 1916 Proclamation, which was regarded by Republicans as the first constitution of Ireland, was tantamount to an embrace of the colonizer. For the feminists, moving away from the initial principles of Republicanism—including equality for women—unequivocally embraced the colonizer's system of discrimination as well.

IRISH WOMEN IN SOCIETY

- Constitutional Inequality
- New Sinn Féin?

Constitutional Inequality

Much of the public outrage concerning the proposed constitution challenged the position of Irish women in society, a central mission of the IWWU. The Irish Women's Workers' Union (IWWU) had been founded in 1911 by suffragettes and members of Inghinidhe na hÉireann. The

Countess, Helena Molony, and Hanna Sheehy-Skeffington held prominent membership in its early years, with Louie Bennett leading the debate in the 1930s. These ladies had worked tirelessly throughout the 1930s to advance legislation that protected working women, secured a decent wage, even the right to work outside the home. In her May 1937 editorial in the *Irish Times,* Ms. Bennett articulated the collective outrage of feminists at Articles 40, 41, and 45 in the proposed 1937 constitution. Writing an open letter to de Valera, the IWWU expressed that "Article 40.1, tends to place women in a different category of citizenship from men and in a different position than men in certain laws. It thus suggests an inferior status for women and gives power to a Government predominantly male (as all Governments now are) to impose legislation on women of which they themselves might strongly disapprove." Allegations of sexism abounded. The wording was picked apart, as was the culture that supported such suggestions. In the end, the following sections in Table 2.3 provided a nexus of feminist obstacles for years to come.

"Women's work" in 1937, in a state of depressed economy, provided much cultural discussion. Of particular concern for the IWWU was the subsequent passage in Article 45, section 4 of the constitution that proclaimed that one's occupation should be suited to one's gender. Bennett recoiled at the thought of such sexism: "Women who think and women who work must all view this clause with indignation and apprehension."[37] Eithne Coyle's Cumann na mBan and Margaret Buckley's Sinn Féin issued a joint declaration conveying their opposition to the constitution as well. The flurry of Republican discontent to de Valera's constitutionalism was penned in a private letter to the president of the Executive Council himself by a group of women calling themselves the Old Cumann na mBan. The responsibility for ensuring an Ireland of equality was in Fianna Fáil's hands:

Table 2.3
1937 Irish Constitution Sections

Article 41.2
Subsection 1: In particular, the State recognises that by her life within the home, woman gives to the State a support without which the common good cannot be achieved.
Subsection 2: The State shall, therefore, endeavour to ensure that mothers shall not be obliged by economic necessity to engage in labour to the neglect of their duties in the home.

Cuman na mBan in Dublin and throughout the country approach Fianna Fáil Parliamentary representatives in their constituencies, [un-
clear text] suppliants; but as women who have taken an active part
in the struggle for National Independence, and whose efforts in no
small measure helped Fianna Fáil to obtain Governmental control [in
1932]. As members of the Government Party, the Fianna Fáil T.D.s'
cannot disclaim responsibility for this unjust treatment of Irishwomen, and as old members of the I.R.A. they know only too well
the part taken by Old Cumann na mBan in Freedom's Fight.[38]

The constitution was not what Republican women had wanted; first, it
was not the 32-county republic for which they had fought, and second, it
was clear that the role of women, though integral to the achievements thus
far, would not figure as prominently in a noncrisis state. This patterned
echo washed across country, and, with dismal levels of approval, the constitution was marginally accepted that December. Historian Margaret Ward
notes that there had been a 31 percent abstention rate, which could have
definitely tipped the balance against de Valera if it had been utilized.[39]

Stuck in the inertia of Irish constitutionalism in 1937, Sinn Féin found
itself on the precipice of social crisis. When World War II broke out in
1938, Ireland yet again attempted to maintain neutrality. The effectiveness
of this endeavor is of much historical debate, as German weapons had a
habit of surfacing in Ireland. The adage "England's difficulty is Ireland's opportunity" afforded a resurgence of IRA initiatives, mainly the commence-
ment of the bombing campaign in 1939, formulated in the midst of the
de Valera-Chamberlain negotiations that produced the Anglo-Irish Pact of
1938. Sinn Féin had also publicly denounced it in a May 7, 1938, statement
in the *Irish Times*. Margaret Buckley's Sinn Féin said:

The disclosures following the London Pact reveal the first fruits of
the notorious so-called Constitution of Ireland, enacted by an oath
bound partition-Parliament of the British Empire, and show how far
the rights and interests of the Irish nation are "safeguarded" by the
great "Charter of Irish Liberty" which subverts the Republic; provides
for the maintenance of the connection with England; the partition of
Ireland, the recognition of the King of England as the King of Ireland,
and accepts as the Church of Ireland one which has never been accepted by the vast majority of the Irish people.[40]

Mary MacSwiney published a Republican response to the various components of the Anglo-Irish Pact in a May 11, 1938, editorial in the *Irish Independent*. Arguing that the position of Irish neutrality was a farce in light of

de Valera's public speeches revealing the obligations of freedom and that de Valera's negotiations defy the Republican lesson of trusting the word of a British negotiator (for there had been many instances where statesmen's promises had been lost in their implementations), MacSwiney rebuked the president for swallowing the status of Ireland. She reminded him of the Republic for which he fought and, in her opinion, abandoned to a fateful partition: "Our main concern, however, is with the surrender of our fundamental liberties—for a surrender this Pact is."[41] The nature of that pact became the confines in which Sinn Féin struggled in the late 1930s and 1940s.

New Sinn Féin?

When Mrs. Buckley became vice president of Sinn Féin in 1935, she served with presidents Father Michael O'Flanagan (1933–1935) and Cathal O Marchadha (1935–1937). At the time, there were 40 some odd members of Sinn Féin and Miss Mary MacSwiney had just left the party. The Sinn Féin presidency, under J. J. O'Kelly (1926–1931) and Brian O'Higgins (1931–1933), had reduced in power significantly. Much like Madam Buckley and the other Sinn Féin presidents of the 1930s, Father Michael O'Flanagan is often omitted from Sinn Féin historical reviews, but in light of his sacramental devotion to the cause, a brief mention is referenced herewithin.

Father O'Flanagan had served as the vice president of Sinn Féin from 1917 on. He was silenced by the Church (first in 1918 and again from 1925 until 1938) for his activities. He had been a curate in Rothscommon/Longford and opposed Eamon de Valera in 1926 to enter Leinster House and Stormont. He led the opposing amendment to end abstentionism, but, despite his best efforts, Fianna Fáil was born. The tension between Sinn Féin and Fianna Fáil was real. Both claimed to be the party of nationalism and heirs to the Irish Republic. Coupled with O'Flanagan's status in the community as a priest, the tension between the parties, and their figureheads, led to much political tension and, interestingly, colloquial *craic* (a Irish term for good conversation). Even though post–Civil War republicanism embodied the aura of "the women and childers" (Erskine Childers) party, many of the prominent Republican women left Sinn Féin with de Valera, perhaps because of the charisma he possessed. A local joke, Ruairí Ó Brádaigh recounts, is that if someone was to cut into swatches the long black coat that de Valera was known to frequently wear, then the women would make it into scapulars (monastic headcoverings).

Mary MacSwiney would have none of this, remaining a steadfast Republican, and de Valera would later refer to her as his political conscience in the 1930s. The de Valera divide could not be healed, so Father O'Flanagan took on the presidency as soon as the Long Fellow (Eamon de Valera) left

Sinn Féin. Father O'Flanagan was president of Sinn Féin from 1933–1935 and supported the Spanish republicans (the Reds) in the Spanish Civil War, a decision that was not popular in Ireland since the Whites were supposed to be the "Christians." Concerning Father O'Flanagan, Ruairí Ó Brádaigh muses over whether these omissions are due the controversial nature of this period in Irish history, specifically the radicalized support of anti-Church republicans during the Spanish Civil War and the anti–de Valera measures in 1926. Sinn Féin in the wake of the Fianna Fáil formation was a dwindling force of post–civil war, Second Dáil–loyal, 32-county Republican members.

When Margaret Buckley became president of Sinn Féin in 1937, there was a tense coexistence between the IRA and Sinn Féin, but by 1950, the relationship had been normalized. Part of the tension arose out of the IRA's experimentation with political process, when it founded political organizations in 1931 called Saor Éire and in 1933 called the Republican Congress. Both attempts were branded as extreme leftist and criticized in the mainstream press and Irish public. In truth, there was as much internal division within Saor Éire and Republican Congress as there was disapproval outside of them. In 1936, Cumann Poblachta na hÉireann, the third attempt at an IRA political agenda, was moderately successful when Count Plunkett, father of Easter Rising martyr Joseph Mary Plunkett, ran as a candidate endorsed by both Cumann Poblachta na hÉireann and Sinn Féin. Since the 1940s, the IRA has maintained a singular nationalist agenda focusing on the armed-resistance strategy.

Continuation of the Republican position on the Irish question was of primary importance to Buckley, and her cooperation in normalizing IRA-Sinn Féin relations was a necessary mend for all Republicans. "This was probably the most important action of her life that she cooperated in" according to Ruairí Ó Brádaigh.[42] In his estimation, she should be remembered in the round, with her work with the Irish Women Workers' Union and as a judge in the Sinn Féin courts, and with the women prisoners in Kilmainhaim, and the Prisoner's Defence League, and her heroic presidency in Sinn Féin (1937–1950). "It required extraordinary fortitude given the circumstances. It is easy when things are going well to be prominent and all that type of thing but when circumstances are very difficult it is a much harder job that requires a much more strong minded person. She should be seen as a strong minded Irish woman who made all these contributions and who gave a need in very difficult times."[43]

CONCLUSIONS

At the conclusion of the 1930s, Sinn Féin consisted of a small dedicated few. The transition to Free State status and constitutionalism left the party

of abstentionism out of the mainstream of Irish politics. Fianna Fáil dominated the political landscape, but the Sinn Féin veterans like Margaret
Buckley and Mary MacSwiney steadfastly denied the politics of English
accommodation. It was an often unpopular position to be in, especially as
the 1940s unfolded, but it was their Republican duty.

Past Republican Sinn Féin president Ruairí Ó Brádaigh recalls the es-
sence of that commitment with a glint of tears in his eyes. He recalls a
visit he made to Mrs. Charlotte Despard's grave to pay his respects. Mrs.
Despard was a Catholic convert and an active Sinn Féin member. She died
in a small town called Whitehead outside of Belfast in 1939. Her work as
a member of the Women's Prisoners Defense League and cofounder of the
Irish Women's Franchise League's suffrage movement is often overshadowed by her reputation for being a Catholic Communist. Mr. Ó Brádaigh
recalls the inscription on her grave in Glasniven Cemetery: "I slept and
dreamt that life was beauty. I woke and found that life was duty." It sums up
his life, he thinks, and it sums up these women's lives. By the beginning of
the 1940s, many in the Republican movement who had formed Sinn Féin
were gone. These women had dreamt of an independent Ireland, the beautiful Éire, and when they awoke, they had found their duty in Sinn Féin.
Even though some of the women choose to follow their destiny in Fianna
Fáil, their contribution to Sinn Féin lived on with Margaret Buckley as she
braved the challenge of keeping Sinn Féin alive in the 1940s.

Chapter 3

PARTITION OF THE REPUBLICAN MIND? 1940s–1950s

I, for one, will have neither hand, act, nor part in helping the Irish Free State to carry this nation of ours, this glorious nation that has been betrayed here to-night, into the British Empire— either with or without your hands up. I maintain here now that this is the grossest act of betrayal that Ireland ever endured.

—Mary MacSwiney[1]

CHAPTER OVERVIEW

If one were to describe republicanism in the 1930s as Uinseann MacEoin did in his biographies of the IRA men active during this period as the "twilight years,"[2] then it would seem appropriate to refer to Margaret Buckley's Sinn Féin in the 1940s and 1950s as an organization of "no importance." Referring to her own self-description as a "woman of no importance," Buckley's cheeky self-deprecation meant to describe how the authorities underestimated her and Sinn Féin. With 26 pounds left in the party's treasury in 1948, Sinn Féin was widely discounted as an organization by authorities in both the north and south. However, in 1955 the organization of "no importance" fielded an MP candidate for Westminster Parliament in the Six Counties who, despite being a treasonous felon, won three elections—each time being disqualified after winning. Both Phillip Clarke and Thomas Mitchell won seats in Westminster, supporting Sinn Féin with 26.3 percent of the vote. Was it a resurgence of support or a miscalculation of Margaret Buckley's Sinn Féin? Perhaps it was a little of one or the other, or perhaps it was a reactionary statement on the course that the Free State was taking.

Chapter Organization

Margaret Buckley was a public figure but also a very personal one. Her nephew only once spoke of her—for history's sake. Her autobiography, *The Jangle of the Keys,* is out of print and is a rare prize to come across in Ireland or the United States. A brief overview of her contributions can be found in Kevin Rafter's *Sinn Féin 1905-2005.* And, hence, it was with this knowledge that Sinn Féin directed the author to Mr. Ruairí Ó Brádaigh. His institutional knowledge on her contributions is largely unwritten, and thus, here within, one finds a unique look into Margaret Buckley's Sinn Féin.

Margaret Buckley's Sinn Féin started out having to prove itself. The chapter begins with an overview of the struggle to prove the continuity between pre–civil war Sinn Féin and post–civil war Sinn Féin. There is little doubt that Sinn Féin failed to dominate the political landscape of the 32 counties in the 1930s. Perhaps it was because it had seemingly been authoritatively crushed like the mythical phoenix that it then arose from the smoldering ashes of Irish discontent. Even while crushed, the spirit of "sinn féin" hung like a misty dew across Ireland.

It seems that Margaret, symptomatic of her organization, may have been underestimated throughout her tenure in the Republican movement. In the opening pages of *The Jangle of the Keys,* Buckley describes her arrest on Little Christmas Eve in 1923: "My arrest was the sequel to a military raid at my home; I always feel a glow of pride and satisfaction when I remember that before the hall door came in, our men had escaped by the back garden, and only I, 'a woman of no importance,' was there to greet the raiders when they trooped in, and dashed through the house, with rifles 'at the ready' and revolvers cocked."[3]

Buckley's description of the perception of women in the 1920s Sinn Féin reveals the security forces' lack of insight into the Republican community. This "woman of no importance" was at the helm of Sinn Féin from 1937 to 1950 and although she would step down from the presidency in 1950, she remained a vice president until her death in 1962. Undetected or unaccounted, the women in Buckley's Sinn Féin constituted a significant part in Republican facilitation. But, in truth, this was nothing new. Republican women had been quite active in their underground efforts, providing safe houses for the IRA and the IRB before them, gunrunning and proselytizing republicanism in the household for a good generation. Women served as the private secretaries to Griffith and Collins, and they had even been delivering dangerous dispatches among leaders. The women were often excellent speakers, found atop many a pile of rubble and often in black widows rags, touring the 32 counties—and even the world—raising funds (and support) for Republican causes. What, then, did the security forces (some of them veterans of the movement themselves) seem to forget as they raided Mrs. Buckley's house in 1923? They overlooked that the hearts and mind of the Republican movement were shaped by "a woman of no importance." How very clever that the strongest threat to de Valera's state was an imposing mind embodied in the so-called frailty of a woman.

It is common to see Sinn Féin in the 1940s described as a small, aged group of committed ideologues. Perhaps this is a fair depiction, but in Margaret Buckley's Sinn Féin, there was continuity of the Republican mind. She and Mary MacSwiney, who died in 1942, were quick to remind Eamon de Valera that Fianna Fáil was a party of deserters. Thus, during some of the darkest days of Republican history, when the de Valera government turned on the residual IRA in the 1940s and the partition of the Six Counties was institutionalized, Margaret Buckley concentrated her efforts on normalizing the relationship between Sinn Féin and the IRA. It was, perhaps, one of her biggest contributions to Sinn Féin history, as many of the IRA veterans had been joining Fianna Fáil and, in 1946, flocking to the newly formed Clann na Pochlachta. Though the 1940s and 1950s were consumed with the Second World War and declarations of a return to Irish neutrality, Margaret Buckley's presidency was punctuated by a few key Republican matters: establishing the importance principle of continuity, enduring the repression of Republicans in the 1940s, protesting the partition, and achieving the normalization of relations with the IRA.

The establishment of the Irish Republic, an independent Ireland, was achieved in 1949. In its creation was embedded a substantive partition, and the implicit acceptance of that partition, of the northern Six Counties of Northern Ireland. The IRA campaign to challenge this partition was known as the Resistance Campaign (often recorded in general history as the Border Campaign). The Republic government declared Sinn Féin and the IRA "proscribed" organizations and began a mass internment of their members. The irony is not lost in Irish history that some of the very same revolutionaries from 1916 incarcerated their former brothers and sisters in arms—in the name of the same ideals for which they once fought side by side: a 32-county independent Republic of Ireland.

HISTORICAL OVERVIEW OF MARGARET BUCKLEY'S PRESIDENCY

- Continuity and the Sinn Féin Monies
- De Valera's Republicanism

- Partition of Ireland—The Republic
- Madame Buckley
- The Resistance Campaign
- 1957 Internment

Continuity and the Sinn Féin Monies

The question of continuity in Sinn Féin was an essential Republican principle for Margaret Buckley. Organizational continuity linked Sinn Féin of 1948 to Sinn Féin of 1905 (or at least of 1922). Hence, it would honor the goals of a Republic proclaimed in 1916: a 32-county independent Irish Republic. Sinn Féin, in many capacities, may not have survived in the darkest years with the many rounds of internments, hunger strikes, and the like without Buckley's leadership and her commitment to the continuity of a Sinn Féin movement. This might be why it was so important to her to pursue the legal case of Sinn Féin monies all the way to the Irish High Court. Her strong personality pushed for the legal recognition of the continuity in the movement by insisting that the reconstituted Sinn Féin (post Free State) was the same institutional organization that Arthur Griffith and others had founded in 1905, the same group that had been awarded funds from the Sinn Féin Funds Act by Eamon de Valera. In Father Michael O'Flanagan's presidential address in 1934, he spoke about the division of Sinn Féin in 1922 where two of the treasurers and vice presidents split into two sides during the Irish Civil War, and the then president (Eamon de Valera) could hardly cut himself into two parts. By Sinn Féin resolution the money, 8,610 pounds, was lodged under de Valera's vestment in January 1922. The money was placed into the chancellery by one of the treasurers and was disputed for decades after the Civil War. Twenty years later, Sinn Féin began a motion to recover the funds; however, in 1947, de Valera moved to absorb the Sinn Féin funds, now amounting to 24,000 pounds. De Valera intended for the monies to be distributed by the Dáil government for either the promotion of Irish language programs or simply for needy persons. Margaret Buckley's objections were heard across Ireland as she filed suit to halt the measure. During the 1948 trial, Eamon de Valera was summoned to testify before J. J. Kelly's questioning and it was reported in the *Daily* news.

At the culmination of the Judge Kingsmill Moore's ruling, the court praised Buckley's persistence and recognized the continuity of Sinn Féin in the 1925 and 1927 organization to which, in Buckley's argument, was still entitled in 1948. The principle of continuity was explained in the High Court's ruling:

A political organisation with the title "Sinn Féin" has been in existence from 1903 to this present day. Leaving aside for the present the crucial question as to whether there was only one organisation of unbroken continuity, or two, or even three organisations discontinuous but in their policy largely identical, we can trace three clearly marked phases in development. The first runs from 1905 to 1917 and is marked by the undisputed guidance of Arthur Griffith. The second extends from 1917 to 1922. During this period Mr. de Valera was continuously President but had associated with him in Council all the Leaders of the National Movement. The third and last extends from 1923 to the present day [1948]. For the first three years of this third period Mr. de Valera was supreme, but after he severed his connection in 1926 control passed to various persons among whom Father O'Flanagan, Mr. O'Kelly, Austin Stack, Judge Art O'Connor and Mrs. Buckley were prominent.[4]

The ruling concluded that there was, in fact, continuity among these three phases in Sinn Féin historical development. Furthermore, the ruling concluded a very important feature of Irish history—the IRA and Sinn Féin, although sharing similar objectives, were two distinctly separate organizations. In 1948, this conclusion was a necessary fact in the Twenty-Six Counties, for it would not have been "proper" to allocate the residual monies, now miniscule after a prolonged legal battle, to an organization (IRA) that had been identified as subversive to the state. Thus, since the now paltry Sinn Féin funds were won by Sinn Féin, it was not a conflict of "democratic" intent. In all, the monies had been effectively spent by the time legal expenses were deducted but it was, after all, a matter of organizational authenticity not money. Though her nephew Seamus Goulding, whom she raised like a son, recalls that she indeed had sympathy for those who had sided with de Valera in the 1926, many of whom were close friends, she had regularly excused people who left Sinn Féin from their posts without anger. Goulding explains: "It [Fianna Fáil] promised everything without ever again having to fight for it."[5] Many people just wanted to stop the fight, but Buckley was committed to the end. Her nephew remembers "[s]he was not a vindictive person, nor could she be, but when it came to the issue of what was known as the Sinn Féin Funds she felt, after much heart-searching, that she and J. J. O'Kelly, Diarmuid O Laoghaire and Seamus O Ruiseal had to grasp the nettle and confront the government and the principals of Fianna Fáil in court."[6] In principle, the legal recognition of organizational continuity had been Margaret Buckley's goal all along.

De Valera's Republicanism

In November 1925, the Sinn Féin Árd Fheis commenced. According to Margaret Buckley's 1956 pamphlet *A Proud History Gives Confidence of Victory*, Eamon de Valera was notably absent from the committee authorized to hammer out the details of the Cahersiveen motion to enter nothing less than a 32-county Republican parliament. Though it was clear that a majority of the Árd Fheis delegates had supported the motion, the committee recommendations were not implemented. At the following Árd Fheis in 1926, de Valera put forth a motion to enter the Dáil Éireann if the oath of allegiance was removed. Father Michael O'Flanagan's amendment to not enter a partition parliament was defeated and the schism within Sinn Féin was apparent: de Valera resigned from Sinn Féin and founded Fianna Fáil that following year. Sinn Féin asked the departing members to tender their resignations and refund their election (TD) deposits back to Sinn Féin, a request that the Fianna Fáil members did not follow.[7] In 1938, all seven of the surviving members of the Second Dáil turned over authority to the IRA Army Council, not the Dáil. A decade later when the Sinn Féin monies were claimed by the de Valera government, Margaret Buckley remained loyal to the Second Dáil. Interesting though not surprising, one of the Sinn Féin treasurers when the Sinn Féin Funds Act had been authorized was Jennie Wyse-Power, who had left Sinn Féin with de Valera. Thus, it was when the fissure of 1927 ruptured that Margaret Buckley's Sinn Féin saw the creation of the constitution in 1937 and the dawn of the Second World War.

Determined to consolidate control over the IRA, the Fianna Fáil Dáil passed the Offences Against the State Act and the Unlawful Organisations Act in 1939, thereby placing Sinn Féin and the IRA on the treason side of the law. Again serving as Eamon de Valera's political conscious, Mary MacSwiney was true to form when, even at the age of 68, she fired off another round of objections. In response to the 1939 Treason Bill, MacSwiney set forth her declarations in a public speech: "The Fianna Fáil Government is guilty of treason by bringing in the Treason Bill to punish those who remained loyal to their oath of allegiance to the Irish Republic."[8] In a somewhat humorous editorial note to the story, the *Irish Press* editor wrote:

> Miss MacSwiney's political views, including those expressed here, are quite familiar to our readers through the repeated publication of her speeches. Her letters have occupied more of our space than those of any other correspondent. About a year ago she wrote saying that she was dissatisfied with our treatment of her correspondence and stated that she would cease sending letters to the IRISH PRESS. Apparently

she has changed her mind and wishes to resume her correspondence with us.[9]

Although humor could be found in MacSwiney's antics, the measures that the Fianna government implemented were of no laughing matter. De Valera's replacement of IRA man P. J. Ruttledge with Gerald Boland as the minister of justice further expressed the intent to purge hard-line Republicans from a Fianna Fáil government.[10]

The so-called emergency powers led to waves of IRA members' arrest. Republicans were interned in Mountjoy Prison at his bequest. His resolve was tested early on when John Plunkett, IRA man and brother of Easter martyr Joseph Mary Plunkett, went on hunger strike with his IRA comrades on February 25, 1940. In a private letter to Mrs. de Valera, Maud Gonne MacBride wrote, "Forgive me for troubling you . . . . Would you as a mother try and save these boys?"[11] Her appeal to Mrs. de Valera did not result in their release, as it became clear that the Taoiseach was prepared to let the IRA men die. In a letter dated March 15, 1940, Josephine Mary Plunkett, John's mother, acknowledged de Valera's response would be his responsibility in their deaths:

To Mr. De Valera

I write as the mother of John Plunkett who, with six other men, are today in their twentyeth day of hunger strike. Lest you may not know the true reason they have adopted this, the only, means of drawing attention to the imprisoning of their comparisons with criminals—it is the same reason that you, with a hundred and twenty others, struck in 1917, where you succeeded in obtaining segregation as political offenders. Your word can relieve these men from the continuance of their fast which is endangering their health and strength and which may even shorten their lives. The responsibility is therefore yours.[12]

Two of the six on strike, Jack (Sean) McNeela and Tony D'Arcy, died that April. The IRA command called off the strike the day of Sean McNeela's death, but a third martyr, Sean McCaughey, would also die on hunger strike over the conditions of his imprisonment in May 1946.

The conditions of arrest and imprisonment were certainly unfavorable, but the lack of a sense of justice as well as the public executions—like that of Dick Goss in August 1941 and George Plant in March 1942 by firing squads or that of Maurice O'Neill in November 1942 by hanging—exposed repression that compromised the hearts of Republicans. Free State authorities, whether in Portlaise Prison or Garda police, were cracking down on IRA men countrywide. Perhaps one of the most infamous tales was that of

Brendan Behan, the playwright who was arrested on April 10, 1942 after a shoot-out with the Garda during an Easter commemoration. He was sentenced to 14 years and served time in Mountjoy before being transferred to the Curragh internment camp in 1943. He remained there with many of the men aforementioned that he eulogized in his poem "The Dead March Past," until given amnesty in December 1946. One of the men that Behan famously envisioned rising to "greet the Easter dawn" was Charlie Kerins.

On December 1, 1944, then IRA chief of staff Charlie Kerins was hung for killing a Special Branch detective, Dennis O'Brien. In the position of chief of staff since 1942, Kerins had executed O'Brien, who had been hunting down his former IRA comrades on behalf of the de Valera government, in September and had lodged his guns and papers at the home of Dr. Kathleen Farrell. Kerins's swift execution sent a clear message from the Fianna government and sent many Sinn Féin members underground.

Those who did not go underground were seen championing other visible causes such as the plight of German war orphans. Dr. Kathleen Farrell was familiar with the impact of war on children, born into a Republican family who understood well the price of being a committed Volunteer: her father was Cornelius Murphy, a founding member of the Gaelic League and later a Fianna Fáil candidate for the Dáil. She grew up with her elder sister Connie and brothers Fergus and Conn in Rathgar just outside of Dublin proper. Her father was a staunch Anti-Treatyite and had served time in Mountjoy, where he organized a hunger strike during the Civil War. Her sister Connie was imprisoned during the same time, serving time in Cork, Kilmainham, and the North Dublin Union. Kathleen attended University College Dublin, where her father had been on staff prior to the war and rose quickly through the ranks of Cumann na mBan, serving as captain while she was in medical school. During World War II, Kathleen formed the Save the Children (Saor an Leanbh) organization for German children orphaned during the war. She married Paul Farrell and had four children, one of whom she briefly served time in jail alongside for their activities. Kathleen remained a tireless advocate for children, regardless of their country of origin, until her death in 1970.

Most certainly, it was not any easier to be a Republican in the Six Counties during this time period. A Cavan County Council meetings record from January 16, 1940, recounted a letter from the Irish Prisoners' National Aid Society regarding the RUC's efforts to control the Republicans:

At intervals the police [RUC] stage a "round up" of all people suspected of being Republicans. They are given no semblance of a trial, no charge being brought against them even. They are simply cast into prison and left to rot. Those at present in the Derry Gaol are to be held, according to Lord Craigavon, for the duration of the war. The only crime of some of the men interned was teaching Irish in the Gaelic League.[13]

The letter depicts a community under siege, where nightly RUC raids to intimidate Republican families for multiple offenses (sometimes only for speaking Irish) included abusive interrogations, the ransacking of houses, and the terrorizing of children.

In 1946, Seán MacBride, son of Maud Gonne MacBride, founded Clann na Pochlachta in the wake of the Republican crisis. His appeal as a direct legacy in the movement was clear, but a miscalculation in the policy of abstentionism may have cost Clann na Pochlachta's success. While the Republicans underwent a reorganization effort, Clann na Pochlachta's support rose due in part to the rejection of the government's treatment of hard-line Republicans. Attempting to preempt any further popularity, Eamon de Valera called for an election in February 1948. The results placed Clann na Pochlachta in coalition governance with Fine Gael, the conservative party of Ireland that had once been associated with the retaining the Commonwealth. Clann na Pochlachta's joint acceptance of the 1937 constitution and coalition with Fine Gael sealed its doomed fate. The hard-line Republicans, though interned throughout 1946, emerged in 1947 to reorganize within Sinn Féin, Cumann na mBan and the IRA.

As Margaret Langsdorf assumed the presidency of Cumann na mBan, Margaret Buckley was busily restructuring Sinn Féin, and IRA men were hurriedly reconstituting the Army Council. Though the Fianna government had done its best to subjugate the Republicans, the hypocrisy of interning, executing, and banning Republicans was not lost on the Irish public. Fianna Fáil suffered for their actions, allowing for a Fine Gael–Clann na Pochlachta government. The newly reenergized IRA Army Council moved to expel any members who joined Clann na Pochlachta in 1947 on the grounds that it recognized the partitionist Dáil and honored the 1937 constitution. Claiming to be the only party to maintain the principles of the 1916 Proclamation, Sinn Féin became the sole heir of the Republican legacy, but it would take Margaret Buckley to have this declaration "proven" in a court of law in 1948.

Meanwhile, the state of Sinn Féin in 1948 was anything but glorious. As Ruairí Ó Brádaigh recounts in an interview with Brian Feeney in *Sinn Féin: A Hundred Turbulent Years*, "the extent of the Sinn Féin organization in 1948 was pitiful: a few Sinn Féin *cumainn* in Dublin, one in Cork and one in Glasgow."[14] The political prisoners of the 1940s had all been released by September 1948, and the IRA decided to cease activities in the Twenty-Six Counties. The surge of antipartitionist sentiment pushed many younger persons, including Ruairí Ó Brádaigh himself, to join the IRA and Sinn Féin in this time period. Young IRA men like Mr. Ó Brádaigh joined Sinn Féin in droves and effectively infiltrated the political party with mission-styled objectives. By November 1950, shortly after Margaret Buckley stepped down, there were cumainn across almost every country in Ireland. The revitalized Sinn Féin was most certainly Dublin based, since the MacBride government was comparatively tolerant of hard-line Republicans, in stark contrast to its predecessor and to the Stormont government in the Six Counties. The result was a reorganized Sinn Féin movement with a tactical focus on the partition of the island of Ireland.

Partition of Ireland—The Republic

With the Second World War over in 1945, the issue that most Republicans saw looming was the continued partition of Ireland. The Anti-Partition League was founded 1946 and served to centralize growing discontent concerning the establishment of the Six Counties. Serendipitously coinciding with the peak of Fianna Fáil's IRA extermination attempts and the founding of MacBride's Clann na Plobachta, the issue of partition was an easier topic to unify Irish discontent. Among the Anti-Partitionists was the all familiar Máire Comerford, who wrote the *Irish Times* on May 5, 1950, stating: "Will anyone deny that neither Arthur Griffith nor Michael Collins would have conceived it possible that such a request would be refused by a native Government 28 years after the signing of the Treaty, which was, from their point of view, intended to give these people the right of self-determination?"[15] Partition, it seemed, could not be stopped and on April 18, 1949, with John Costello as Taoiseach, the product of many of de Valera's negotiations came to fruition—that being a Republic of Ireland, the 26-county version. Having left the Commonwealth, Ireland left an irredentist Six Counties remaining in the clasp of the United Kingdom and the Six Counties formally became known as Northern Ireland.

Hard-line Republicans systematically refused to acknowledge the provisions of the 1948 (Republic of Ireland) Oireachtas Act that announced the 26-county republic. This was still Margaret Buckley's Sinn Féin and she would not allow Republicans to legitimize a subversion of the loyalty to the 1916 Republic. With relations on the mend with the IRA by 1949, Sinn Féin became a political mouthpiece for this Anti-Partitionism, although the fruits of their labor would be six years in the making during the 1955 Westminster Parliament elections. The IRA Army Council, however, immediately initiated the formulation of the Resistance Campaign, which it rolled out in 1956.

Madam Buckley

At her final Árd Fheis speech as president of Sinn Féin in 1950, Mrs. Margaret Buckley addressed a faithful yet small audience, including a shy young first-year student at University College Dublin named Ruairí Ó Brádaigh, who would later be the president of Sinn Féin. "Well, we're back here together again, despite the begrudgers" she is reported to have said.[16] Ó Brádaigh recalls that his first Árd Fheis was held "in number nine Parnell Square which was the headquarters of Sinn Féin and it was in the big front room which accommodated everyone . . . . [T]there weren't that many of us you know but it was quite an occasion."[17] In awe of someone that he had been reading about, Ó Brádaigh found her to be more manly than many of the men; not masculine per say, but of "a push up and go to" indomitable spirit. After the Árd Fheis, Margaret Buckley, or "Madam Buckley" as the younger members of the Ard Chomhairle would refer to her, stepped down to the role of vice president until a fateful Saturday evening at nine o'clock in 1957.

When Margaret Buckley delivered her final presidential address at the Árd Fheis in 1950, it was neither her last presidential speech nor was it the end of her involvement. Ruairí Ó Brádaigh, Sinn Féin president from 1970 to 1983 and founding member of Republican Sinn Féin in 1986, remembers that well after she retired as Sinn Féin president, Margaret Buckley would participate in Sinn Féin public meetings. The public meetings were held outside the Lower Abbey Street and O'Connell Street outside the Elvery's sports shop, and Mr. Ó Brádaigh can still recall Mrs. Buckley sitting atop the lorry quite regally, speaking to protesters. On the occasion of the 1951 arrest of Republicans in Belfast, he recounts that Mrs. Buckley personally saw to it that a black flag was flown outside the Sinn Féin headquarters to protest their weeklong internment.[18] Far from demure and quiet, Margaret Buckley remained a perennial, looming, and influential feature of Sinn Féin throughout the 1950s Sinn Féin presidencies. Padraig MacLogan served as president of Sinn Féin from 1950 to 1962 (with the sole exception of a one-year term served by Tom Doyle in 1953–54). MacLogan, like most of the Sinn Féin Ard Chomhairle, was on the IRA Army Council, and the fact that the IRA had infiltrated Sinn Féin seemed to suit both organizations. Some accounts depict this as a passing of the old guard in Sinn Féin while some relegate this to a military style takeover of the political party. If the roar of the IRA lion seemed to overshadow the electoral engineering of Sinn Féin, it was most certainly influenced by the proscription of Sinn Féin and (when not proscribed) its policy of abstentionism, a topic that would once again divide Republicans in the 1980s.

The 1950s were a challenging time to be a Republican in Ireland. The North had just been partitioned to the central objection of Republicans, and both governments, North and South, were unwilling to tolerate an IRA or Sinn Féin presence. In the 1940s, the Six Counties had been dominated by the B-Specials and the RUC. There were many internments and many arrests but of all the executions and internments it was that of 19-year-old IRA lad Tom Williams that many of the ballads enshrine. Captured shortly after a shoot-out in Belfast at a banned Easter commemoration parade that resulted in the death of a Catholic RUC man, Williams took responsibility for his entire six-men, two-women unit and was sentenced to death. His cellmate in the Crumlin Road Jail was Joe Cahill, who went on to be a key figure in the IRA and an honorary vice president of Sinn Féin. On September 2 1942, Williams was hung by the RUC and thrown in an unmarked grave on the jail grounds, where he remained until 2000 when he was reburied outside the prison walls. It was the way of Republican life— and death—in the North and as the '50s unfolded, Tom Williams's story was replicated across the Six Counties. In the end, the defining moments of the decade boiled down to the actions of the Resistance Campaign and the 1957 internments.

The Resistance Campaign

Growing discontent with the IRA seemed to concentrate efforts in two strategies: an armed ambush of targets by the IRA and focusing Sinn Féin efforts on Westminster elections, as opposed to Dáil or Stormont elections. The shift to Westminster politics was deliberate: Sinn Féin candidates had not been put forth in the Dáil due to the oppressive Fianna Fáil tactics and though Sinn Féin itself was soon to be a proscribed organization again in the Six Counties, independent Republican candidates for Stormont would not take the required oath of allegiance to assume office even though they could run prior to 1953. Stormont then began to pass legislation that restricted the Republicans or nationalists from even declaring candidacy. In 1951, the Public Order Act made it illegal for persons to take part in an unlawful procession (a demonstration march) and in 1953 passed legislation that has prospective candidates take an oath of allegiance before nomination, which Republicans would not do. Furthermore, the 1954 Flags and Emblems Act outlawed the use of the Irish tricolor. Curiously, Westminster parliamentary elections did not require the oath of allegiance for candidacy that Stormont elections did and Republicans took full advantage of this:[19] in 1955, Sinn Féin fielded Republican candidates Phil Clarke in Fermanagh/South Tyrone and Tom Mitchell in Mid-Ulster. Surprisingly, both men won but were then disqualified on the basis that they had been convicted of treason felony legislation.

In the midst of the electoral strategy, the story of Jimmy Drumm, husband of future Sinn Féin vice president Máire Drumm, suddenly captured the plight of the dedicated Republicans in the Six Counties, having first found prison in 1938 at the tender age of 17. He was released from the Crumlin Road Jail in 1940 only to be interned shortly thereafter while his fiancé Máire visited him until 1945. In 1956, Jimmy was interned for a second time without trial and remained in jail until the conclusion of the Resistance Campaign. Unabashedly committed to a Republican destiny, Jimmy returned to his post and was an unfortunate target during the Operation Demetrius sweep of August 9, 1971. Máire was left to raise five young children during his stay in Long Kesh.[20] The price was high for these Republican men and women, both for those in the field and for those supporting them at home.

The Resistance Campaign lasted from 1956 to 1962, but it is often said to have been comprised of two parts. From 1956 to 1959, the campaign focused on procuring weapons from barracks in the Six Counties, then from 1959 to 1962 operated as the Border Campaign. Ruairí Ó Brádaigh, the IRA chief of staff at the conclusion of the Resistance (or Border) Campaign, was the author of the 1962 IRA statement ending said campaign. He explains the political meaning of the Resistance terminology: "The Republican view is that this was a general resistance campaign. The British institutional perspective was that it was a border campaign since this recognized the partition."[21]

Though little has been written concerning it, Ó Brádaigh reveals that "Cumann na mBan were a vital component of the general resistance campaign; if one were to examine the numbers of Republican prisoners during this time, it would be clear that the men were interned while the women, by and large, were not. This left them, as it had during the internment of Charles Stewart Parnell and the Irish Land League experience, to pick up the pieces of organizational activity."[22] A few of the women did not escape the swift arm of internment: in 1956, Bridie O'Neill was interned in the North for a full seven months and in the South, Tessa Carney, secretary of the Prisoner's Dependents Fund, was taken into Mountjoy for refusing to pay a fine. The fact that neither woman's imprisonment raised a public outrage was symptomatic of the political times.

The 1956–1962 "Operation Harvest" campaign was planned by IRA Army Council chief of staff Seán Cronin. On December 12, 1956, four IRA columns, some 120 men, attacked bridges and military targets in the Six Counties. Perhaps one of the most commemorated missions was the 1957

Brookeborough raid. Though not generally or operationally successful, it raised a significant level of support for Sinn Féin and the IRA. In a January 2007 speech honoring the two men killed in January 1957, Sinn Féin president Gerry Adams retold the story of Republican lore:

> I remember at a commemoration in Monaghan how Daithí Ó Conaill enthralled us all with his account of the Brookeborough raid.
>
> As he recalled it that day there was snow on the ground and in the hills. 14 IRA Volunteers set out in a lorry from Bunlogher at around 7pm to attack the RUC barracks in Brookeborough village. 11 volunteers lay in the back of the truck. They were armed with a mixture of weapons, including two Bren guns, two Thompsons, and 303 rifles. They also had two mines, six grenades and six Molotov cocktails.
>
> The two mines were placed at the front door but both failed to explode. In the gun battle that ensued Feargal Ó hAnnluain and Seán Sabhat were mortally wounded.[23]

Following the immortalized legacy of the Brookeborough martyrs, a Dáil election was called for March 5, 1957. Four Sinn Féin TD candidates were elected, all men, including Ruairí Ó Brádaigh for Longford/Westmeath. In the same election, de Valera became Taoiseach again and reintroduced internment that July.

1957 Internment

The Curragh internment camp had cement floors in the huts. The jail had formerly been the cavalry stables of the British Army, and the bowls for washing had been the animals' food containers.[24] The dehumanization of the Curragh internment camp a few miles outside of Dublin and the "security measures" of the camp produced the outrage captured in a 1958 Sinn Féin publicity document: "At the moment a further 'security' restriction is being implemented. This consists of steel or strong mesh over the windows of the huts in which the men are billited or which they use for other purposes. With the erection of this mesh the way for escape from the huts in the event of fire is confined to a single doorway."[25] With Fianna Fáil back in power and the Curragh camp reopened for prisoners, de Valera's controversial tactics were reintroduced. Just as they had been in the 1940s, the tactics were once again illicit and deliberate: root out the Republican threat to the Fianna government.

On the Saturday evening on the first weekend in July of 1957, internment of prominent Republicans swept the Twenty-Six Counties. Much like their comrades in the Six Counties that previous winter (including Jimmy

Drumm), most hard-line Republicans found themselves in jail. The Curragh internment had been cleverly planned: the 26-county Dáil had just gone into recess for the summer and security forces descended upon a regular meeting of the Ard Chomhairle as the head office in Dublin was swept by security forces. All 12 of the men on the National Executive were imprisoned minus the sole woman member, Mrs. Margaret Buckley. Although her ill health and not her gender may have been the reason for her freedom, the "woman of no importance" went straight down to the Sunday *Press* to give a statement about the sweep of Sinn Féin officers, though the government maintained that it was a meeting of the IRA Army council. Mr. Ó Brádaigh, having trained the Teeling Column of the IRA in the West of Ireland, found himself in Mountjoy initially and remembers that Madam Buckley was "equal to the occasion" to continue Sinn Féin activities in the Ard Chomhairle's absence. Her quick thinking and masterful response saved many senior Sinn Féin members from the sweep.

Ó Brádaigh chuckles as he tells the story of one such member.[26] Mick McCarthy was out fishing with his family outside of Cork City when someone advised him to read the Sunday *Press* statement that Buckley had issued. In it, Buckley detailed the most recent sweep and stated that the Garda gave no explanation for the incident. She was quoted as saying: "We are completely at a loss to know why our members were taken into custody."[27] She additionally noted that no documents were taken in the raid even though there were papers on the table in preparation for the meeting. Her mastery over the power of news communication served as an early warning for other Republicans. Alerted of the price on his head, Mick McCarthy fled and it was a full 15 months later when the Garda caught up with him!

That fall with Sinn Féin president Padraig MacLogan still imprisoned, Mrs. Buckley, serving as the vice president, delivered the presidential address to the Árd Fheis in Dublin. She reiterated that Sinn Féin was still committed to the Republic proclaimed in 1916 and that she was pleased with the recent by-election results, especially in the Dublin North Central district, which was not heavily republican.[28]

As support for the Curragh internees rose, de Valera's confidence seemed to retreat. By the fall of 1958 when Ruairí Ó Brádaigh was the chief of staff of the IRA, Eamon de Valera was poised to release the internees and in March of 1959 the Curragh internment camp closed.[29] Though public support appeared to be behind the Republican prisoners, this did not translate into Sinn Féin electoral support and the October 1959 Westminster elections produced abysmal results for Sinn Féin. By February 1962, Ruairí Ó Brádaigh was once again serving as IRA chief of staff and as such penned the letter ending the Resistance Campaign.

CONCLUSION—THE END OF AN ERA

By 1960, Margaret Buckley was quite ill and retreating from her active public life. Most of her Republican efforts in these years were spent writing articles under the name Margaret Lee. Her Sinn Féin had orchestrated an attempt at electoral politics and the IRA's Resistance Campaign would shortly come to a close, but if one thought that Sinn Féin would fade away on the pages of Irish history, they would be mistaken. In June 1959, Eamon de Valera took his bow as Taoiseach leaving Sean Lemass, who downplayed the nationalist rhetoric that preceded him, at the helm of the partitioned Republic. Margaret Buckley, the "woman of no importance," had been ever so important. Throughout her presidency, Buckley's efforts to keep Sinn Féin engaged produced a solid declaration of Republican continuity and normalized relations with the IRA. She passed away on July 24, 1962, just a few months after the Resistance Campaign had ceased, leaving behind her the great legacy of the Sinn Féin movement. She was truly a woman of extraordinary importance to Sinn Féin, who made a 32-county Irish Republic her life's duty. Though discouraged by splintered movements and derelict status during the difficult 1940s and 1950s, Margaret Buckley's Sinn Féin had not been snuffed out into historical obscurity. Though it redefined what a Republic would be in the 20th century, the partition of the Irish State had failed to permanently partition the Republican mind.

Chapter 4

VOICES OF EQUALITY, 1960s

What allowed us to survive and to increase was the fact that they [the British government] tried so often to separate us as revolutionaries or as freedom fighters from the community and they failed miserably you understand—we were the community. It was the community sons and daughters. They could never have succeeded in separating us from the community, and that still holds true today. We are these people.

—Eibhlín Glenholmes[1]

CHAPTER OVERVIEW

There is something instinctive about a mother protecting her child. Whether through forces of nature or animalistic fury, the woman feels the child's pain and is inspired to do anything to stop that pain. It is compelling and powerful. It is amazing, then, when a mother tempers the surge of biological impetus and surmounts the looming threat with a mental sea of calm to protect her young. The passion is channeled into focus and determination, perhaps even into vision. Transcending defensive urges, the woman sees clearly a path to the normative solution of steadfast compassion. In the eye of the storm, she rises above the turbulent waves of her environment and, still recognizing the eminent danger to her child, the mother plunges into a whirlwind of danger to take her stand on her principles. It is an inspiring feat of survival to raise a family in a war zone.

By the end of 1960s, life for a Republican child in the Northern Six Counties of Ireland was full of possibilities—the possibility of being shot by a stray bullet, the possibility of being detained and interrogated by the British Army, the possibility of visiting a father or mother in jail, the possibility of losing a friend or a sibling, the possibility of receiving an inferior education and living in substandard facilities, the possibility of not having enough to eat each day. In the midst of physical and psychological terror, these children faced daily stress and intimidation. There is a saying that each time a parent argues in front of their children, that it changes who they are. If this is to be believed, then imagine how much these children were changed by the arguments taking place in Northern Irish society.

Chapter Organization

The 1960s was a turbulent decade. The discrimination against Catholics in the North bubbled over. Unequal access to basic citizenship rights— voting, political representation, social services, and the like—erupted into social protests. The second-class citizenship status paralleled the plight of African Americans in the States, and from the U.S. civil rights movement, Irish community organizers learned the importance of neighborhood patrols, marches, and national demonstrations. The IRA and Sinn Féin had long since dwindled, but in the awakening consciousness of political activism, they came to the defense of communities under siege.

This chapter recounts the context of the rise of republicanism in Northern Ireland and the street politics of the 1960s. As the RUC police came for the men, the Republican women faced the impossible task of staging protests, organizing hen patrols and bin brigades, and tending to their families. Meanwhile, Sinn Féin undertook a not-so-concealed resurgence as "Republican Clubs." As the Troubles ignited in August 1969, the female voice of Sinn Féin had been projected through megaphones and on box platforms. The "hens" and "wags" included many local women, hitherto unknown to Republican politics, but forever known after as community legends. Among them were the Gildernews, Bernadette Devlin, Mary Nelis, and Marie Moore. Individually, these women were hens on patrol in their communities, but collectively, they are a legendary force for change.

HISTORICAL OVERVIEW

- Community Organization
- Reorganization in the North
- The Troubles Ignite

Community Organization

The Republican woman faced the same challenges; but, coupled with the overwhelming concern for her family's well-being, tending to her household obligations, and struggling to achieve or maintain employment, her challenges must have seem enormous. But it was here, in the midst of turbulent times, that she rose up and plunged into the stagnant inertia that oppressed her.

Daily concerns of second-class citizenship dominated the political landscape of the 1960s. Torn by the injustice they were surrounded by and the demands placed upon you at home, many women bravely chose to act. Forming Women's Action Groups (WAGS) to confront the issues, Catholic (and Republican) women took to the streets to raise awareness and call for action. But social action took organization and time—time that a mother, for example, may not have had in plentiful supply since childcare and money were scarce. Thus, the sacrifices were great, but the cause even greater, since their actions were meant to improve the future for their community.

Those women who were employed outside of the home faced daily intimidation and often discrimination from their Unionist colleagues and employers. Although there were organized unions in place, they seemed to only represent the interests of one community—the Unionist one. But community, for Sinn Féin, was inclusive not exclusive. It is a lesson of acceptance and of community connection that Sinn Féin understood. The first national coordinator for gender equality, Eibhlín Glenholmes, explains:

> We are the community. We identify with these issues because we live them. We want changes because that's our mommy or daddy lying in that hospital. It's our kids going to these schools so we want the best education system. And that's why we have the policies that we'll deliver for everyone because we will never do this . . . , that's the fear of Unionists that we will inflict on them what they inflicted on us if we ever came into power, and that is absolutely the polar opposite of everything that we represent. We would be called the oppressors, and that is a role that we would never be happy in and we would never ever consider. I think of Bobby Sands: 'our revenge will be the laughter of our children.' He was so far ahead of us. We're still catching up.[2]

The community was dwindling as well. The 1961 census returns in the Republic reflected the lowest level of population since the Famine. Emigration rose, as did unemployment. Those who were fortunate enough to hold jobs eked out a meager wage that could not sustain a family. It was a dismal economy with a dismal forecast, and in the midst of it all, Sinn Féin struggled to respond to the community's basic needs of food, shelter, jobs, and fundamental human rights.

In 1962, the Irish Republican Army called off the Resistance (border) Campaign. It was a whimper of an operation that had been plagued with low recruitment, success, and community support. Reflecting this low level of support, at the Árd Fheis conference in November of 1960, Sinn Féin president Padraig MacLogain railed against the Twenty-Six County police for their treatment of conference attendees. In a November 7, 1960, article in the *Irish Press,* he equated the Garda detainment of the Árd Fheis attendees and the seizure of their printed agendas and reports to that of the Stormont authorities. Furthermore, the arrests and detentions of Sinn Féin members, he argued, was an attempt to demoralize members and starve their dependents.[3] Attempts to continue the Resistance Campaign continued throughout 1960 and 1961, with little success; in February 1961, a woman named Mary Nolan was arrested in Liverpool for smuggling explosives to Dublin. Intercepted at a Dublin rail station, Garda police found a trunk containing over 100 gelignite sticks and an envelope with her Liverpool address on it. According to the *Irish Times,* a search of her home in Liverpool produced several more gelignite sticks, four bullets, and over 20 letters from Dublin.[4] Under interrogation, she revealed that she had joined Sinn Féin in 1958 and been given the three boxes in which to mail materials to Dublin. She additionally revealed that the letters used the words "golf balls" as a code for bullets.[5] The sensational nature of the story, covered in the *Irish Press* and *Irish Independent* as well, demonstrates that it was a substantial stash of weaponry for 1961.

Meanwhile, as the IRA wound down the Resistance Campaign, tensions began to rise to the surface in the North. Keenly aware of the situation in the Six Counties in the early 1960s, the Republicans prioritized reorganization to cope with the needs of the Catholic community. Establishing the Wolfe Tone Societies in Dublin and in Belfast enabled Republicans to refocus and reengage. The state of Sinn Féin had not been much stronger than the IRA in the 1960s. Daisy Mules, a Derry schoolteacher who has served on the Ard Chomhairle, described the relationship: "After the civil war until about 1970, Sinn Féin was in existence almost exclusively as a support network for the armed struggle. During the civil rights movement in the six counties, Sinn Féin was initially tied into support for the armed struggle in terms of selling republican newspapers and propaganda, but it did not really have a political agenda as such."[6] Keenly aware that it needed to be reinvigorated, the Sinn Féin Ard Chomhairle, now dominated by IRA men, responded to the social needs of the Irish community. At the Árd Fheis in 1962, Sinn Féin discussed the prospects of developing a new economic and social platform, one that reflected the extreme leftist elements of some of its Ard Chomhairle. Though it was quite divisive, it was against the provisions of IRA membership to be a Communist.[7] Under the direction of Sinn Féin president Tomas MacGiolla (1962–1970) and IRA chief of staff Cathal Goulding, and shaped by the ideas of Roy Johnson, the Sinn Féin men sought to reconcile the ideology of Marxism, the crises facing Irish North and South, and traditional republicanism.

In 1963, Pope John XXIII died and Terence O'Neill became prime minister of Northern Ireland. Not that the two events were interrelated, but the overarching state of flux across Europe certainly affected the course of Irish history in the 1960s. In the midst of the Vatican reorganization, Sinn Féin developed the Social and Economic Programme, approved at the 1964 Árd Fheis, which, although true to Arthur Griffith's initial vision of republicanism, seemed protectionist in the climate of global free trade. As the unification of what would later become the European Union took root on the continent, trade relations between Ireland and England seemed to be echoing the modern, regionalization trends. However, the state of the Irish economy, North and South, and Sinn Féin's efforts to promote rural cooperatives, factory-worker *cumainn* (basic organizational unit within Sinn Féin), and egalitarianism did not seem to mesh. Refreshed with a political agenda, Sinn Féin identified the social protest trend sweeping Europe and the United States—sit-ins, demonstrations, marches, and fish-ins became the primary tool of Republican action. It was clear that contemporary issues of inequality and injustice, across many areas of policy, were to become the agenda dominating Sinn Féin politics in the 1960s. The swell of populist strategies breathed new life into a defunct military agenda by activating persons across all communities to action.

Due to the proscribed status of Sinn Féin in the North after 1964 and the relationship with the Séan Lemass government in the South, many of its initiatives appeared on the political stage without credits, though the authorities had little doubt who had played the part. Housing Action Committees sprung up in Dublin and in Derry. Republican Clubs, organizing speakers, debates, and student protests, cropped up at universities across the 32 counties. And in October 1964, the product of the bicentenary of Wolfe Tone's birth, the Wolfe Tone Society was founded in Dublin. Orchestrating a discourse on the intellectual values of republicanism (and hence reinforcing the move away from the armed struggle as the exclusive strategy), the Wolfe Tone Society's offered a forum for the dissemination of the Sinn Féin's Social and Economic Programme. The societies also cleverly opened up an arena for "protestant, catholic and dissenter" to engage in public discourse on the crisis of contemporary issues. The point was not lost in the North, where some Protestants joined the Belfast Wolfe Tone Society too.

Reorganization in the North

Awoken from the "twilight" slumber of the 1950s, Sinn Féin heeded the call of a community intolerant to their second-class citizenship. This, however, was no easy task, for, as Ruairí Ó Brádaigh explains, "what happened was that in the end of December 1956 Sinn Féin was banned in the Six Counties, and there was a group of students in Omagh that were jailed by the RUC for putting up Sinn Féin posters. 'Don't emigrate Join Sinn Féin Find your Corner' read the posters."[8] With RUC forces on the heels of IRA members breeching the border, active Republicans often found themselves in jail. Ó Brádaigh himself was among them, from 1956 to 1958, when he and Daithí Ó Conaill escaped.

And so it was that, in 1962, the Republican Clubs were used as a cover name for Sinn Féin until they were banned in 1967. In elections, people were called Republican candidates and ran as "Independents," as in 1966 when Ruairí Ó Brádaigh stood for the Fermanagh/S. Tyrone seat. The "Republican party" was the way the press referred to them, but everyone knew it was really a Sinn Féin candidate. Sinn Féin gravitated to a heavier Marxist ideology during this time. Roy Johnson had formed an intellectual society he called the "Wolfe Tone Society," (discussed earlier) and very quickly, the socialist ideologies took over Sinn Féin as they had in the 1930s. By the mid-1960s, it seemed that RUC were no longer enforcing the Republican Club ban, so in 1969, when the split with the Officials occurred, Provisional Sinn Féin dropped the Republican Club name. Official Sinn Féin continued using the Republican Club banner until the ban was removed in 1974.

In 1969, the split heard round Ireland occurred. In addition to the rising wave of Marxist ideology, the issue of abstentionism—a core principle of Arthur Griffith's Sinn Féin—had torn the party in two. Those who favored abandoning abstentionism were called Officials, including Roy Johnston (or Stickies for the Easter lilies that they would stick to their lapels). Those who held fast to the principle of abstentionism, headed by Ruairí Ó Brádaigh, adopted the name Provisional Sinn Féin. The Sinn Féin headed by Gerry Adams lays claim to this lineage. More concerning the Provisional-Official split in Sinn Féin is examined in the conclusion of this chapter.

Meanwhile, the issue of civil rights became a national issue in Ireland. Systemic abuses of disenfranchisement of Catholics in the North dominated daily life. In 1964, Conn and Patricia McClusky founded the Campaign for Social Justice (CSJ) in Dungannon. Documenting the plight of the housing crisis and demanding the acquisition of civil rights for all Catholics in the North, CSJ became a catalyst for the civil rights movement. The double standards of British democracy in Northern Ireland placed Catholics in the role of second-class citizens in their own government. Facing many of the same social and economic issues as persons in the South, the situation in the Six Counties was exacerbated by the political (governmental) treatment of republicanism laden with socioeconomic inequalities. Treated as inferior by the Unionist government, Catholics were denied social services afforded their Protestant neighbors, such as housing. Since housing was a requisite for voting (One House One Vote), this further disenfranchised them in the electoral arena as well. Hence, the discrimination of social and economic policy was institutionalized, even reinforced, by the fact that they had no outlet for political recourse.

The Derry March was held on October 5, 1968. Organized by the Derry Housing Action Committee and blessed by the Northern Irish Civil Rights Association, the march was scheduled to be a nonviolent protest of the housing policies in Derry. As the protesters approached their route, they were greeted by RUC forces in riot gear. Images of the RUC charging the unarmed crowd with batons was eerily reminiscent of the Alabama police in the 1950s in the States. Rioting over the incident raged for two days after the protest. Many historians refer to this march as the beginning of the Troubles.

Bernadette Devlin was watching the events on television that day. Her outrage was immediate and swift. The Queens University Belfast student formed People's Democracy, a student-based organization, and began planning a four-day march from Belfast to Derry for that following January. The People's Democracy march also ended in violence, for as the marchers approached the Burntollet Bridge right outside Derry, they were greeted by Protestant protesters who attacked them. Many were later revealed to be off-duty RUC men. But the resolve to persist in the protest against injustice remained.

The movement that Sinn Féin was making toward a rights-based social agitation harnessed the energy of the disaffected into protest action and would expose the Stormont government's dubious discrimination. Furthermore, community-based agitation opened up a fertile opportunity for women, often bearing the brunt of the social ills and discriminatory practices, to take to the streets to be heard.

The Troubles Ignite

On August 12, 1969, the Apprentice Boys (a historical organization that celebrates the Apprentice Boys of 1688 who supported Williamite forces in the Siege of Derry) held a commemorative march through the Derry city center. Two days earlier, the Derry Citizens Defense Association, a group of community activists, had approached the Apprentice Boys asking them to delay or cancel the march as it would be provocative to nationalists within the barricades of Free Derry. Their requests were unheeded, and the commemoration proceeded as scheduled. Coming to the edge of Free Derry while nationalist protesters jeered and threw rocks at the marchers, the tension mounted until around seven o'clock when the RUC attempted to push the nationalists back behind the barricades and into the Bogside. What happened next was broadcast around the world, as a full on engagement exploded. Over 1,000 cans of CS gas and 14 gas grenades were thrown into the Bogside over the three-day battle; close to 1,000 casualties were treated by first aid responders during the Battle of the Bogside, according to the Museum of Free Derry. As Nell McCafferty recalled in a 2000 speech during the West Belfast Féile, "I saw my mother, a deeply, respectable woman of 58, strip a blanket from the bed, go down to the Free Derry Corner, join a line of other 50-year-old women to run a petrol-bomb making factory. She did what she had to do."[9]

According to the Bloody Sunday Trust, over 500 women and children had to be evacuated to nearby Donegal on the first night. By morning, a hodgepodge collection of young girls and boys were perched at the top of the Rossville flats with petrol bombs meant for the Unionist rioters and RUC forces. Violence erupted across towns in the Six Counties. By the 14th of August, the British Army had assembled to impose a cessation to the civil violence. The rapid mobilization of young girls and women was a method of community defense that had become, in a way, necessary due to the impact of the suppression of nationalist/Republican men in the years before the Battle of the Bogside. Former Deputy Mayor of Belfast, Marie Moore recalled:

> Because naturally enough, women, with so many being in jail, they were the steadfast person within the house; they were the mother, the father, the breadwinner in some cases. And of course were naturally frightened that they could be next and the family would be left without anyone. Psychologically, your children come first and your family comes first, and everything else that you see comes after that. I think that's in most women: make sure my family's all right and then I'll do what I have to do.[10]

Mobilized to relieve the RUC and quell the disorder, the British Army arrived in the Six Counties on the 14th and 15th of August 1969. Sinn Féin activist Chrissie McAuley grew up in West Belfast. During the late 1970s and 1980s, she wrote for *An Phoblacht/Republican News*. She recalls the initial occupation:

> That August, when the RUC and the notorious B Specials led loyalist mobs on attacks into nationalist areas, burning houses in their hundreds and shooting dead several innocent people, and my family fled from our home [in West Belfast's Lower Falls area], was a turning point in my life. Little nine-year-old Patrick Rooney from Divis Flats in the Lower Falls was shot dead as he lay sleeping in bed. I remember thinking that it could have been anyone. Any catholic was, and remains today, a potential victim of such sectarian hatred.[11]

Sectarian violence, coupled with the imposition of a British occupation, led to the erection of barricades on the streets and in the hearts of the Six Counties. Chrissie further explains that "[d]uring the subsequent years, the widespread raids on houses again brought women onto the streets in protest, banging bin lids and blowing whistles. It became common practice for women, outnumbered and confronted by heavily-armed soldiers, to pull and free arrested teenagers from jeeps and saracens."[12] The waves of threats crashed onto the shores of the Bogside community in Derry and the Falls Road in Belfast and, soon, all throughout the Six Counties. By September 9–10, the "peace line" went up overnight in Belfast, dividing the communities in an ideological fog of war. In this sea of conflict, many a Republican woman stood firm to protect any semblance of normalcy for her family and to protest the encroachment on her dignity.

HENS AND WAGS

- A Female Voice
- The Gildernew Family
- Bernadette Devlin McAliskey
- Mary Nelis
- Marie Moore

A Female Voice

Feminism, though principally intertwined with the ideology of republicanism, suffered fleeting attention throughout the 1960s. An international movement to reexamine, even reformulate, social gender roles merged into the Civil Rights Movement in Northern Ireland. Though many saw ethnic equality and gender equality in two spheres of organizational goals, for

Sinn Féin, equality encompassed both arenas. More largely stated, there was a crisis in human rights and an evidence of human suffering that came to define the Republican agenda. Equality meant complete equality, and as women emerged onto the forefront of the Civil Rights Movement, Sinn Féin harnessed their energy.

In truth, it was both an organizational necessity and an ideological complement. Most of the Republican women were not yet identified by the police (both the RUC and the Garda). The realization of female leadership in the Republican movement had been known to Sinn Féin all along, especially during the Markievicz, MacSwiney, and Buckley days, but in the rank and file, the consciousness of one's individual capabilities to transform a society *as an individual agent of change* surfaced in the 1960s. Mary Nelis, a community activist during this period, describes the political awakening of Catholic women in a turbulent social and political environment:

> I can see now in retrospect that that's where women actually came into their own in Derry, because they have never gone back. A lot of women whose roles were cut out for them—be a good wife, be a good mother—because of the influence of the Catholic Church, decided 'No, that's not what my life's about. I'm a woman first. I'm a human being. There's other things about, not just sitting at home looking after children and being denied any option.' So the role of women has changed tremendously, because women became involved in every campaign that was going, from the civil rights movement right through the bin lids. And women paid a high price for it.[13]

Though the price was high, the recourse was silent submission in an unjust society. Former Sinn Féin publicity director Mairead Keane sees lessons in the holes in female Republican activism. In a 1991 interview, she states: "A lot was lost, certainly in terms of the development of the movement from those years from 1926 to 1969. What women have learned today from those women's experiences of fighting in the uprising and actively participating at the turn of the century is that women must put their demands on an agenda in a strong, coherent manner."[14]

Finding one's voice in a society that reinforced your gender, ethnicity, and social class as inferior must have been a seemingly insurmountable task, but four such women's experiences lit the path to social activism: Annie Gildernew, Bernadette Devlin, Mary Nelis, and Marie Moore. Standing tall amongst their supportive peers, these Republican women called international attention to the plight of women in Ireland and helped to shape the course of civil rights in Northern Ireland. Their accomplishments and their voices rang clear across the country, though it was only through the countless unnamed supporters and their communities that this was done. They were their communities and would be among the first to credit others.

The Gildernew Family

On June 18, 1968, Annie Gildernew and Mary Theresa Goodfellow, Sinn Féin MLA Michelle Gildernew's grandmother and aunt respectively, were evicted by the bailiffs and RUC forces from council housing assigned by the Dungannon Rural Council housing authority.[15] The eviction left the mothers and their small children without a home. Assigned to a single woman, the house was prioritized for Protestant occupancy, despite the current resident's inconvenience or family status. The event flared tensions around the North, because it exposed the overt nature of discrimination. A house meant more than just a shelter in Northern Ireland. A house meant a legal means to a vote. No house, no vote. Thus, the housing discrimination produced concrete interference with suffrage. And without the ability to freely vote, the housing conditions would remain intact. Fueled by government insensitivity to the crisis, the Catholic community was galvanized into a Civil Rights Movement. As Annie Gildernew explained in *Women in a War Zone,* these women knew what must be done: "We were only fighting for our rights. What we did not know at the time was what we were starting . . . and, if it was tomorrow, we'd do it again."[16]

Austin Currie, a nationalist MP for the Dungannon area, staged a publicity "squat" to call attention to the comprehensive lack of equality. He then consulted the newly created Northern Ireland Civil Rights Association for assistance in a protest march on the heels of the Dungannon squat. In 1966, the Dublin Wolfe Tone Society held a conference to discuss the organizational path to raising awareness of the breach in civil rights in the Six Counties. Led by Betty Sinclair—the first chairperson, the Northern Ireland Civil Rights Association (NICRA) was the outgrowth of these discussions; it was founded to combat official, state-sanctioned discrimination against Catholics. Inspired by and often patterning itself after the Civil Rights Movement in the United States, the NICRA campaigned against unjust social policies in areas such as housing, education, and employment. Committed to a passionate voice of social activism, the Irish Civil Rights Movement brandished nonviolent, social protests to awaken a social consciousness. Bravely singing "We Shall Overcome" along protest marches, male and female activists alike endured threats and charges. Annie Gildernew had been joined by a host of Derry women in her fight against social injustice, among them being newly elected (2007) MLA Martina

Anderson's mother and grandmother. The activism, though challenging, energized a community of women to aspire to more for their families. It is fitting, therefore, that Martina Anderson and Michelle Gildernew have followed in the path of their family legacy and serve as elected representatives for their communities.

Bernadette Devlin McAliskey

Though she has never been a member of Sinn Féin, Bernadette Devlin McAliskey is a deeply committed Republican who has shaped the lives of so many Sinn Féin women. She was born in Cookstown in 1947, educated in Dungannon, and attended Queens University Belfast in the 1960s. She became active in left-wing politics and the civil rights debate while at Queens. Leading street demonstrations to call attention to the plight of the oppressed, frequently imprisoned for her speeches, almost killed in her own home in January 1981 and serving as the youngest female member of Westminster Parliament, her persona seems far too large to be contained by a political party. Her disagreements with Sinn Féin may have dissuaded her from joining the group, but the political ends of an independent Ireland would have been the same as the ones she endorsed. Her street politics unleashed a powerful voice into the Civil Rights Movement. She was a prominent activist with a formidable presence, one that spoke of equality and justice in a way that shamed those who suppressed it. She was a key figure in People's Democracy, the radical university group, and NICRA. She championed equality for the all, regardless of label, and passionately participated in the first civil rights march from Coalisland to Dungannon on August 24, where the marchers were prevented from entering Dungannon by the RUC forces. She then traveled to Derry for the Derry march of October 5, 1968.

Reminiscent of the Southern Christian Leadership Conference marches in the southern United States, the Derry march was organized by activists Eamonn McCann and Eamon Melaugh. Sponsored by the Derry Housing Action Committee and several other ad hoc Derry groups, the march coincided with a Loyalist commemoration. Residents turned out for the march, including Ivan Cooper, John Hume, Gerry Fitt, and Eddie McAteer (the latter two Nationalist MPs in Stormont were beaten by RUC forces later that day). Ordered to disband by the county inspector, the marchers continued on to Duke Street. A brutal confrontation between nonviolent protesters and the overzealous police forces erupted. With police batons and newly deployed water cannons, the police rained down on the protesters until they retreated into the Bogside neighborhood. Immortalized in the still images of news reels, one can still see women and children attempting to run to safety. Close to 1,000 civilians were injured (some cite this number much higher during the entire Battle of the Bogside), and rioting broke out later in the evening in Bogside. In *The Price of My Soul*, McAliskey, arriving at ten o'clock that night after the march, captures the moment of altercation that evening in the Bogside:

> Suddenly, a boy yelled, "My God, they're coming!" Everybody stopped dead. It was one of the most horrific sights I have ever seen. High above us, the city wall was lined with a great silent mass of black figures. Slowly, the mass started to move, down through the walls, into the two roads still not barricaded, and when the two battalions of police met, they joined forces and started a stomp toward us, beating their shields with their batons and howling dreadfully, in the manner of savages trying to intimidate their foes.[17]

It was the beginning of "the Troubles."

Bernadette Devlin McAliskey's zealous outrage over injustice and inequality secured enough support to be elected as the youngest member of Westminster Parliament in 1969 as a 21-year old Unity Party candidate. Infamous for her antics on the floor of the House of Commons, Devlin has not swayed from the pursuit of equality and the eradication of discrimination. The PR spokesperson for the National H-Block/Armagh Association, she was a vocal opponent of the conditions the prisoners were kept in made her a target of a Loyalist death squad. Riddled with bullets in 1981, she fought for her life in the manner in which she fought for civil rights. For a week, she clung to life support; by March, she and her husband, shot several times as well, were home and back to the street politics. She remains a constant fixture at local community discussions and inspired to realize a society in which opportunity is afforded every child and social responsibility eradicates systemic discrimination. In one of her speeches, this one to a union in New York City, she explains that education is the premise upon which injustice can be fought:

> It is interesting to note that the rebels who formed the leadership of the civil rights movement in the late 1960s, in No Northern Ireland, were from the first and second generations of Catholics to whom education on the highest level was opened on a mass basis. This shows that there is nothing more dangerous than an oppressed people who acquire the first weapons of education and organisation.[18]

Devlin's political awakening in the 1960s was, according to Derry mother of nine Mary Nelis, typical of the effect of the weight of discrimination— women were compelled to act, to take to the streets with the only weapons they had . . . their minds, their hearts, and their hands.

Mary Nelis

Mary Margaret Elliott was born in the Bogside in 1935, grew up in the Bogside, and fell into community activism shortly after she married William Nelis in 1955. When she moved to the Foylehill side of the Creggan in the 1960, she was pleased to have an indoor bathroom and toilet but was quite conscious of the fact that the Creggan was an institutionally enforced slum.[19] As the community was overwhelmed with the hateful plumes of unethical indignation, Nelis took to the streets as a "pregnant petitioner" to protest the treatment of Catholic women and families. Pushing their babies in buggies or still pregnant, the petitioners would walk door-to-door collecting signatures protesting the conditions of Catholics in Derry. Nelis, along with Brigid Bond and Fionbarr O'Doherty, assisted with the organization of the Derry Housing Action Committee. The committee's focus was to eliminate slum housing in the Bogside, but it evolved into a full Civil Rights Movement. Staging a six-week squat in the Guildhall building, the Derry women called attention to the plight of Nellie Gorman, a mother of five children kept in a one-room house. Nelis explains that "[t]here was a chain reaction set up then. There was no going back, people were actually up off their knees, thinking, challenging, and you knew yourself that you were going somewhere."[20]

Mary was not, in her own mind, political per say, just conscious of fairness and decency. She briefly joined SDLP in 1974 before becoming active in the Derry branch of the Relatives Action Committee, for her son Donnacha was in jail, placed on remand in 1976 just two months after special category status had ended. He went on the blanket in the Crumlin Road jail, where he was not allowed visitors for a month. When she was finally able to see him, he was badly bruised with what looked like cigarette burns on his back. She describes the impact of prison visits on the families in a 1996 booklet entitled *A Diary from Derry*:

It was my first visit to a remand prison. It was really bad. Dirty, old, you'd always hear the iron gates closing, it had a depressive atmosphere, the place looked like a dungeon. It was a prison in every sense of the word, it had that atmosphere about it. The remand prison searches were terrible. It was women searchers when you went in, at the beginning you didn't know any better, there was something about it, you knew that some of them actually enjoyed what they were doing. The searches always caused distress, sometimes after you'd go through the search, there would be women crying, wains as well, it was all over the searches. It was something we used to talk about going up and going down on the transport. The women were being searched, private parts of their bodies and being left feeling dirty.[21]

Along with other members of the RAC, Mary Nelis went on the blanket, like her son. The "blanket women" of the Relatives Action Committee traveled across Ireland, Europe, and even to the United States to expose the conditions that Mary's son, and the other political prisoners, were facing. The camaraderie among the women she traveled with is something she remembers fondly: "All the women were great, they were just like myself, with families, some grown up, who had nothing. Just poor women, who had nothing."[22] With many of the husbands away in England for work, these women were mother, father, sole nurturer, and advocate—torn apart by seeing their children lying in their own waste in a prison cell. Her connections with the families of other political prisoners, and the subsequent Hunger Strike, drew her closer to Sinn Féin, which she joined in 1981. A committed community volunteer, Mary taught adult literacy programs through the Derry Reading Workshop and, in 1984, helped to set up the Dove House, a resource center in the Bogside. In the 1990s, she would serve two elected terms on the Derry City Council before becoming an MLA in the Northern Ireland Assembly. Mary Nelis's contribution to the peace process is further discussed in chapter 7. Stepping down in 2004 to care for her husband, Mary now writes a weekly column in *An Phoblacht*.

Marie Moore

Marie Gilmore (Moore) was born into the Clonard area of West Belfast in 1936. Her life was filled with moments of heroic activism, perhaps shaped by her childhood experiences. At the tender age of six, her baptism celebration became a moment in Irish history when IRA member Tom Williams was captured as he lay bleeding in her family home. Kneeling down beside her grandparents, the six-year-old Marie had a RUC gun pointed at her head during the ensuing interrogations. Later, when the Civil Rights Movement began to bubble, Marie was at the epicenter of the resistance, alongside Máire Drumm. In August 1969, she organized the Sinn Féin *cumann* in Clonard and assisted in the evacuation of Republican families under siege by Loyalist mobs. Current Sinn Féin president Gerry Adams explains the centrality of Marie Moore:

Marie said that she didn't get her republicanism from that event [the gun at her head at the age of six]. She got it from songs, from ballads, from the injustices around her, from all that she could see. She was involved in the civil rights movement. She was on the first march

from Coalisland to Dungannon. She was active in the events leading to the Battle of the Bogside and then the Belfast pogroms which
followed that. She was in Clonard when Bombay Street was burned.
She was out in Belfast when St. Mathews Church was attacked. All
of these iconic events in the recent republican history of this city of
Belfast and of the north, Maire Moore was there.[23]

In the 1970s, Marie was a tireless Republican activist and supporter of
prisoner rights. While on hen patrol in 1972, she was shot by the RUC during the Falls Road Curfew. Her injuries left her with a limp for the rest of
her life. Several of her comrades did not survive the attack. As a member of
the Sinn Féin POW Department, which she briefly headed up, during the
No Wash Protests and Hunger Strikes, she was a comm (communications)
courier between Republican prisoners and the outside. Marie understood
the life of a political prisoner—she had been one, as a woman on remand
for treason in 1978–79. The communication task was quite daunting—
dried cigarette papers were smuggled in and passed to the prisoners, all
under extreme scrutiny and high watch.

Marie continuously served in various roles in Sinn Féin throughout
her life. While balancing raising three children, and grandchildren, Marie
served as a member of the National Executive in 1979, helped to develop
the Women's Department in the 1980s, and served as Gerry Adams's personal assistant when he was elected MP in 1983 and again in 1988. She
was such a trusted member of the party that Gerry Adams used her house
in the 1980s to conduct secret meetings with elders in the Presbyterian
Church. In 1993, she was elected to the Belfast City Council (pre-peace
process) where she served until she was elected Deputy Lord Mayor of Belfast in 2000—the first Sinn Féin woman to hold that post. In March 2009,
after a bout of ill health, Marie Moore passed away.[24]

CONCLUSIONS—THE TROUBLES CAUSE TROUBLE

The epic Battle of the Bogside may not conjure up images of World War I
trench warfare or World War II maritime ambushes, but in the hearts and
minds of the Republicans in Ireland it was both a heroic stand of their
community in Free Derry and a spark of decades of direct military occupation. It also coincided with a rift in the Republican ranks over the
political course of Sinn Féin and the Irish Republican Army. Back in 1965,
a motion had been put forth at the Sinn Féin Árd Fheis to change the IRA
standing orders and Sinn Féin constitution to allow the party to recognize
Leinster House, allowing the party to assume any seats it was elected to in
the Dáil. It was a motion to end abstentionism, a central tenant of Arthur

Griffith's Sinn Féin. Although the motion failed to receive the necessary two-thirds majority required to pass, it is, through hindsight, clearly the beginning of the 1969 Republican split. On the heels of B-Specials undisciplined charge on the Bogside and the British Army deployment to the Six Counties, the political realm was no longer of substantial concern for the majority of Sinn Féin members by the January 1970 Árd Fheis. Ruairí Ó Brádaigh led the group of those opposed to the nonabstentionist motion, and Provisional Sinn Féin was born. Citing the failure of the previous Sinn Féin leadership as heavily Marxist and identifying their failure to protect the nationalist community in the North, Provisional Sinn Féin refused to acknowledge the Dáil, Stormont, or Westminster, hereby honoring the policy of abstentionism and redirecting the movement to assist in the armed struggle before it. And so it was, at the conclusion of the 1960s, that the Troubles begat more trouble in Sinn Féin.[25]

Chapter 5

HUNGER FOR JUSTICE, 1970s

You clench your teeth to try to keep your mouth closed but they push a metal spring device around your jaw to prise it open. They force a wooden clamp with a hole in the middle into your mouth. Then, they insert a big rubber tube down that. They hold your head back. You can't move. They throw whatever they like into the food mixer—orange juice, soup, or cartons of cream if they want to beef up the calories. They take jugs of this gruel from the food mixer and pour it into a funnel attached to the tube. The force-feeding takes 15 minutes but it feels like forever. You're in control of nothing. You're terrified the food will go down the wrong way and you won't be able to let them know because you can't speak or move. You're frightened you'll choke to death.

—Marian Price[1]

CHAPTER OVERVIEW

The 1970s were the deadliest days of the Troubles, with waves of troop deployment, sectarian violence, and increased military activity rippling across the northern counties of Ireland. The violence occasionally spilled over into the Republic, with assassinations, imprisonments, and even paramilitary activities cropping up across the island. During the peak of violence in 1972, an estimated close to 500 people lost their lives, according to a National Archives report released in 2003. The pleasures of daily routines were often disrupted, making most Irish women—regardless of their identities—focused on the challenges of survival in the midst of a military siege in the North. Those who had become politically apathetic were reawakening to the injustices and loss of life around them; in the midst of some of the tragic moments of Irish history, a revival of Irish identity emerged. During the Civil Rights Movement, the gross inequalities of Catholics in the North had been brought to the surface, and with the reinstallation of direct rule in 1972, a keen awareness of one's Irishness shone through the darkness. Across the Six Counties in particular, the harmonious sounds of the Irish language signaled independence, perhaps even defiance, in a state where rights and liberties were becoming increasingly scarce. With the British Army and the Royal Ulster Constabulary (RUC) assuming the role of the jailer of the Six Counties, Republicans found that the embrace of Irish language and Gaelic culture became the keys to enlightenment and strength. As Mary Corcoran explains in *Out of Order: The Political Imprisonment of Women in Northern Ireland 1972–1998,* the gaol (jail) became a "–tacht" (place) where Republicans provided self-instructed courses in language, history, theory, and social discourse.[2] Standing firm in their principles and confident in their identity, women like Máire Drumm, Sinn Féin vice president from 1972 to 1976, raged against injustices imposed on them, sharpening their wit, as they struggled to survive.

Chapter Organization

The decision to pick up a gun can be a difficult, or easy, one, depending on the impetus for that decision. In Ireland, that decision was complicated with layers of hatred, discrimination, systemic inequality, and injustice. Many Republicans, including hitherto "normal" mothers, housewives, sisters, and daughters, made that choice in the 1970s. The hardship of their decision, and subsequent actions, is a legacy of war. Another legacy is the fluctuation of statistics during the fog of war; accordingly, there will be refined information available within the renewed commitment to establish assumed responsibilities from all stakeholders.

With the outbreak of the Troubles in August 1969, Sinn Féin was not fully equipped to cope with the realities of a martial society under British occupation. The lull of the 1950s and the proscription of IRA and Sinn Féin as illegal organizations had muted the mouthpiece for resistance. But the events set to unfold in the early 1970s reinvigorated the Republican base for social agitation. Thus, the chapter begins with a historical overview of internal Republican debates and the creation of a military state in Northern Ireland. Several key events in the decade would contribute to the escalation of violence, including the policy of internment in 1971, the tragic events of Bloody Sunday in 1972, and the mainland bombing campaign in 1973. The challenges facing those who joined the armed resistance were many, including the conditions of Armagh and Maghaberry prisons, but the streamlined recruitment of Cumann na mBan (hitherto the female branch of armed resistance) into the IRA as a engendered force led to many Republican women joining the IRA itself. Not all Republicans joined the IRA in the 1970s, though admittedly many saw this as their primary avenue of action. Those who remained in Sinn Féin supported their Republican brothers and sisters in the cause of a free and equal Ireland.

The 1970s was the era of Máire Drumm. Her heroic efforts to defend her community under siege have been immortalized in Irish Republican memory. Her life, and her death, captures the struggle of a Republican woman in the 1970s. Following the beat of the "Drumm," her Republican sisters forged a mix of infinite patience and impassioned outrage into a line of community defense. This chapter profiles the lives of Máire Drumm, Peggy Deery, Marian and Dolours Price, Liz McKee, and Mairéad Farrell.

There were so many contradictions in the 1970s. As the violence peaked, so did the voices of women affected by that violence. The peace movement evolved, largely the work of women unwilling to accept the turbulent conditions in which they found themselves. In turn, the plight of the woman in Ireland found itself center stage with each passing news story broadcast around the world. The rise of feminism worldwide and of social activism in general empowered the women in Ireland. But, in the end, the challenges of living in a war zone meant enduring increasing levels of human rights abuses and daily violence.

HISTORICAL OVERVIEW

- Republican Debate
- The Military State
- 1971: Internment of Women
- 1972: Blood on the Streets
- 1973: An Explosive Year
- Female POWs
- Cumann na mBan

Increasingly, levels of injustice through the intimidation, interrogation, and imprisonment of their community terrorized Republican women in the Six Counties; for these women, British withdrawal was the only solution. Cries of "Brits Out" rang out from the Catholic ghettoes, and a resolve was established to not fall victim to the indifference of the status quo. *Imeacht gan teacht ort.* (May you leave without returning.) It was all about survival . . . the normal routines of daily life in the 1970s were disrupted with the threats of random street-side detainment, security interrogations, and extended stays in prison at the Crown's will. A woman in the Six Counties would have daily feared for her family, perhaps herself, as she circumvented the obstacles to a normal existence. By the end of the decade, she could be detained for seven days without explanation of her whereabouts or the status of her imprisonment to her family. The psychological warfare used during interrogations attempted to dehumanize the "target" and intended to verbally, sometimes physically, terrorize women. Chronic roadside detentions, intimidating house searches, and high-tech surveillance normalized the criminalization policies in the Six Counties. "The early '70s were a political awakening for women who normally had taken on a traditional role of mother, housekeeper and in a great many cases, breadwinner as many women worked in the mills."[3] As the British Army became the entrenched presence of an unwelcome guest who has overstayed an enforced hospitality, a new manner of Republican resistance was organized.

Republican Debate

Sinn Féin itself faced a public debate over the course it was taking at the outbreak of the Troubles. Fresh from an internal split in 1969–70 between the Stickies (Official Sinn Féin) and the Provos (Provisional Sinn Féin), Republicans, actively engaged in the Troubles, had to regroup and to re-strategize. Those who saw electoral politics—deeply affiliated with leftist socialism—as a necessary component of the Republican campaign violence formed what became known as Official Sinn Féin. The group now known as Provisional Sinn Féin (PSF), lead by Ruairí Ó Brádaigh, emerged as the heir to the Republican legacy in the 1970s. PSF would develop an *Eire Nua* policy in 1971 that guided its party development, specifically on social and economic matters, throughout the late 1970s and early 1980s.

The other half of the Sinn Féin split, the Officials, begat more factions. In 1972, the Official IRA (OIRA) declared a cease-fire that effectively concluded its activity, until in 1975 when Official Sinn Féin was effectively crippled with yet another split. The political offshoot of the offshoot was the Irish Republican Socialist Party (IRSP) while the armed divisions of the Irish National Liberation Army (INLA) shared the left-wing politics of it. With two forces competing for the Republican mainstay of support, the OIRA spiraled into a pattern of intra-sectarian violence, attacking Provisional IRA (PIRA) and INLA forces. Meanwhile, as leftist ideologies overtook Official Sinn Féin and Provisional Sinn Féin was still adhering to the policy of abstentionism, the political field was wide open for the formation of a centrist political party.

In August 1970, Gerry Fitt and John Hume founded a "moderate" alternative of electoral choice, the Social Democratic and Labour Party (SDLP). Appealing to a moderate Catholic and broadly stated nationalist base, SDLP sought a constitutionalist solution to the crisis in the North. Sinn Féin struggled to garner electoral support throughout the 1970s, as it grappled with being an illegally proscribed organization until May 1974. Furthermore, Sinn Féin's abstentionist policies disallowed a member from taking a seat in elected government in any British institution (and also in the Dáil since it was the product of British partition). These dimensions allowed for SDLP to garner political support from many Catholics, who might be wary of Republican tactics. However, as the decade continued to unfold, support for Sinn Féin would resurface, as a moderate political solution was not viable for many living in the escalating cycle of violence. A significant factor in the manifold increase in Republicanism was the presence of the British Army, and their "civil-military relations," in Northern Ireland.

The Military State

Deployed on August 14, 1969, the British military reasserted its imperial shadow across the Irish Sea onto the Six Counties, and under its weight, a new series of concerns emerged. Treated as second-class citizens by their neighbors and government and now occupied by military forces, Republican women became overnight interlockers for (Provisional) Sinn Féin and the Irish Republican Army. As strong as the intimidation was, so was the Republican woman's strength, for she was the heart and mind of the resistance. The North of Ireland was now a war zone. Sinn Féin councillor Chrissie McAuley described the conditions in her 1988 article "Nationalist Women and the RUC." Pinned beneath the weight of the political ghettoization of their community, women observed the security forces institutionalize terror. "While women universally suffer discrimination in all its forms in every society nationalist women in the North are doubly discriminated against. We bear the brunt of bringing up children amidst the RUC/British Army harassment. We can be arrested, interrogated, imprisoned and even be killed at any time, given the right excuse, by the crown forces."[4] The systematic use of intimidation bullied women, who were increasingly targeted for their roles in the resistance.

Having lost her appeal to prevent detention, Bernadette Devlin was arrested on June 26, 1970, and began serving a six-month sentence for her activities during the Battle of the Bogside. Political activism, at the end of a megaphone or a bin lid, now meant the security forces, often using the threat of taking a woman's children into protective custody to intimidate them, led to the specific targeting of women. In addition to the physical force imposed on the community, much of the war was psychological. Fear, both imagined and real, was manipulated to secure subdued conquest, but the women boldly balked at their oppression. The breech of the Falls Road curfew has become an iconic symbol of female insubordination to the British Army.

On July 3, 1970, the Falls Road curfew was introduced in Belfast. During the summer of 1970, the Catholic community on the Falls Road in West Belfast had organized to protect the community from the security threats that surrounded them. Republican activities spiked as British Army security measures were imposed on the community. One such measure was to place a curfew on the Lower Falls Road, one of the strongholds of the Republican neighborhoods. For three days, armed British soldiers imprisoned families in their own homes. Intolerant of the civil liberties suspensions and undaunted by the intimidation tactics in house searches and roadside interrogations, Máire Drumm, a mother of five children, organized the breech of the curfew to collect groceries and household necessities. The march was a proud act of defiance played out in a peaceful organization. Facing gun-toting patrols staring down the streets, these women, some pushing baby prams or holding their children's hands, set out to carry on a routine need without giving into the intimidation of their occupiers. It calls to mind the peace activists in the United States that inserted daisies in the barrel of military guns, to effectively silence them under the weight of community disapproval. These Falls Road women were unarmed, unafraid warriors against a military garrison, and they would have their groceries that evening. Lily Fitzsimmons recalls:

> We filled prams with bread, milk, baby-food and other necessities we could lay our hands on. We assembled at several points along the route, where we were joined by hundreds of others at the junction of Glen Road and Falls Road, the Whiterock, Beechmont and finally the Royal Hospital. . . . While most of the soldiers could only look on in amazement as we made our way past them, a few smart ass squaddies made crude sexual gestures. Some of the younger women responded with the two finger victory sign. The feeling among the women was one of great exhilaration and triumph at breaking the Falls curfew.[5]

It was an epic moment of female solidarity with the female David standing firm against the Goliath garrison, often retold with a twinkle in the eye of the storyteller. The success was short-lived, however, as new, more aggressive military tactics took root.

On August 2, 1970, rubber bullets were introduced across the Six Counties. Over the course of approximately five years, an estimated 55,000 bullets were fired in the name of crowd dispersal and instilling civil order. When the rubber bullets were finally banned for their deadly repercussions in 1975, plastic bullets replaced them. The safety of plastic bullets is still widely disputed, even though they are still found in routine riot police countermeasures around the world. According to *Women in a War Zone*, over 110,000 rubber and plastic bullets were fired between 1970 and 1989. "The overwhelming majority of those killed [17 people total] were shot in 'non-riot' situations yet according to the British government the weapon is only supposed to be used in 'riot' situations."[6] Since women and children constituted a large part of street demonstrations, prayer vigils, and street meetings where these rubber and plastic bullets were fired, they often became the victims of them. One such victim was Emma Groves. Emma was patiently awaiting the completion of some routine house searches, and arrests, in her community in the relative comfort of her own home in West Belfast on a November morning in 1971. She reportedly put an Irish rebel song on her radio as a sign of defiance. Unexpectedly, one of the British soldiers eight feet away fired a rubber bullet through an open window, hitting the mother of 11 children in the face and blinding her for life.[7] The doctor, deeply concerned about how the news of the surgical loss of her eyes and blindness would affect her, solicited Mother Teresa to deliver the news. Emma Groves dedicated her life to raising awareness of rubber and plastic bullets, testifying before the European Parliament, founding Relatives for Justice in 1984, and appealing directly (in person) to the manufacturers in the United States and in Scotland to cease production. Known as the First Lady of Belfast, Emma Groves was a formidable human rights activist who brought international focus to the carnage of rubber/plastic bullets. Although she received a compensation payment of 35,000 pounds for her loss, she died on April 2, 2007, without any formal admission of responsibility declared.

The first death from a rubber bullet was in April 1972. Francis Roundtree was an 11-year-old boy walking home in West Belfast, when a soldier shot him from five to seven yards away. In 1973, plastic bullets, also known as baton rounds, became a component of the antiriot arsenal. The transition from rubber to plastic bullets was complete by 1975 and had been done to reduce this sort of tragedy . . . it did not. Over the course of 21 years, an estimated 17 people, more than half of whom were children like Francis, died. The list of victims continues to be refined in the post-Agreement North, but it also includes children like 12-year-old Carol Ann

Kelly, who went out for a pint of milk on May 22, 1981, and never returned home. Rubber (or plastic) bullets were not, however, the only ammunition used by security forces. Live rounds were fired at targets across the North, targets that increasingly began to be female.

1971: Internment of Women

In 1971, the profile of the "security threat" appeared to change. On August 9, 1971, Operation Demetrius commenced. The military objective was to target the Republican security threat by rounding up IRA operatives. There were 450 on the initial list, but the list had been formulated on outdated intelligence. Some 350 people were detained, and many were released within 48 hours. The policy of internment, as it became known, lasted from 1971 until December 5, 1975, during which time 1,981 people were detained, of which 1,874 were Catholic or Republican. With close to 95 percent of the internees recorded as nationalist, one wonders how many Loyalists remained on the outside, in collusion with security forces, to reign terror on the Republican community. Fearful of their neighbors in the Loyalist paramilitary, the RUC, and the visiting British soldiers, the Republican community, left largely unemployed in the ghettoes and slums, was under siege. Belfast Sinn Féin councillor Marie Moore recalls that with husbands, brothers, and fathers in jail, the women took to the streets. "[W]e actually fought hand to hand with the paratroopers that morning in the Clonard. We were struggling with their rifles and pulling them off them and getting beat."[8] Barricaded into their communities, the women organized food deliveries, street maintenance, and rubbish collection. In an effort to collectively warn the communities, women created the "binlid brigades" to warn of impending security raids or civil discontent.

Originally known as "hen patrols," the women would shadow British military patrols around, often squawking or blowing whistles to announce their presence. Hen patrols became known as binlid brigades when "women who came onto to the streets when they heard the army or RUC coming in and rattled their binlids and blew their whistles to warn people who may be staying in houses, that the raids were going on."[9] The community action raised awareness of the women as activists and made them targets. A seemingly deliberate strategy to dissuade women from engaging in binlid brigades occurred when in the span of a few months Marie Moore, Rita O'Hare, Dorothy Maguire, and Maura Meehan were shot. Although Moore and O'Hare both survived, Maguire and her sister Maura did not.

On Saturday, October 23, 1971, 30-year-old Maura Meehan and 19-year-old Dorothy Maguire were shot dead by the British Army in the Lower Falls area (Cape Street) of West Belfast while attempting to warn their neighbors about security raids. They were in a car sounding a siren to protest the raids when they were shot in the back of the head. Their deaths cemented the reality that street politics could make one a target. Dorothy and Maura, members of Cumann na mBan, had grown up in a strong Republican family. The sisters were the generational offspring of Ned Maguire, who led the IRA rooftop escape from the Crumlin Road jail in January of 1943. Their brother Ned would later be interned in the Cages of Long Kesh in 1974, and their second cousin Kieran Doherty would die in the 1981 hunger strike. Thus, it was of little surprise that Dorothy and Maura were intent to play their part in the struggle as well. The early warning signals of the "binlid brigades," such as the one the Maguire sisters participated in that day, would alert wanted persons to go on the run and warn of the impending harassment of the families, including the ransacking of houses and the detention of anyone over the age of 17. Statements collected from witnesses on the scene suggested that both women were unarmed.

1972: Blood on the Streets

Tensions exploded in 1972 in an event that would define military-civilian relations for four decades. On January 30, 1972, in the Bogside community in Derry, British Army paratroopers opened fire on protesters demonstrating against the internment policy introduced the previous August. Organized by civil rights activists, the Derry Civil Rights Association march had been frowned upon by the authorities, as many of the Derry events before it. Many of Éamonn McCann's civil rights activists were prepared to be arrested to call attention to the second-class nature of their citizenship, but facing arrest at the base of Free Derry Corner was not what they would encounter. Unlike previous skirmishes at demonstration events, the British Paratroopers were to use deadly force to in a crowd-dispersal maneuver. With organizers Bernadette Devlin and Ivan Cooper standing in the lorry prepared to speak to the marchers behind them, a hail of live rounds were fired at the demonstrators. Fourteen unarmed civilians were killed on Bloody Sunday in Derry, and, despite the outrage splashed across the headlines around the world, not one soldier present that day has been held accountable for these deaths.

Wakes and funerals began that February for those killed. In the Creggan Chapel, a funeral mass was held on February 3 as the trauma of the incident began to sink in. Overcome with the emotions of the day, a riot resulted in the British embassy being burned to ground. The flagrant injustices of Bloody Sunday, and the subsequent "investigation" released in the 1975 Widgery Report, drew international attention to the plight of civil rights in Northern Ireland. Civil disorder continued to mount and, on March 30, 1972, direct rule was reintroduced.

That summer, Billy McKee and other Republican POWs engaged in a hunger strike for special category status, which was granted by Secretary of State William Whitelaw on June 19, 1972. Special category status designated those held on political offenses as distinct from the criminal prison population; among the various concessions for political prisoners were personal clothing, regularized visits, and educational programs. The day after special category status was granted, secret meetings between Sinn Féin (represented by Gerry Adams and Daithí Ó Conaill) and British government representatives Frank Steele (MI6) and P. J. Woodfield began, culminating in an IRA cease-fire on July 7, 1972. The ongoing negotiations, and cease-fire, were shattered on July 21, 1972, known as Bloody Friday, when 22 bombs exploded across the North in under 75 minutes. The increased level of violence is demonstrated by the fact that in the three years prior to Bloody Sunday (August 1969 to January 1972), 210 people had been killed; in the 11 months after Bloody Sunday, 445 people died.[10]

On July 31, 1972, in the wake of such palpable conflict, Operation Motorman commenced. It was the largest British military operation since the Suez Crisis. The focus of the mission was to breach the no-go areas in Derry and Belfast with over 12,000 troops. Some 12,000 troops were assigned to the slightly over 14,000 kilometers of Northern Ireland; that is, almost one soldier per kilometer in the Six Counties. The barricaded areas in Derry and Belfast were homespun, erected out of rudimentary local supplies and designed to protect Catholic communities from various Loyalist, RUC, and military threats. Manned by community volunteers and patrolled with scouts, the barricades served as a primitive form of community defense in comparison to the looming power of 12,000 soldiers. Overwhelmed with thousands of British military troops, it became clear that Operation Motorman thinly veiled tactical objectives to minimize or to eliminate the IRA's ability to facilitate operations. The operation resulted in the widespread continuation of arrests, or detainment, of key Republican figures across the Six Counties. In an attempt to cut off the head of the proverbial snake, the Republic cooperated by netting several key leaders in the South. The strikes were swift and netted Máire Drumm herself on November 5, 1972. On November 19, the head of the IRA Army Council, Seán MacStíofáin, was arrested in Dublin, followed by Martin McGuinness on December 31. Perhaps the most problematic for Sinn Féin logistically was the December 29, 1972, arrest of Ruairí Ó Brádaigh (then president of Sinn Féin). The following January, under the Offences Against the State Act in the Twenty-Six Counties, Provisional Sinn Féin was banned from entering its offices in Dublin.

Although many of the detentions were temporary, the waves of arrests provided an operational challenge for the Republican leadership. In January of 1973, with Sinn Féin President Ruairí Ó Brádaigh jailed in the Republic, Máire Drumm, fresh from her own internment, became the second woman to serve as president of the political party (in an acting capacity). Elected at an outdoor meeting outside of the Kevin Street Sinn Féin offices that had been closed by the Dublin police, Drumm was thrust back onto the national stage. Balancing a family of five children, one son whom was interned in Long Kesh at the time, and intermittent sentences in Armagh and Mountjoy, she was steadfast in her commitment to Sinn Féin. According to *The Guardian,* she is quoted as saying, "It is not enough to throw stones and bottles, and it is a waste of time shouting 'up the IRA.' The important thing is to join. Sure we want to see the British soldiers go home, but we want them to go home in their coffins."[11] She was described by the reporter as "a woman of great charm and friendliness, well salted with a sharp wit."[12] By those who knew her, she is described as defiant, convicted, and devoted.

1973: An Explosive Year

In March of 1973, two important events defined the scope of events that year: the London car bombs on March 8 and the border poll. Timed to coincide with the border poll, an IRA team deployed to London to plant four car bombs in strategic places outside the Scotland Yard office, British Forces Broadcasting Office, Old Bailey, and Whitehall army recruitment center. Two of the four bombs were defused before the scheduled detonation. The devastation produced over 200 casualties and one death. Two of the 10 persons detained that day were Marian and Dolours Price.

The '73 bombings signaled a rebirth of an aggressive mainland bombing campaign in Britain, one that had embedded sleeper Active Service Units (ASUs) activated throughout the 1970s. Two of the most infamous bombings were the October 5, 1974, bombing in Guilford, killing five people, and the November 21, 1974, bombing in Birmingham, killing 21 persons. The bombings were tragic, as were their consequences. The British calls for retributive justice resulted in the false imprisonment of the Guilford Four and Birmingham Six. Although the "Balcombe Street gang" of the PIRA took responsibility for the events in Guilford, the Guilford Four and the surviving Maguire Seven remained in jail until their release in 1990. The following year, the Birmingham Six returned home, free after close to 16 years in prison. In the campaign against the miscarriage of justice, the plight of Northern Ireland and the questionable proceedings of the British Courts made front page news around the world.

The IRA operations in the fall of 1974 had immediate ramifications, some not made public until recently. In the wake of close to 30 deaths and hundreds more injured, the British government moved to swiftly halt the IRA's active service unit (ASU) activity, resulting in legislation impacting all citizens in the United Kingdom. On December 5, 1974, the Prevention of Terrorism Act for NI became effective; the act extended the duration and terms of detention under the Special and Emergency Powers Act, thus widening the scope of state terrorist allegations. And then on December 10, 1974, a Republican delegation held secret talks with some Protestant clergymen at Smyth's Village Hotel in Feakle, County Clare.

The Feakle talks were attended by a group that included Ruairí Ó Brádaigh, Daithí Ó Conaill, and Máire Drumm. The Protestant delegation included Dr. Arthur Butler, Dr. Jack Weir, Reverend Ralph Baxter and Reverend William Arlow. The Protestants presented the Republicans with a document allegedly from the British government.[13] Drumm's presence at the meeting recognized not only her position within Sinn Féin but also the roles that Republican women had adopted. No longer solely the fundraiser or street activist, women were integral to the strategic process of the movement. In previous rounds of negotiations with the British (notably the ones that produced the Anglo Irish Treaty of 1920), Sinn Féin women had accompanied the male negotiators as assistants or secretaries; now, in 1974, Máire Drumm, a woman, was a principal negotiator alongside her male comrades. Later that December, the IRA declared a cease-fire, and Sinn Féin reportedly began secret talks with the British government on February 17, 1975. A series of secret talks with the various representatives of the British government would continue to occur over the next two decades.

The second event, on March 8, 1973, that would shape the Troubles for the next 30 years was the border poll. Ninety-eight percent voted in favor of retaining the link with Britain. This was largely influenced by a nationalist boycott, since it recognized the partition of the Six Counties. Subject to an abstentionist policy, most Catholics did not participate. Thus, only 57 percent of the eligible electorate voted. The merits (and demerits) of the abstentionism policy were hotly contested throughout the 1980s, and it eventually was abandoned by the Sinn Féin Árd Fheis in 1986. This produced yet another split within the Republican movement (in 1986) when Ruairí Ó Brádaigh, maintaining that this was a breach of central Republican principles, formed Republican Sinn Féin in protest. The controversial decision to boycott the 1973 border poll is still debated within nationalist circles, but the core effect of it was to reflect a disproportionate, perhaps inaccurate, level of support for the Union. The June 28, 1973 elections to the Northern Ireland Assembly and the December 9, 1973 Sunningdale Agreement reflected the assumptions of the level of support for the Union.

Under the Sunningdale Agreement, the Northern Irish government would consist of a Council of Ministers and a Consultative Assembly. Consisting of seven members from the Northern Ireland Executive and seven members of the Irish government, the Council of Ministers would have limited executive powers. Comprised of 30 members from the Northern Ireland Assembly and 30 members of the Irish Dail, the Consultative Assembly would have advisory functions. The experiment in devolved, consultative government was brief, as direct rule was reintroduced on May 28, 1974, after a tumultuous 14-day Ulster Workers' Council (UWC) strike. During the UWC strike, there was a surge of Ulster Freedom Force (UFF) and Ulster Volunteer Force (UVF) activities across the 32 counties that targeted Catholics. Then on July 3, 1974, Máire Drumm announced that Sinn Féin would engage in talks with the UWC. Demonstrating openness to their Unionist counterparts may not have been reciprocated on the issue of Irish independence, but Sinn Féin did share common concerns about POW conditions with Loyalist paramilitary representatives, a point that was not lost on Ulster Defense Association (UDA) leader Andy Tyrie when he approached Sinn Féin for talks in late 1974.

Female POWs

Since 1970, the Crumlin Road jail in Belfast had been bubbling at the seams with POWs and detainees. The overflow flooded other nearby facilities, including the Armagh Jail. Prior to the arrival of the British Army, the Armagh Jail had been used as a borstal prison for young men and rarely housed more than a handful of women. After security operations began to employ detention, interrogation, and remand tactics, the jail population swelled from two women in 1972 to over a hundred in the height of the internment phase (1972–1976). According to Father Raymond Murray, then chaplain of the Armagh Jail, 32 of these women were held without charge (on remand) courtesy of the Diplock courts.[14] When the Long Kesh facility, later known as the Maze prison, was opened in August of 1972, several male internees were moved into the H Blocks there. In May and June of 1972, the women engaged in a hunger strike aimed at the designation of a political status for internees. They won. From 1972 until 1976, the political prisoners, including men and women, were given special category status—which allowed prisoners to wear personal clothes and participate in educational programs. Many POWs learned or expanded their knowledge of the Irish language, increasing the Gaeltacht (Irish speakers) population inside the prisons, and reinvigorating the use of Irish in the Republican community as a whole. However, the educational programs and special category status concessions did not conceal the blatant disequilibrium of ethnic discrimination disproportionately targeting Catholic women. In his 1973 status report, Father Murray noted: "During the past year 12 women were interned. To work in a Catholic community is to realize the sense of injustice created and the intense dislike of the police this fosters. How? This 12 is balanced against the total number of loyalist prisoners interned (10) in Long Kesh, and this is in spite of the assassination of 137 innocent Catholics, the blowing up of Catholic churches, schools, halls and parochial houses."[15]

As a special category prisoner in Armagh, one would have been convicted by a juryless court and subject to military-grade security in the prisons. There were still others on remand awaiting trials and those interned without trial. In a period of "relative containment," Mary Corcoran explains in *Out of Order: The Political Imprisonment of Women in Northern Ireland 1972–1998* that political prisoners were easily organized around prison issues. The quality of food, recreation in a mud-soaked yard, washing and cooking rights were so poor that it served as an easy platform for collective organization.[16] Prison conditions had become a constant source of debate, producing the blanket protest by Ciaran Nugent and other blanket men beginning in September 1976. Many prison riots, including the one on October 15, 1974, in which male prisoners set fires that burned huts in the Maze, and demonstrations of contempt, such as the October 16, 1974, "detention" of the Armagh prison governor held hostage by female Republican POWs, were the direct result of prison conditions. Additionally, the remedialization of the educational programs during the 1970s, while allowing women courses in Irish, politics, and history, redirected prisoners into vocational programs such as dressmaking and handicrafts rather than academic courses.[17] Even so, the special category status allowed Republican women to formalize their prison structure and speak with one united voice on behalf of their community.

Laurence McKeown, author of *Out of Time: Irish Republican Prisoners Long Kesh 1972–2000,* echoes this sentiment in his assessment of the Republican POW leadership structure. A prisoner in Long Kesh for 16 years and a participant in the 1981 hunger strikes, from which he was called off when he slipped into a coma, McKeown states that the impact of internment was to reorganize the POW leadership—from the formerly used hierarchical model to a more communal and cooperative one.[18] Although there are those who cast dispersions on the cooperative model's full implementation, citing evidence of vertical punitively imposed measures for breaching the POW code in Long Kesh, there is less evidence of this with the women prisoners. Mary Corcoran's interviews of 12 unnamed former female POWs in the late 1990s, substantiate that although internal pressures to advance the collective consensus were present in Armagh in the mid-70s, the vertical elements of the leadership had faded by the 1980s. The shift to "supportive" or consensus model of leadership may have been driven by the need to shore up a wide base of support across the Republican/nationalist community rather than the democratization of it all. That is, as Corcoran suggests, the hierarchical model may have become too dangerous in revealing dissent among personality-based leadership or forced compliance with it.[19] Corcoran does footnote that two of her interviewees later sided with Ruairí Ó Brádaigh in the 1986 split.

By 1974, when the new policy of criminalization was being phased in across the justice system, the A Company of the IRA in Armagh, demonstrating Laurence McKeown's Long Kesh experience, had consolidated the three sections into one negotiating body on behalf of their POWs. When the borstal program for younger, nonpolitical boys was terminated at Armagh in 1975, the Armagh Jail became the premier institutions for female Republicans to be held for often brutal interrogations and intimidation practices that reportedly included "Chinese torture" tactics. These practices inflicted on political prisoners were of grave importance to human rights activists worldwide, and the Republican O/C (Commanding Officer) in Armagh became the voice for those targeted by the tactics.

Criminalization would lead to the revocation of special category status in 1976 and ignited vast protests among the Republican community. Enacted by the Treatment of Offenders Act for Northern Ireland in 1976, criminalization ended internment and increased remission (time served for sentence) from 30 to 50 percent time served. In *Sisters in Cells: Two Republican Prisoners,"* Áine and Eibhlín Nic Giolla Easpaig, imprisoned in Durham Jail in 1975, explain the impact that their political status had on them: "You are on your own. . . . The person who is detained has no idea what is in store for him, what comes next, when he can go free, if he can go free. And of course, the permission one must get to do almost anything cultivates a dependence on others around one that is neither healthy nor right."[20] When special category status was discontinued on March 1, 1976, the female POWs joined their male counterparts in protest. The women initially refused to comply with the policies of the new system in a non-cooperation protest, resulting in restricted solitary confinement for many female POWs like Mairéad Farrell.

Cumann na mBan

Outside the prison walls, Cumann na mBan was absorbed into the Irish Republican Army by 1977–78, when women became full members. Many women in the 1970s had joined the IRA directly, rather than Cumann na mBan. Thus, the gradual demobilization was logical. Referenced in the

"Staff Report" found on IRA Chief of Staff Seamus Twomey in December 1977, the tactical use of female volunteers was a high priority in the 1970s. In a chapter prepared for *Irish Women and Nationalism,* Rhiannon Talbot suggests that women had been transporting and placing bombs and guns since the 1970s since they were less likely to be stopped and searched by the British military or RUC forces.[21] There is additional documentation that between 1971 and 1972, female volunteers participated in active service unit (ASU) ambushes as well as courier and messenger duties.[22] *AP/RN* reporter Chrissie McAuley, a committed Sinn Féin activist and councillor, describes the evolution of the role of Republican women's resistance of British policies: "The brutality of Internment steered increasing numbers of women onto the streets in protests and into the ranks of Cumann na mBan, Cumann na gCailini and Óglaigh na hÉireann (the IRA). The women Volunteers undertook every kind of role: intelligence gathering; transporting weapons to and from operations against the enemy; making and planting incendiary devices and bombs against commercial targets; training other Volunteers in the use of weapons and explosives."[23]

In May 1977, the Ulster Unionists attempted a second work strike. Unlike the Ulster Worker's Council (UWC) strike of May 1974 that had brought down the Sunningdale Assembly in protest of power-sharing in the North, the 1977 version appeared less focused. Known as "Paisley's strike" as the Reverend Ian Paisley was a chief architect, the United Unionist Action Council (UUAC) failed to mirror the momentum of an increasingly organized IRA and Sinn Féin.

REPUBLICAN WOMEN AND THE BEAT OF THE DRUMM

- Máire Drumm
- Peggy Deery
- Marian and Dolours Price
- Liz McKee
- Mairéad Farrell

Máire Drumm

Republican resistance in the 1970s can be epitomized by the life of one woman—Máire Drumm. In her life, she empowered women all around her, and in her tragic death, she defined their cause. Máire McAteer (Drumm) was an ordinary Catholic woman born on November 22, 1919, in Killeen, South Armagh. Her mother had been a strong-minded Republican woman in the 1920s. Shortly after her schooling, she moved to Belfast where she worked in a grocery store on the Crumlin Road. In 1940, Máire joined Sinn Féin and became a committed Volunteer. She regularly visited the prisoners at the Crumlin Road Jail, where she met Jimmy Drumm, whom she married in 1946. The mother of five children, Séamus, Margaret, Catherine, Séan and Marie Óg, she, shortly after Jimmy was interned for another four years without trial, became active in the Civil Rights Movement in the 1960s and rose through the ranks to became the vice president of the party in the 1970s. By all accounts, she was a quintessential Republican who was deeply admired by her community. Referred to as the "mother of the prisoners," her commitment to republicanism was only rivaled by her love for her family and community. Marie Moore, the first Sinn Féin member to serve as deputy mayor of Belfast in 1999–2000, recalls her as an "icon for women, as a wife to Jimmy as a mother to her 5 children as a political activist to women everywhere. I remember her talking to myself and Mary McGuigan [a former member of the Ard Chomhairle], she said: 'Women are at last breaking the chains of being slave to slaves. We must make sure they never go back to being slave of slaves; but be the leaders and policy makers of a new Ireland.' "[24]

Drumm was a prominent opponent of the British occupation, and her spirited activism shaped a generation of young women. Images of her standing on street corners with unwavering defiance are depicted across Belfast in political murals. She famously led the breach of the Falls Road curfew in 1970 and the anti-internment rallies in August 1971, in January 1973, and in August 1975. Her political activism is a thread throughout the 1970s, demonstrating the peak of community organization and the valley of sectarian assassination. Deeply affected by the sacrifices a politically active woman made, Máire endured long years of the internment of her husband, as well as some of the five children she was raising. She herself was in and out of prison, mainly for her fiery speeches, which typically earned her a few months' stay in prison for inciting (or inspiring) a crowd. The extraordinary zeal she inspired was known throughout Ireland.

Referring to her as his "political wife," Ruairí Ó Brádaigh remembers:

> She was a very straight, very direct person. You always knew where you stood with her. She wasn't someone who suddenly rose up with what happened in 1969. Maura Drumm was a member of Margaret Buckley's Sinn Féin, as she used to say herself. Back in 1939, she had been working in Dublin and she worked in England and she was involved there and in Cork with Cumann na mBan so there was no hesitation about her at all and I think that she emphasized no hesitation in repeating it. She was no way sectarian in no way of any of her utterances, public or private, could it be said that she every said anything that could be misinterpreted in that regard. Her opposition was

to English rule and the English government and the English Army, and she was very, very clear about that. She inspired an extraordinary degree of affection. As a result of her situation, she was looked on as a strong woman, direct, forthright, honest. There was no two ways about her. People could always make an educated guess as to what her attitude would be to situations and so on. What she said publicly is on the record. I found her a great source of support and of strength. Her passing was a terrible loss.[25]

In 1976, she was struggling with her eyesight and sought medical treatment. That October, she was admitted to Mater Hospital on the Crumlin Road in Belfast for cataract surgery. On October 28, 1976, while resting in her hospital bed, Máire Drumm was shot and killed by Loyalist paramilitaries. The indignity of her death ignited the entire community. Máire's legacy has become the generation of young women, and indeed men as well, she inspired to lifelong republicanism. Speaking with the author in the spring of 2007, Ard Chomhairle member Eibhlín Glenholmes remembered that her father took her to see Mrs. Drumm speak in Dunville Park:

My God, that woman was inspirational. She was a gifted orator. She was a woman who didn't see her own gender. It wasn't even a consideration. Maura Drumm was just there, in your face. Maura Drumm probably did more for young women growing up around her time. She was prepared to take on the British Army. She was prepared to take on the British establishment. She was a loving mother and married to her dear husband Jimmy, who was also a lifelong republican. The woman just never stopped. You just looked at her and went of course it's tough but this is what you do. Everyone my age wanted to be Maura Drumm when they grew up. She went to jail for what she said. And she was very very conscious of the age of most of the women in jail at the time, they were very young. Maura was so kind to them, you know, mentoring and motherly. She always made very sure that you know she was Maura Drumm. She was Sinn Féin. She was Sinn Féin.[26]

In her life, she was a perennial thorn in the Crown; and in her death, she was a martyr.

Peggy Deery

Speaking at the West Belfast Féile in 2000, Derry-born journalist Nell McCafferty recalled the story of Peggy Deery, the only woman shot on

Bloody Sunday. She was a neighbor of McCafferty's who, like many nationalist women, lived in the squalor of a Derry slum with 14 children. Her husband was dying of cancer, she often went without heat, and she died in debt. But as McCafferty recalled in Laura Friel's report for *An Phoblacht/Republican News,* she was so hopeful that that she would one day become a first-class citizen that she named her 14th child after Bernadette Devlin.[27] Dressed in her Sunday best, the recently widowed Peggy Deery left her children at home to go march with her neighbor Michael McDaid, a young barman with a promising future, for her civil rights. According to the compiled interviews given to *Ireland on Sunday* and BBC by the Troops Out Movement, Peggy Deery was near the car park on Rossville Street when she was shot in the legs by a trooper.[28] The assailant approached her, and she begged for her life in the name of her children. The Para (soldier) ran off, leaving Peggy bleeding on the street until a group of men, including 24-year-old Patrick McDaid, carried her to safety.

Although she lived to endure 16 more years of stark poverty, Peggy spent considerable time in the hospital clinging to death, the back of her legs torn open. When she returned home, Peggy Deery, like many of the survivors, was never the same—for she lived in fear of her children's safety. Her 22-year-old neighbor Micky did not make it home at all; he was one of the 14 shot in the face while he stood beside the barricades. Peggy's remaining children also became victims of the Troubles. In 1986, her son Michael died after a fight. In 1987, her son Patrick died as he, and a fellow IRA volunteer, were working on a bomb. The pain was crippling; in January 1988, Peggy died at the age of 53.[29]

Marian and Dolours Price

The Price sisters grew up in West Belfast in a prominent Republican household. Dolours, born in 1951, and Marian, born in 1954, were the children of Albert Price, a dedicated IRA man. The sisters entered the movement in the late 1960s–early 1970s. Marian joined when she was just 17, and she left nursing school to join the IRA's mainland campaign. She, Dolours, and Gerry Kelly were among the IRA unit captured on March 8, 1973. A police detective who detained her at the airport has said that she glanced at her watch as the bombs were scheduled to detonate—and she smiled.[30]

Convicted in November of the Old Bailey and Whitehall bombings that March day, Marian and Dolours Price began protesting their confinement to a British jail. Maintaining their POW status, the Price sisters went on a devastating day hunger strike (some sources claim 167 days, others 206 days) to secure a transfer to an Irish jail. During their hunger strike, the prison officials force-fed them with plastic tubes down their throats in a manner that is reminiscent of the American suffragette Alice Paul in 1917. The Price sisters were accustomed to the life of Republicans. Their West Belfast parents had been active in the 1930s. Their aunt Bridie Dolan had been blinded, losing her hands as well, in 1938, while moving ammunition she was hiding for the IRA. Thus, within two years of joining the IRA, Marian and Dolours were on the Republican front line on an operation in London. Their arrest was swift, almost a swift as the sentencing. Unable to attend their mother's IRA-flanked funeral in February 1975, the Andersonstown natives finally won a transfer to Armagh Jail in March of 1975 and were eventually released in the 1980 on medical grounds (both suffered from anorexia).

Marian remains committed to her actions in 1973, and in a 2003 post–Belfast Agreement interview with *The Guardian,* she explained that she would not condemn people of her daughters' generation to pay the same price.[31] Now a member of the 32-County Sovereignty Committee, once headed by Bobby Sands's sister (Bernadette Sands McKevitt), Marian feels betrayed by Gerry Adams's Sinn Féin. Still passionate about the conditions of her former comrades, Marian is the spokesperson for the Irish Republican Prisoners Welfare Association.

Her sister, Dolours, is a mother of three and still retains a similarly hardline Republican public life. Having divorced actor Stephen Rea in 2003, she now contributes regularly to Anthony McIntyre's online journal *The Blanket.* In a July 17, 2004, article entitled "Once I Knew a Boy," Dolours conveys criticism of the path of Gerry Kelly, now Sinn Féin MLA for North Dublin, who had once been her comrade in 1973. She summarizes what she and her sister Marian sacrificed for while in the English jails:

> When we starved together it was not "to move the process forward", it was not for seats in a British Government, it was not to be treated as "equals" in a Stormont Assembly. It was, I like to think, because we had a shared passion for justice and freedom for this island, the whole of this island of Ireland. I believe that we were dedicated to the old struggle to rid this land of any British interference, that our wish was to regain our dignity as Irishmen and women never again to bend the knee, never again to lie down except in death after a good fight. Death would never have been our defeat—living on our knees, now that is defeat![32]

The sentiment reflects the Price sisters' motivations for an Irish Republic, but Marian explains she was too physically and mentally exhausted to rejoin when she was released from jail. She was content to watch Sinn Féin politicians take on the responsibilities, until her father pointed out to her that Gerry Adams would sell her out. "I told him [her father] to give Sinn Féin a chance. I was wrong."[33] Both sisters have recently come to much controversy; in November 2009, Marian Price was detained on charges related to Real IRA (RIRA) activity concerning the murders of two soldiers at the Massereene Army Barracks. She was released two days later. In February 2010, her sister Dolours was quoted in the *Irish News* as having personally transported Seamus Wright, killed by the IRA, across the border to be executed and buried in 1972. She went on to admit that she has been treated for Post Traumatic Stress Disorder (PTSD).

Liz McKee

On January 1, 1973, Elizabeth (Liz) McKee became the first female prisoner detained under the Detention of Terrorists Order of November 1972 in the Armagh Jail by then Secretary of State William Whitelaw. Her arrest that previous December (the 29th) had been based on the suspicion that she assisted in the escape of a male IRA comrade from Lagan Valley hospital. McKee, then 19 years of age and from Andersontown, was held for interrogation at Castlereagh until being sent to Armagh. Accused of being a "lilywhite" recruit new to the (Provisional) IRA's Cumann na mBan, McKee was a lesson in the British policy of strategic detention of female imprisonment. It was clear, to both the British and the Republicans, that the strength women possessed was an asset to the Republican movement. Political agitation, whether in the form of military activities, soapbox speeches, or early warning networks, opened up the realm of patriarchal politics for the female voice. From 1981 to 1984, Liz worked with Bairbre de Brún, and others, on a West Belfast benefit and also on the "Right to Fuel" campaign to combat fuel-based poverty.

Gerry Adams recognizes the sacrifice that Liz made. "Liz is a wonderful, generous, kindhearted human being, a republican of standing in her own right. She too was imprisoned without trial and suffered, maybe even more than Alex, enduring in the way that women do, all the tribulations visited upon herself, her husband and their family."[34] Liz McKee is now married to Alex Maskey, MLA for South Belfast and the first Sinn Féin mayor of Belfast (in 2002–2003), and is the mother of two children.

Mairéad Farrell

Mairéad Farrell was born in 1957 in Belfast. A bright student with a soft-spoken nature, Mairéad became principally focused on republicanism. Although her grandfather was engaged militarily during the Black and Tan War, she did not come from an overtly activist family, though many of the greatest patriots have been converted by various key events or personal experiences. Miss Farrell joined the IRA around the time that she left school, although some sources speculate her recruitment to be as early as age 14. In April 1976, she was arrested for her involvement in planting bombs in the Conway Hotel in Dungiven and interned in Armagh Jail. Well respected and disciplined, she quickly became O. C. (Commanding Officer) of the Republican POWs. Denied special category status under the new policy of criminalization, Mairéad would not wear the prison uniform. The coat she wore is now on display at the Irish Republican History Museum in Conway Mill. Mairéad's lucid direction organized the Armagh women. As the "no work" protest of prison work (1977) and nonconformity (1979) policies were introduced into the prisons, the Republican prisoners prepared. The No Wash and hunger strike protests in 1980 were an outgrowth of this outrage. Meanwhile, the security forces escalated the imprisonment of younger females with roundups typified by Operation Petticoat in August 1977, in which approximately 100 Catholic girls were arrested for a firebomb campaign across seven towns. As the female prison population swelled, so did the protests inside the jail. The last female political internee with special category status was released in 1984, three years after the introduction of the "normalization" policy that attempted to depoliticize the penal policies with the goals of bureaucratic normalcy. Her brief life after her release, a mere four years, is profiled in chapter 6.

Normalization, it seems, might have been the match held to the nationalist flame. The women in Armagh, and the Republican community itself, viewed the Troubles as a political and military war. Their actions to this effect were, thus, acts of resistance and war, not crimes. The criminal status denied the recognition of their acts as politically motivated and institutionalized the treatment of Republican women as "normal" criminal prisoners. Even though the British policy had been designed to equalize IRA assassination of a British civil servant, for example, with the homicide committed in the name of money, "criminalization" would even further politicize Republicans to collective action rather than subjugate them. Representative of the focused spirit of all these women, Mairéad Farrell coordinated the female participation in the 1980 hunger strike with Mairéad Nugent and Mary Doyle. Later, in 1986, the remaining women were transferred to the new Maghaberry facility in Lisburn. When Mairéad was released that year, after a 10½-year imprisonment, she continued her studies at Queens University Belfast until she went to Gilbratar, Spain, in 1988.

CONTRADICTIONS IN THE DECADE

- Peace People
- Rise of Feminism
- Human Rights and Violence?

As the 1970s came to a close, the impact of the Troubles was weighing heavily on the international community. The Civil Rights Movement of the 1960s had erupted into war and produced a military garrison state. Republican women had taken to the streets, tended to the needs of increasing numbers of POWs and their communities, and even taken up arms to defend themselves against occupation. Although many have described the Troubles as a low-intensity conflict or civil violence, it was—for the women and children especially—a war zone. Faced with the reality of a comprehensive crisis of liberty, women joined Sinn Féin to secure a voice in the midst of CS gas, flying bullets, and internment. Activated by the awareness of the frailty of human rights protection in the North, Republican women mobilized into political action as armed soldiers and community activists in the midst of a war. These roles of women in Irish society were a catalyst for some interesting off-shoots of ideological feminism and conflict resolution.

Peace People

As the world sat watching the events unfolding in the Six Counties, the war stirred up a movement for peace that spilled out onto the world stage. In October 1977, Betty Williams and Mairead Corrigan, founding members of the Peace People, were awarded the 1976 Nobel Peace Prize. The Peace People was an organization born from the tragic events that previous August. Mairead Corrigan's sister Anne Maguire was walking with her eight-year-old daughter, two-year old son, and six-week old baby in West Belfast when a chase occurred between a Republican man named Danny Lennon and the British Army. The British shot Danny in the head, and the car veered straight into the Maguire family, killing all three children. Severely injured and deeply troubled, Anne later committed suicide. The high level of visibility of both Anne's sister Mairead and social advocate Betty Williams, along with Ciaran McKeown, introduced a discourse on peace and empowered a language of nonviolence. Suspicious of a pacific embrace of occupation, however, many in the Republican community were not eager to sign on to a movement, with well-respected goals, that could ensure the continuation of second-class citizenship under Unionist domination.

Rise of Feminism

In the 1970s, women across Ireland emerged as agents of collective action. In addition to the Peace People, whose efforts had captured the attentions of the world community, there were numerous organic community groups flourishing across the 32 counties. This was not without controversy, as the debate among feminists and republicans produced a series of organizational splits and ideological divides. Debates abounded over the source and agents of gender inequality, and each community group seemed to corner a market of an answer. It is a debate echoed within feminist circles even today, with much divisive opinion. Perhaps the genesis of the feminization debate, and indeed the seed for the Peace People, was the Northern Ireland Women's Rights Movement (NIWRM). Formed in May 1975, the NIWRM served as an umbrella organization to link Protestant and Catholic women in all issues that affect women. Its efforts produced concrete policy results, including the 1976 Sex Discrimination Order and divorce and abortion rights. In 1978, the organization held the first International Women's Day celebration, which celebrated the awakening of gender empowerment. The NIWRM opened a center in March 1980 with Belfast City Council funding on Donegall Street; these ties to the Unionist-dominated council revealed a latent trust issue for Republicans. In its policy, the NIWRM was, in fact, anti-Republican in that it held that sectarianism was yet another tactic of oppressing women. The organization tended to cast community issues in a broad antiimperialist and feminist light. The NIWRM center's funding source only reinforced misgivings about its previous efforts. Despite thinly veiled confidence issues with Republicans, the NIWRM was quite effective in organizing a collective consciousness about changing social roles for Irish women.

The Socialist Women's Group (SWG), however, was unabashedly pro-Republican. The SWG had split from the NIWRM after it publicly criticized the Troops Out Movement (TOM) in 1976. SWG became closely affiliated both the Belfast Women's Collective and the Relatives Action Committee (RAC). Initially comprised of relatives of POWs, the RAC was founded on Easter 1976 to support the campaign for political status and organized street protests. Chaired by Father Piaras O Duill with Bernadette Devlin as its spokesperson, the RAC's efforts included "blanket women" who traveled across Ireland and Britain draped in blankets like Ciaran Nugent and his comrades to raise public awareness of the POWs prison conditions. As the stench of the No Wash campaign permeated Irish and British society, the RAC movement centralized its organization in 1978 and began to organize public marches. With the advancement of a new electoral strategy in

1981, the RAC branches consolidated into a national organizational front known as the National Smash H Block/Armagh Committee in the 1980s.

Although the SWG had been perceived with an air of radical feminist socialism and quickly disbanded, many of its members reconnected to form the Belfast Women's Collective in 1977. From its inception until 1980, the Women's Collective highlighted an engendered perspective in its "Women's Action" paper and focused on activism that most deeply affected female prisoners such as visitation rights, education programs, dependent care, and prison brutality and intimidation techniques. Although it was short-lived, the Women's Collective worked closely with the Republican community to liberate women from imposed gender roles and empower them to act collectively.

Founded in April 1978, Women Against Imperialism (WAI) linked Irish feminists to their female counterparts across the world. WAI argued that Irish nationalism was itself a feminist issue since it was only through national liberation that social liberation could transpire. The WAI's journal *Saorbhean* (Free Woman) contained articles maintaining the premise that pre-Victorian Brehon laws had been superseded by inequality embedded in British institutions. Unapologetically Republican, WAI joined organizational efforts with Sinn Féin in 1981. The tension and successive factions of feminists with Republicans was often cast as a tug-of-war over prioritization. For Sinn Féin women, it was quite simple. Inequality was imposed by the British and was not limited to a gender struggle. It was a war of independence first, since one cannot have an equal society without patriarchal patronization until British occupation is eliminated. WAI authors reverberated sentiments similar to the leftist Peoples' Democracy in its *Unfree Citizen* newspaper. Peoples' Democracy activist Bernadette Devlin famously articulated this in her comments when she said that "[w]e are not oppressed simply because we are women but also because we are working class women and because we are working class republican women."[35]

Human Rights and Violence?

The globalization of the social inequality debate in Northern Ireland took on a human rights dimension at the conclusion of the 1970s. In 1972, Lord Diplock had authorized the creation of a special court system for those accused of terrorist offenses in Northern Ireland. On the pretense of overcoming jury intimidation and witness tampering, the "Diplock courts" were juryless trials under the authority of one judge. The policy of "criminalization" was aimed at a legal distinction of paramilitary actions as criminal—not political—and scaled away the political status of Republican, and

Loyalist, prisoners. Then, in 1974, the British government had passed the Prevention of Terrorism Act (PTA) that enabled authorities to detain anyone under suspicion of terrorism for seven days, the later five of which had to be "authorized" by the home secretary (in the UK), without access to legal representation. The combination of internment, phased in Diplock Courts, and increased security powers led to many egregious cases of human rights abuses. Amnesty International began logging complaints in 1972 and accusing the British government of an unjust legal system. On January 18, 1978, the European Commission on Human Rights ruled against the British government for violating basic human rights with the policy of internment and interrogation practices. The excitement of judicial vindication in the decision was hampered by the election of Margaret Thatcher in the spring of 1979. Her conservative position on the North reaped a downward spiral of violence in the 1980s, notably her lack of concessions during the 1981 Hunger Strike.

CONCLUSIONS

The 1970s entered with the bang of bin lids across the North and exited with the explosions of bombs across Ireland and mainland Britain. Ireland has spiraled into an escalating civil violence, inter-sectarian killings, and a renewed war against the British. Republican women put down their aprons and picked up picket signs. Sinn Féin women forged the POW Department in support of their comrades and the Relatives Action Committee (RAC) for their families. These women were called to action and enacted new methods of community defense and street politics in defiance of an unjust systemic of discrimination and intimidation. The names of the women— Máire Drumm, Bernadette Devlin, Marie Moore, Mary Nelis, and the like—are enshrined in the Republican consciousness, for they inspired future generations to stand tall in the face of injustice. They were ordinary women, with families and children, who had hopes of a better society and a community of freedom and equality in which to raise their families. Some of them embraced hurling sticks and others grabbed their guns, all in the name of Ireland.

And so it was, that in the fall of 1979, history was made. That September, Pope John Paul II visited Ireland. He began his visit to Phoenix Park in Dublin on the 29th. He then traveled to Drogheda, 30 miles from the Six Counties, and turned the discussion to the Troubles. In this speech, he addressed the papal concerns with Republican violence: "On my knees I beg you to turn away from the paths of violence and to return to the ways of peace. . . . Violence only delays the day of justice. . . . Further violence in Ireland will only drag down to ruin the land you claim to love and the values you claim to cherish. In the name of God I beg you."[36] In the escalation of sectarian violence and security force terror, the Pope's appeal was not heeded. A stand of epic, heroic proportions was on the horizon and would change the course of Irish history. On March 6, 1980, Frank Maguire, the Westminster MP for Fermanagh-South Tyrone died; the decision of whom to slate for the by-election would bring the Troubles to the international stage.

Chapter 6

OPPRESSED FLOWERS, 1980s

I joined Sinn Féin [in 1981] because I could see that it was a political party of ordinary people, made up of the people in my community. They weren't just politicians, you could identify with them. They understood the problems of the community because they were experiencing the same repression.

—Lily Fitzsimmons[1]

CHAPTER OVERVIEW

May 5, 1981 changed everything. It transformed people, impacted society, in a way that only a handful of days in history have. And it was one young man from Twinbrook who brought the world to its knees in shock and horror. No more would Irish Republicanism be unfamiliar. No more would the plight of sectarian oppression be relegated to unconsciousness. No more would Sinn Féin's voice fall on deaf ears. Bobby Sands, and his comrades on hunger strike, made a contemplative protest for a united Ireland as British prime minister Margaret Thatcher watched 10 men die.

Bobby Sands was, in many ways, typical, but his wisdom was anything but typical. He was keenly aware of his sacrifice, and of the role that his female comrades played in this struggle.

But there are none more courageous, nor sorrowful, than those oppressed flowers in the Armagh Gaol. Irish women who, unlike the flowers of the wild, refuse to bow before the foreign winds of torture and inhumanity. The beauty of the nation is being scarred by pain and hate, it has been buried in dark dungeons; hidden from the light of day without which no flower can survive. It can be heard screaming in a tormenting agony that wrecks the heart. Yet these flowers refuse to be broken![2]

As Bobby Sands was on hunger strike in the spring of 1981, his comrades in Armagh Jail sent letters to sustain his spirit. His mother did, too, though they were often blackened with censored lines. He, and the other strikers, had been smuggling communications out on small bits of toilet paper (bog rolls) and shared a concealed miniature pencil among them. Members of Sinn Féin's POW Department, chaired by Marie Moore and Tom Hartley through the 1980s, and the Relatives Action Committee (RAC) facilitated a support network for the Republican prisoners. It was a dark time, one described by Eibhlín Glenholmes as "1981 is the year. Everything changed. Forever."[3]

The 1980s crystallized the potency of the Irish struggle across the world. Though the ultimate sacrifice of the 10 hunger strikers would become the central linchpin of the struggle for freedom, Republican women supported the development, implementation, and coordination of the hunger strike and the election of Mr. Bobby Sands, prisoner 1066. Bobby Sands reminded the world that every Republican had a part to play, and the women of Sinn Féin understood that they were the oppressed flowers who remained unbroken. These women were hunger strikers in 1980, strip-searched Armagh comrades, POW Department members, RAC support systems for prisoner's families, grassroots community activists, Republican electioneers, communications smugglers, and IRA operatives armed with armalites and car bombs.

Chapter Organization

This chapter seeks to place Republican women in the events of the 1980s. First, the key events in the Republican movement and Anglo-Irish governance are examined. This decade is often researched, and the author wishes to recommend additional reading for a more detailed coverage of particular events and subjects from this pivotal point in Irish history.[4] Much of the events of the 1980s, like that of the 1970s, occurred in the Six Counties of Northern Ireland. This is reflected in the 1983 election of Gerry Adams as Sinn Féin president, which symbolized a shift from a Dublin base, which had been under the leadership of Ruairí Ó Brádaigh, to Belfast where Adams resided. Once the key developments of Sinn Féin party history and Anglo-Irish governance have been examined, then the central roles that Republican women played are discussed—founding the Sinn Féin's Women's Department, sustaining the hunger strikes, supporting Sinn Féin's POW Department, enduring strip-searching, nurturing families with the Relatives Action Committee (RAC), arming in the resistance, recording history in *An Phoblacht/Republican News* (AP/RN), and agitating for justice. There were many women who played these roles, shaped their part of Irish her-story; a few are known to history, but far too many are not. This chapter provides profiles in courage of five women, whose stories tell the very difficult choices made in a time of war.

It must be noted that in the wake of the death of Bobby Sands, MP, many people in Ireland joined Sinn Féin and/or the Irish Republican Army. The overlap in membership, combined with the development of the armalite and the ballot box strategy in the mid-1980s, makes the designation of "Republicans" murky. Thus, the author wishes to acknowledge that some of the women profiled within this chapter may have been members of both organizations or only a member of one. In general, those Republican women who were convicted of paramilitary offenses against the state were accused IRA members. Those women on the streets and in the community supporting the Republican movement were more likely to have been Sinn Féin. That said, in the end, these women were sisters in a struggle much larger than organizational territories.

HISTORICAL OVERVIEW

- Prison Protests and the Hunger Strike
- Internal Party Fissures
- 1982
- Sinn Féin Elections?
- Abstentionism?
- Sectarian Violence in the 1980s
- Toward a Lasting Peace?

Prison Protests and the Hunger Strike

In 1976, special category status for Republican political prisoners was revoked. Known as the policy of criminalization, the revocation led to Republican POW protests, especially in the H-Blocks and at Armagh Jail. Prisoners refused to accept criminal uniforms, going "on the blanket." A "No Wash" protest coincided, where the POWs were not granted bathing privileges and their chamber pots were not emptied. The result was a feces-ridden, urine-smelling, maggot-infested existence. The women, denied sanitary napkins, had menses in their cells as well. The No Wash protest in the Armagh Jail was described by Mairéad Farrell's mother in 1980: "I think it's inhuman that the girls are being forced to live in these conditions. I think it's absolutely desperate that such conditions are allowed to continue. Mairead says the flies are terrible and there are some kind of fleas and other insects hopping about the cell."[5] And so it was, in early 1980, that Republican prisoners were still on the blanket, though the women in Armagh were allowed to wear their own clothes, and on the No Wash protest—all for better prison conditions and special category status privileges.

The year 1980 opened a Pandora's box within Sinn Féin and the contents spread across the world. Table 6.1 details the key events related to Sinn Féin party development and Irish history during this time period. The Hunger Strikes of 1980 and 1981 demonstrated a resurgence of protest campaigns against the prison conditions of Republican political prisoners. The No Wash and Blanket campaigns of the 1970s had been targeting the revocation of special category status in 1976, and in the Irish tradition of hunger striking, Republican prisoners in the H-Blocks and Armagh Jail (women) united to bring their five central demands back to the British government.

Table 6.1
Key Events of the 1980s

November 1980	"Women in a New Ireland" document passes the Sinn Féin Ard Fheis. The document calls for a Women's Department, contraception, and gender equality.
April 30, 1980	Marion Price was released from Armagh women's prison; she had been suffering from anorexia nervosa. Her sister, Dolours, was released a year later in 1981.
October 27, 1980	Seven male POWs, Brendan Hughes, Tommy McKearney, Raymond McCartney, Tom McFeeley, Seán McKenna, Leo Green, and John Nixon, go on hunger strike, protesting the revocation of special category status. Their strike lasts 53 days.
December 1, 1980	Three women, Mairéad Farrell, Mairead Nugent, and Mary Doyle, join their male comrades in the Armagh Jail. They remain on the strike one day past the men.

Table 6.1
Key Events of the 1980s (*Continued*)

January 16, 1981	Bernadette McAliskey and her husband are the victims of an attempted assassination.
Fall 1981	Danny Morrison gives the "armalite and ballot box" speech at the Árd Fheis party conference. This becomes the foundation of a move away from abstentionism.
March 1, 1981	Bobby Sands and his comrades begin another hunger strike. Bobby's strike would last 66 days.
April 9, 1981	Bobby Sands, H-Block prisoner number 1066, becomes the MP for Westminster Parliament from Fermanagh and South Tyrone.
May 5, 1981	Bobby Sands is the first to die on the hunger strike. His comrades soon follow in his path: Francis Hughes (59 days on strike); Raymond McCreesh (61 days); Patsy Ó Hara (61 days); Joe McDonnell (61 days); Martin Hurson (46 days); Kevin Lynch (71 days); Kieran Doherty (73 days); Thomas McElwee (62 days); and Michael Devine (60 days).
1982	Falls Road Centre opened.
1982	Policy of strip searching women institutionalized.
October 20, 1982	Northern Ireland Assembly (a power sharing devolved institution) elections are held. Sinn Féin stands in the election, earning 10.1 percent of the vote, and earns five seats, which they do not take.
July 20, 1982	A series of bombs is detonated in London, including Hyde Park, renewing the IRA's Mainland Campaign.
May 30, 1983	The Fine Gael-Labour Irish Government, reelected in November 1982, establishes the New Ireland Forum to seek a peaceful solution for the North. Sinn Féin is excluded.

(*continued*)

Table 6.1
Key Events of the 1980s (*Continued*)

June 11, 1983	Gerry Adams wins the Westminster MP seat for West Belfast. He does not assume his seat due to abstentionism. That fall, Adams is elected president of Sinn Féin.
June 1984	Second election for European Parliament is held. Sinn Féin does not win a seat.
October 12, 1984	The IRA bombed the Conservative Party conference in Brighton, England. Five people were killed. Margaret Thatcher was there.
November 15, 1985	Anglo-Irish Agreement is signed by Margaret Thatcher and Garrett FitzGerald. It recognizes mutual government interest in Northern Ireland but establishes that no change in the status shall occur without majority consensus of the people.
Novembers 1985–86	At the 1985 Árd Fheis, a motion to end abstentionism is proposed. The matter is taken up that following November, when the majority of the delegates voted to drop abstentionism. Ruairí Ó Brádaigh led the delegation that objected, and he left with Daithí Ó Conaill to form Republican Sinn Féin.
March 1986	Maghaberry Prison is opened for female prisoner transfer. Most of the Armagh women end up in Maghaberry.
June 1986	Northern Ireland Assembly is dissolved.
November 8, 1987	An IRA bomb interrupts the Enniskillen Remembrance Day, killing 11.
1987 Scenario for Peace	Sinn Féin demonstrates a party platform for peace, conditional upon the withdrawal of the British troops and disbanding of the RUC police.
January 11, 1988	John Hume, leader of SDLP, and Gerry Adams meet to discuss mutual interests in a peaceful Ireland.
March 6, 1988	IRA Volunteers Mairéad Farrell, Séan Savage, and Daniel McCann are shot dead by the British SAS in Gilbraltar, Spain. The three were unarmed at the time.

In the fall of 1980, a hunger strike based on five demands began. The male POWs in the H-Blocks of Long Kesh were joined by three females (Mary Doyle, Mairéad Farrell, and Mairead Nugent) in Armagh Jail. Their five demands were honed and publicized by the Smash the H-Blocks Campaign. The cornerstone of the campaign was a five-pronged set of demands: (1) To be able to wear nonprison clothes; (2) To not participate in prison work detail; (3) To have freedom of association with other POWs; (4) To be eligible for full remission of sentences; and (5) To organize educational and physical programming along with regular mail privileges. The 1980 hunger strike was eventually called off, and Republican leadership began refining the strategy for a second strike for the same demands. That second strike would become the 1981 Hunger Strikes that acutely reminded the world of the dedicated passion of Republican volunteers. And so it began on March 1, 1981, when Bobby Sands refused his food. He knew the price he would pay and how the burden of his martyrdom would impact his family. He wrote in his journal that day:

My heart is very sore because I know that I have broken my poor mother's heart, and my home is struck with unbearable anxiety. But I have considered all the arguments and tried every means to avoid what has become unavoidable: it has been forced upon me and my comrades by four-and-a-half years of stark inhumanity.[6]

He wrote a letter to the girls in Armagh Jail that day. He knew the price that they had paid in their commitment to republicanism and freedom. The Sands family was indeed distraught, and the British would get his pound of flesh.

In late March 1981, Bobby Sands was placed on the Anti-H Block ticket for the Westminster seat for Fermanagh/South Tyrone. The seat had been vacated with the death of the sitting MP, Frank Maguire. Sands knew a good campaign, and election, would not secure his release. He was prepared to die. On May 5, 1981, some 40 days after being elected as a Westminster MP, Bobby Sands died. His death sent shock waves around Europe, even as the remaining hunger strikers, one by one, began to succumb to their fate. In the midst of the continued hunger strike and the media frenzy following it, Sinn Féin activists that had worked the streets in Fermanagh/South Tyrone for Bobby Sands would do the same in constituencies in the Republic (Twenty-Six Counties) as well. The Dáil elections of June 1981 are less recorded in history, but nine republican prisoners stood for election. Two, hunger striker Kieran Doherty in Cavan/Monaghan and blanket man Paddy Agnew in Louth, were elected. Perhaps even less known is the election campaign for Mairéad Farrell, one of the three female Armagh hunger strikers in 1980, stood for election that June 1981 in Cork North Central. Maura McCrory describes the passion that drove her to campaign for Mairéad Farrell: "My son [who was in the H Blocks] was not on hunger strike and I knew the anguish my own family was suffering. I could only imagine the pain of those mothers and families whose sons, brothers and sisters faced a slow death. I knew I had to work for them, to go on fighting. During Mairead Farrell's election campaign in Cork I was out of Belfast for a month. My daughter was to make her First Communion. I just made it back in time."[7] Despite the efforts of her supporters, like Maura McCrory, Mairéad Farrell was not elected.[8]

The mood permeating the elections was dark. Sinn Féin activist Mary Nelis remembers that when Bobby Sands died, it was like their own child had died. Though the Hunger Strikes raised awareness about the plight of the POWs and conditions in the North, it was not a nexus for feminism. She says that she joined Sinn Féin during this time, but that "Sinn Féin was a male dominated organisation, so joining Sinn Féin wasn't the panacea for your own liberation, your own freedom, your own recognition as women. We had to fight our way in Sinn Féin, and we're still doing that. The decision-making is so entrenched among the male comrades, you know, that you still have to remind them all the time: 'Here we are boys, we have our rights.'"[9]

Internal Party Fissures

Within the party structure of Sinn Féin, there was also a fissure brewing. The Republic-based party had developed a federal governance proposal, under the authority of Ruairí Ó Brádaigh and Daithí Ó Conaill. The proposal for a national, federal model of Irish government was swiftly defeated at the 1979 Árd Fheis, which had been held in January 1980. That same year, Ó Brádaigh introduced a proposal for a Women's Department and the consideration of contraceptive policies within it proved quite controversial. This, combined with the growing strength of leadership in the Northern anchor of Sinn Féin, headed by a young man named Gerry Adams, proved to be the beginning of an irrevocable split for Sinn Féin in 1985-86. The Adams-backed (1985) Árd Fheis proposal to end abstentionism proved to be a final straw for Ó Brádaigh, who had resigned his presidency in 1983. As the new Westminster MP for West Belfast, Gerry Adams had had little problems rising to fill Ó Brádaigh's vacancy. The former Long Kesh prisoner had a particular charisma, an "electability" factor that propelled him onto the international scene. His notoriety was not unnoticed; Loyalists paramilitaries from the Ulster Freedom Force (UFF) attempted to assassinate him on March 14, 1984. His car was riddled with over 20 bullets, but he survived to lead Sinn Féin into the next phase of postabstentionist party politics.

1982

In the wake of the Hunger Strike, the world became more focused upon the events in Northern Ireland. Interestingly, as the world looked more closely, the conflict became more intense. In 1982, the policy of strip-searching female Republican POWs was institutionalized. It was a suffering and violation that only women could know. Even female visitors were subject to the policy. It was a vile act to remove a visitor's tampon or a grandmother's girdle, but this was, in the eyes of the prisoners, an act of war, of inhumanity. Those victimized on their visits and those seeking support for the daily trauma they endured began to raise their voices and gather in resistance. However, on the inside of the prisons, Rule 25 for remand prisoners allowed the prisons to impose solidarity confinement for an indefinite period; Siobhan O'Hanlon, who would become Gerry Adams's personal assistant, had once spent a month in solidarity under Rule 25.[10] In such conditions, the solidarity for the prisoners and their families was quite important. The POW Department of Sinn Féin, led by the gentle Marie Moore, was there to assist, as was the Relatives Action Committees (RAC) and, in 1982, the Falls Community Center was formed to provide additional support. In 1984, former prisoners Mary Doyle and Linda Quigley, along with Sinn Féin POW representative Chrissie McAuley, announced they were forming the Stop the Strip Searches Campaign.[11] With an active, energized community, Sinn Féin began to reflect on the electoral success mobilized during the 1981 hunger strikes, and the party shifted to participate, once again, in elections across Ireland.

Sinn Féin Elections?

The support could not have prepared Republicans for what was to come, including the reconstitution of a "powersharing" authority called the Northern Ireland Assembly. Convened in late 1982, the Assembly ostensibly included fair elections, and Sinn Féin even won five seats, but the concept of "powersharing" was a farce. It never did materialize as a true institution. Frustrated with the lack of progress, the British dissolved it in June 1986. In the meantime, elections in the Republic were held, pushing the Fine Gael-Labour party coalition out and then back into control of the Dáil. Sinn Féin's electoral efforts were not solely centered in the Twenty-Six Counties, perhaps as a matter of their marginalized status in the Republic or perhaps as a part of a national campaign strategy. In 1983, Gerry Adams was elected to the West Belfast seat for Westminster Parliament. But given Sinn Féin's position that the British government was an illegitimate authority in Ireland, he did not take his seat. European Parliament elections were held in 1984, but once again, Sinn Féin failed to make an electoral gain.

Abstentionism?

At the Árd Fheis in November 1985, there was a vibrant discussion of the electoral success in the North (with Sands and Adams's elections) and the policy of abstaining from Leinster House in the Twenty-Six Counties. Could it be that Sinn Féin's limited success in the Republic was overshadowed by the policy to abstain from actually taking the seats if won? After all, the Irish in the South had a functioning legislative institution, and perhaps in the refusal to accept it as an interconnected partition chamber was preventing Sinn Féin from entering its governance. Could more advancement toward a 32-county Ireland be made from within Leinster?

The debate did not produce a formal motion to change the party policy. Perhaps the Adams contingency (including Pat Doherty, Danny Morrison, and Martin McGuinness) needed more time to network the idea or maybe the IRA Army Council needed time to have internal discussions. No matter the reason, the motion was delayed for proposal until the next Árd Fheis. Hence, on Sunday, November 3, 1986, motion 162 was opened for debate. Some 54 speakers later, a vote was called with 429 voting to amend the Sinn Féin party constitution to end abstentionism in Leinster House and 161 voting against.[12] The necessary two-thirds affirmation was met, and Ruairí Ó Brádaigh led the dissenters out to form Republican Sinn Féin.

Sectarian Violence in the 1980s

A Republican in the 1980s had many threats to their lives—the British Army, the RUC, the Irish National Liberation Army (INLA), the Ulster Freedom Force (UFF), and the Ulster Defense Association (UDA) among them. Being active in Sinn Féin (or the IRA) made one a target. The bloodshed was high, even though violence had peaked in the 1970s, and tensions were high. The IRA was armed and active. Reprisal killings between the UFF/UDA and the IRA were one strain of activities. Targeting British military establishments and "economic targets" in the Six Counties and the UK was another.

In the wake of the Belfast Agreement in 1998 and the process of decommissioning, the precise nature of bombing activities, IRA armament, and the affiliated death/causality statistics are being reexamined. Included here are the best estimates of documented activities and statistics. Hitherto, Tim

Pat Coogan's 1994 book, *The IRA: A History,* has provided much referenced material on the IRA and its capabilities and campaigns, The author additionally recognizes that Richard English's 2003 book, *Armed Struggle: The History of the IRA,* contains well-documented accuracy in regard to IRA activities, especially during the 1970s and '80s. Out of respect for those who lost their lives and were harmed in the campaign, the best information that could be documented is referenced in this chapter. Where possible, statistics have been additionally verified with accounts posted through the International Conflict Research Institute (INCORE)'s Conflict Archive on the Internet (CAIN) Web site project.

In the 1980s, the IRA's bombing tactics would become more refined. The IRA was no longer limited to an arsenal of home-mixed explosives. Having access to Lybia's steady supply of Semtex and syncing it (allegedly) with remote detonation, or with timed devices such as a VHS timer, increased the safety in its production. In the late 1980s, the IRA began using fertilizer and gas-based pyrotechnics with cell signal detonation. The targeted goal was to cause maximum economic damage to the British establishment with little to no collateral human cost . . . unless it was of British soldiers. The goal did not always meet reality. In October 1981, the IRA placed a nail bomb at Chelsea Barracks that killed two innocent civilians. In the 1982 Hyde Park and Regents Park bombings, a gelignite bomb was detonated via radio signal in Hyde Park and a timed device went off in Regents Park, killing a total of 11 soldiers and seven horses (from the mounted cavalry unit). In December 1983, Harrod's department store was car bombed, killing 6 and injuring over 90 civilians. In October 1984, the IRA targeted the British Conservative Cabinet and party officials, including Margaret Thatcher herself, with a pre-set timer bomb. Five were killed.[13]

In 1985, the IRA was set on "legitimate targets," meaning British (including the RUC) security forces, government institutions, and economic targets. The February 1985 attack on the Newry RUC Barracks was conducted with homemade mortar attacks launched from a lorry bed. Nine RUC members were killed and over 30 were injured. Not civilians; just security forces. In general, targets would be given to the British media and police with a minimum of 45 minutes to an hour prior notification. And then there was the tragedy in Enniskillen. That November 1987, an IRA bomb detonated in a building near a Remembrance Day ceremony. Eleven were killed; 63 were injured. All were civilians, and there were 13 children among the injured. Gerry Adams condemned the attack as it undermined legitimate IRA targets, but the tide of public opinion began to turn against such Republican efforts. The 1996 bombings, of Canary Wharf that February and in Manchester city center in June, implemented lorry fertilizer-based bombs mixed in South Armagh. Two died, and close to 40 were injured, at the Canary Wharf bombing, and close to 300 were injured in Manchester. Though the procedure had been refined ostensibly to limit casualties, the IRA activities cost Sinn Féin a place at the peace table.[14]

Inter-sectarian and intra-sectarian violence was another hallmark feature of the Troubles in the 1980s. Tit-for-tat reprisal killings, assassinations, kidnappings, and intimidation schemes existed between the UFF/UVF/UDA Loyalist paramilitaries and the IRA, as well as between INLA and the Irish People's Liberation Organisation (IPLO). Feuding between INLA and the IPLO commenced in December 1986 and claimed 11 lives before its conclusion in March 1987. Feuding between the Official IRA and the Provisional IRA hit a fever in the late 1970s but was effectively over when the OIRA ceased military activities in the 1980s. The Ulster Volunteer Force (UVF) concentrated its efforts on undermining fellow Loyalist paramilitaries in the Ulster Freedom Fighters (UFF) / Ulster Defense Association (UDA), along with Sinn Féin activists and Republican paramilitaries in the 1980s. But the flow of armaments continued among all parties to the conflict. The 1984 interception of guns aboard the *Marita Ann* in November 1984 revealed the IRA's continued attempts to procure Republican weaponry. It was a complicated clandestine world, made even more conspiratorial with the infiltration of British "supergrasses" swarming across Northern Ireland from 1980 on and worming into each group (the IRA, INLA, IPLO, UFF/UDA, UVF, etc). "Loose lips sink ships" was a constant warning in the North; perhaps with a mutual exposure, the inter-sectarian divide would move to political means? Both Loyalists and Republicans in the late 1980s seemed to be issuing signals that there might be a political solution.

Toward a Lasting Peace?

In May 1983, the Irish Taoiseach Garrett FitzGerald convened the New Ireland Forum in Dublin. Composed of parties across the political spectrum and the border, the New Ireland Forum sought to discuss purposeful solutions to the status of Northern Ireland. It did not include Sinn Féin. Curiously, the party of the incoming Westminster MP from West Belfast, elected two weeks later, was not allowed entry into these talks.

When the New Ireland Forum issued its recommendations in a 1984 report, it suggested three proposals for Northern Ireland. a unitary state of 32 counties; a federal/confederal state for Northern Ireland, or joint authority for the British and Irish governments. Even though Margaret Thatcher's reaction to the report was not across the board, the report's recommendation number three (joint authority) may have indeed laid the foundation for the Anglo-Irish Agreement of 1985 and the peace process of the 1990s.

The peace process of the 1990s was built on the foundation of the late 1980s. Sinn Féin had embraced the ballot box and ended abstentionism in Leinster House (Republic). Gerry Adams was an abstentionist member of Westminster Parliament. Sinn Féin had earned enough vote share to have five seats in the Northern Ireland Assembly (which it did not take). And in 1986, Gerry Adams published *The Politics of Irish Freedom*. In the final chapter of his book, Gerry Adams explored the possibility for peace in Ireland. Removing the source of the imposed inequalities (the British) remained the primary step for freedom, but in his reflections he offers insight into the prospects for a peaceful solution: "These objectives can only be achieved when ordinary people identify with them. This support can only be achieved nationally when it is worked at the local level. This can only be done by hard work, for example, through dialogue and by linking the local problems where they belong—as part of our British problem and at the door of both partitionist governments."[15]

Dialogue it was. In January 1988, John Hume of the Social Democratic and Labour Party (SDLP) met with Gerry Adams to discuss the common principles that united Nationalists and Republicans. Their meetings paved the road for joint statements indicating that the marginalization of Sinn Féin could no longer be allowed. The interests of all parties must be addressed in crafting a political solution. Talks concluded between SDLP and Sinn Féin in August 1988. The following March, Gerry Adams announced that Sinn Féin would entertain a political path to peace. A new secretary of state for Northern Ireland, Peter Brooke, was appointed that July. In November 1989, Peter Brooke gave a speech in which he would not rule out the inclusion of Sinn Féin in talks toward peace.[16] And so, the 1980s came to a close with hope—hope for peace in Ireland and for Sinn Féin to be a party to it.

WOMEN IN THE 1980S

- Women's Department
- Republican Women and the Hunger Strikes
- POW Department
- Strip-searching—Suffering in a Way That Only Women Can Know
- Female Soldiers
- Recording Her-story in *AP/RN*
- Social Agitation—Armalites, Ballot Boxes, and *The Politics of Irish Freedom*

Women's Department

The Women's Department was born in 1980, after support from then President Ruairí Ó Brádaigh and the Sinn Féin Árd Fheis discussion of the "Women in a New Ireland" document. Republican women suffered greatly in the 1960s and 1970s, as the violence and daily intimidation of living in conflict grew. Maura McCrory recalls that "[w]e, women, still have to cope with the daily oppression and humiliation and grief that it brings. We, women, are still running to the jails, still fighting on community issues, for our children's future, for our environment."[17] As mothers, daughters, sisters, and partners, the women in Sinn Féin knew the power of sisterhood and solidarity in struggle. They cared for each other's children, offered a shoulder when the grief and suffering became overwhelming, and took to the streets in protest of inequality, prison conditions, and injustice. Anyone who has met these women notices their sharp minds, keen insights, passionate hearts, and glints of suffering in their eyes. The bond forged among the female Republican community in the North is evident.

And so it was, in the midst of the Hunger Strike, electioneering, and activism, that Sinn Féin solidified a network of women. It was not without controversy, however. The perception that Sinn Féin was a male-dominated patriarchal organization abounded. Many felt that the Women's Department empowered women; others felt that it segregated and subjugated them. There was also concern that pushing a women's agenda would interfere in the national liberation movement. That is, that is would detract attention, time, and resources from the primary goal of an independent Ireland, sans the British. The policies that the Women's Department discussed and researched were often controversial too. Though the policy documents produced by the Women's Department provided an engendered perspective on conflict issues and social problems, this valuable, insightful discussion was often dismissed as radical feminism, the rants of crazed women. Whether this is true or not, the discussions were hardly ineffective. They reflected a global awakening to the role of women in society—contraception, abortion, and women's rights in general among them.

Mairead Keane, head of the Women's Department from approximately 1987 to 1993, described the purpose of the Women's Department as twofold. She described the purpose as: "one, to raise and maintain consciousness around women's oppression and to influence within the movement; and two, to raise the issues of Partition and British occupation outside the movement, and to show how this is linked to women's oppression in Ireland."[18] Policy development occurred both bottom-up, from the local *cumman* to the Árd Fheis, and from the top national level of the Women's Department presenting reports to the Árd Fheis.

The success of the Women's Department was fledgling. In 1983, the party adopted a policy whereby one-quarter of the National Executive (Ard Chomhairle) was to be women. But, it was notably hard for women to rise through the ranks from the *cumman*. Those who did serve as a core force within Sinn Féin included Lucilita Breachnach, Bairbre de Brún, Rita O'Hare, and Jennifer McCann. But the early 1980s was the time of the hunger strikes, the crises in Armagh Jail, and strip-searching. Efforts to combat those injustices were led by the Anti-H Block/Armagh Campaign, the POW Department, and the Stop the Strip Searching Now Campaign. So, what then was the Women's Department to do?

The decision was clear—work on what they could. They began formulating policy drafts and holding discussions on key women's rights issues. They published discussions in "Women in Struggle" and wrote articles for *An Phoblacht*. They developed a network of solidarity of oppressed women by traveling abroad (many women also worked in the International Department) and nurtured International Women's Day commemorations. And they pushed forward several key motions to the Árd Fheis.

At the 1984 Árd Fheis, the party discussed the party position on divorce and abortion. Recent proposed changes to the Irish Constitution and soaring statistics of domestic violence paired with revocation of conception counseling centers and right-to-choose debates resulted in a two-year rise and ebb of support for a liberal feminist agenda. When the dust settled in 1986, it was clear that Ireland—and Sinn Féin—was not ready to defy tenants of their Catholic heritage. The distaste of the debates lingered, and many sought to blame the progressive proposals of abortion choice, open contraception availability, and divorce accordance on those "crazed feminists" in the Women's Department. As a result, many of the initial supporters of the Women's Department moved on, leaving a leadership vacuum until Mairead Keane was appointed chair of the department.

Mairead Keane brought a vision to the Women's Department. In a 1992 Sinn Féin Women's Department policy document, Keane described her vision to increase communication between women and the Ard Chomhairle, bring women's issues to the forefront for discussion, and to increase the prominence of the Women's Department. She then began trotting the world promoting global female solidarity for the women.[19] In 1987, Sinn Féin published *A Woman's Voice,* which, for the next few years, would contain stories such as a 20-year history of women in the North, a tribute to Mairéad Farrell—killed in Gibraltar in 1988, and the role of Sinn Féin councillors. In November 1988, Sinn Féin organized a women's conference in Dublin. Open to the public, three sessions highlighted the challenge facing women in Ireland, the impact of Irish membership in the European Economic Community, and the impact of prison conditions and imprisonment. Mairead Keane remained a significant force in Sinn Féin through the 1990s, and her role is further discussed in chapter 7.

In the January/February 1989 issue of *A Woman's Voice,* Lily Fitzsimmons and Theresa Holland discussed the role of Sinn Féin councillors: "In our work we come across the usual day-to-day problems of bad housing, homelessness, inadequate health facilities, anti-social problems like joyriding, severe poverty and physical and sexual abuse."[20] The results of much casework, a "Sinn Féin Manifesto" on women was published in 1989; in addition to having a gendered discussion of equal opportunity at work, equal pay for equal work, violence against women, health care and child care, it chronicled how the current education system reinforced sexism and stereotyping that allowed for a continuation of oppressed women in Ireland. Three national conferences later, the Sinn Féin Women's Department had a national spokesperson, a stronger women's branch in Belfast with full-time party activists, and a Dublin base that paralleled efforts to incorporate women's history into the Education Department programming.[21]

Republican Women and the Hunger Strikes

The No Wash protest in Armagh occurred around February 7, 1980, and would last approximately 13 months. The protest occurred shortly after a row in the Armagh Jail that resulted in swift, punitive action for the female prisoners. During a particularly traumatic engagement in the Armagh Jail in 1980, the prison went into lockdown. Riot police were called in, and the Republican POWs were cornered in their cells and beaten. The "swat" team was looking for black skirts and berets that Republican POWs wore to hold parade demonstrations in the prison courtyard. Eileen Morgan described what transpired in *Women in a War Zone:* "I was sitting in my cell when the door burst open and three male screws, with riot gear, came charging in. One of them jumped on top of me and kept punching me on the arms and chest, while the other held both my legs, swung my legs round so that I was lying flat on the bed. One sat on my legs and another on my chest while another put his hand over my nose and mouth so that I could hardly breathe. I was kept this way for a few minutes."[22] After having eight female prison officials hold her in the air with her clothes pulled up around her neck while four men watched, she was tossed back into her cell on her head. Toilet privileges were revoked for the prisoners, and thus, the no-wash/dirty protest began in the Armagh Jail.

Martina Anderson was first arrested at 18 years of age shortly after the 1980 hunger strike. When she arrived at the Armagh Jail, what she found shocked this very public Republican activist. The No Wash protest had a particular female dimension—menses:

I felt that I particularly had not done enough to speak out about, or even had the awareness of, what was happening in Armagh gaol to women—menstrual cycles and all that entailed. You had women on the no wash protest and they were not getting the sanitary protection. They were not getting washed, and they had to deal with all of that. I wasn't as aware, and I didn't feel that as a community even we had been aware. I suppose growing up in the 1980s you didn't actually mention periods, you didn't mention menstrual cycles. That was something that women snuck off in a room and dealt with in all the ways we had to, and I suppose that to a certain extent they still do. But I felt that because that was something that the system had as a weapon to use against our prisoners that we should have been more mindful of the impact on them. Bobby had started the hunger strike when I was in Armagh, and we had also the three comrades [Mary Doyle, Mariead Nugent, and Mariead Farrell] that had been on the first hunger strike. They were remarkable women. Mary Doyle and women like her were women that we looked up to . . . we had nothing but the utmost respect and admiration for them; they showed us the way as young people coming in. They taught us. In the small time that I was there, they encouraged us to get involved in the education programme, to discuss and debate, to become aware of the empowerment out of which we came and the war.[23]

Eibhlín Glenholmes explains that these women were the community's Countess Markieviczes, Mary MacSwineys, and Máire Comerfords.

To see someone prepared to do that for you, for their country. . . . These were our friends, our comrades. 1981 was our 1916. It instilled upon us that never again, never ever again, is this going to happen to us. And this is probably one of the biggest motivators. Gerry Adams put [it] very well once when he was explaining to me the negotiations with the British. It's almost unfair, that they have these politicians and civil servants at their side, and we have the delegation that we have. We have the hunger strikes, Mairéad Farrell, Máire Drumm . . . so it's the necessity, the imperative to deliver. Our people deserve it, and to ensure with us in the back of our heads that we will take our people, all the people in our society, where 1981 will never happen again.[24]

Nell McCafferty, a Dublin-based feminist writer, was outraged at the complacency of the Irish feminist to allow such transgressions against women in the No Wash campaign. She wrote a scathing article in 1980 for the *Irish Times* entitled "It Is My Belief That Armagh is a Feminist Issue."

Her opening line was potently painful: "There is menstrual blood on the walls of Armagh Prison in Northern Ireland. The 32 women on dirt strike there have not washed their bodies since February 8th 1980; they use their cells as toilets. For over 200 days now they have lived amid their own excreta, urine and blood."[25] With the introduction of institutionalized strip-searching in November 1982, the prison conditions in Armagh would go from inhumane to worse yet.

On December 1, 1980, three of the Armagh women joined their male comrades on the strike. Despite the men calling off the strike due to signs of British acquiesce, the women remained suspicious and remained on strike for another day. Though they did not join them again on the strike in 1981, they sent regular communications to the men to offer their solidarity.

During the Hunger Strikes of 1981, there were no women on the strike, but Republican women across Ireland rallied support for the men. Female POWs sent letters to the men to encourage them in their fight, and Sinn Féin councillors provided support to the prisoners and their families. Lily Fitzsimmons and Teresa Holland described how these 1981 activities extended throughout the 1980s. They provided housing assistance to the prisoner's families, pushed for social security benefits for the families, and facilitated child care for the women visiting their partners or families in jail.[26] These services, including planning protests to raise awareness of the prisoners' conditions, were often coordinated by Sinn Féin's POW Department.

POW Department

Sinn Féin's POW Department, championed by Marie Moore during the 1980s, served an immeasurable impact of kindness for the political prisoners. "They loved. They cared. They minded. They did everything beyond the call of duty for our families," Martina Anderson recalls.[27] The contact was especially important to Anderson because her family "who had to travel to England, could not have coped and managed either financially or mentally without the helping assistance of that department."[28] The support was also logistically important for the women on the inside. Martina explains that "[i]t also, in terms of prisoners, would have been looking after our welfare, as well as our families, and ensuring that any reading material and documentation and keeping us abreast because there was a disconnection for us who were in England."[29]

Communication was a lifeline for a POW. Martina recounts how valuable visits were: "Everything that you were hearing was sometimes almost a story twenty-four hours old. It was never when it was happening. And the news over there didn't carry the effects of the contact and the way it was being carried over here, so you would only get snapshots of information.

And so by the time you would get the daily papers over, you were always trying to play catch up and wondering what the effects of all of that were."[30] The POW Department facilitated visits, which also provided, if possible, a smuggled gift such as a small crystal radio, cigarette papers (for writing), and shortened pencils. The POW comms (communications) would then have to be smuggled back out, many appearing in *An Phoblacht* for general supporters.

In 1976, the families of Republican POWs formed Relatives Action Committees (RAC) across the Six Counties. In protest of the revocation of special category status, the POWs had begun Blanket and No Wash protests. The prison conditions continued to deteriorate under these circumstances, and the families refused to accept the inhumanity in which their relatives lived. Many Sinn Féin activists were involved in the RAC movement, wearing multiple hats in their activism. Sinn Féin women were on the front line of RAC planning for marches, demonstrations, speaking tours, and (later) the electioneering of the H-Block candidates. In 1978–79, a national network of the Anti-H Block Armagh Committee had been established, and activists took to the streets with leaflets and pamphlets about the prisoners, their conditions, and plans for action. Long before the election stand of Bobby Sands and his comrades, members were chaining themselves to the rails of government buildings and walking the streets in blankets and bare feet.

The plight of the POW families was bleak. Coordinated efforts by An Cumann Cabhrach and the Prisoners Dependents' Fund sustained them as much as possible. An Cumann Cabhrach had been founded in 1953 and rejuvenated in 1975. The organization would provide funds to the families of prisoners during the POWs incarceration. This could be decades, and within that time, many children and women lost a family member in the struggle. An Cumann Cabhrach also assisted them.

Strip-searching—Suffering in a Way That Only Women Can Know

"Remove your clothing."

I was hustled into a small cubicle, the curtain closing behind offering a sickening attempt at consideration of privacy, except the curtain only emphasizes the ritual. My jaw set, I slowly removed my jumper, jeans, shoes and, een more slowly, began to undo the buttons of my shirt—this last vestige of normalcy.

Normality—what a joke!

Outside the cubicle I could hear the twittering of the four Screws and thought of how I'd face them.

"Remove your bra and pants."

I refused to allow her note of jocularity to understate what was happening to me. Eventually the curtain was thrown back . . .

"Ready? Good."

No, I'm not ready, my brain replied. And I never will be ready!

A sheet was hanging across the cubicle to lend emphasis to, rather than cover, my nakedness. Her eyes staring at a space about six inches above my head, I was motioned to leave the temporary security of the cubicle.[31]

The act of strip-searching is ostensibly about security. When the act becomes a ritual, often repeated multiple times a day, it is clear that there is another objective. Eibhlín Glenholmes was subjected to strip-searching while she was on remand. She describes it as an act of war. "It was a violation but most certainly I was in the hands of the enemy. I expected nothing less from them. . . . I knew that given the nature of the war we were engaged in, this was not a Chile situation, it was not an Argentina."[32] The psychological effects were extreme. It compromised modesty, provoked anorexia, and emerged as physical stress. The Republican POWs would often band together to deflect attention from a particularly distraught comrade by creating a behavioral disturbance that would make them, and not their comrade, the focus of the ensuing attentions. When one refused a strip search, they would hold you down and perform it anyway.

Sometimes, Ms. Glenholmes recalls that up to 14 screws (prison guards) would be in the room watching to intimidate and reinforce mentally the balance of power. Eibhlín describes how her comrade Mary's periods stopped as a result of the stress of strip searches, but she personally "just registered myself out of it. I thought Bobby Sands had died. There was nothing they could do to touch me inside. And that's where I went to inside my head and it was happening outside. It was an act of war. They were the enemy. They had me at that moment, but they weren't going to have me forever. It was just a part of war, that's what it was. It had nothing to do with being strong. . . . I never cried when I was strip searched, but I cried for my friends."[33] Martina Anderson recounts: "We underwent a number of strip searches daily, sometimes six times a day. On remand, it was just a regular feature of remand. In fact, I would say that we spent our remand period not concentrating on our trial at all, but trying to challenge the system to give us the space to survive in a prison."[34]

Being on remand in the 1980s was the equivalent of a guilty sentence. There was no feeling of a democratic process. Martina clarifies: "It was always limitations as opposed to what most all the remand prisoners do [which] is to actually get their depositions and their papers and to prepare for their trial. We didn't have the space to do that because we were constantly cell searched, strip searched. It was an ongoing battle in remand and that was for thirteen months. We left Brixton after experiencing hundreds and hundreds of strip searches. We moved after we were sentenced to life imprisonment to Durham jail. And in Durham jail, the strip searches continued, not in the same number as was before. However, every time when you had visits or when you had a cell search, so on a weekly basis or on a monthly basis, you were still experiencing strip searches. I think, in terms of the effects of strip searching on women, it's something akin to, it can be, to a sexual assault on one's body."[35]

Eating disorders, she says, were a frequent side effect of the assaults.

> I think as a woman, that you tried to, when you were getting them in such numbers, that we tried to block out what was happening to you. You had to learn to almost bring some shutter down in your brain and go through it procedurally, to try not to—emotionally. It would destroy you. I think if I was being honest about it, that the thirteen months on remand, there was a period of time where emotionally it was impacting on our well-being; particularly getting six strip searches a day, you wanted to do lights out, you were getting annoyed, you were getting angry. . . . It was uncalled for, it was unjust; everything about it, it was done to degrade you. It was making me very angry, and it came to a point of realizing, of sensing your own anger and sensing how this was changing you as an individual and I felt I had to psychologically deal with that in my own head so that the system wasn't going to change me as a person and destroy me and eat me up and to have me as some angry individual because of what they were doing to me.[36]

Fighting the courts on the treatment of Republican prisoners did not yield much fruit, so the focus became raising the political consciousness and public awareness on the outside of the women's plight. The strip-searching policy enraged many of the English women's groups, to which Martina Anderson expresses sincere appreciation. She remembers that every Saturday, there was a protest outside the Brixton prison, and on International Women's Day, there were a number of women's groups protesting outside Durham jail as well. On the Irish front, the Relatives Action Committee (RAC) and the Stop Strip Searching Movement spoke for these women, when they did not have a voice that the British establishment would hear. Even RAC members were subject to strip-searching. Lily Fitzsimmons tells the story of harassment of a female visitor in October 1980 where she was forced to remove her sanitary napkin when the guard realized she was menstruating and of an elderly woman who was forced to remove her corset in order to visit her grandson.[37]

In Ireland, the radical feminist left refused to support the Armagh Republican prisoners on the No Wash and Stop the Strip Searching campaign. Eibhlín Glenholmes says that this stemmed from the feminist perspective that the POWs belonged to a male-dominated organization. The POWs, however, "saw themselves as soldiers first and then women. . . . The women of Armagh jail needed the support of their sisters. The time to debate the issue was post-protest, not then."[38] Since her return to Belfast in 2001, Eibhlín herself has been reaching out to the radical feminist left and attempting to reengage them with Sinn Féin.

Even after the transfer of the women to Maghaberry Prison, beginning March 18, 1986, the policy of strip-searching continued. Maghaberry was a 30 million pound prison with 17 remand prisoners, yet strip-searching was used for security, even though it was high-tech facility.

Female Soldiers

In the 1970s, Cumman na mBan (the armed women affiliated with the Republican struggle) had been disbanded. The female soldiers of Cumann na mBan were eligible to be full members of the Irish Republican Army. In this capacity, women transitioned from supportive roles to integrated members of IRA units. Martin Dillon, author of *The Dirty War,* describes the younger members of the IRA Army Council's willingness to utilize the "honeytrap," where young female IRA members would lure security forces with the promise of sex. Once in a secured location, the soldiers would be killed by their male comrades.[39] The "honeytrap" was apparently used throughout the seventies and early eighties.

Since the IRA had employed a nongender-based membership, many young women joined the IRA directly to channel their Republican efforts, after special category status ended in 1976. Volunteer Mairéad Farrell, previously profile in chapter 5, was one of those women. Mairead Keane recalls that "it would be respected and accepted that Mairéad Farrell was an IRA volunteer. Women, as well as men, are IRA volunteers, and that is definitely accepted."[40] She was arrested shortly thereafter and imprisoned in Armagh Jail. As one of the three female hunger strikers in 1980, Farrell rallied her comrades in solidarity. While the men went on strike in 1981, Farrell organized negotiations with the prison governor for more visits with family and rallied the women as their O/C (Commanding Officer). She took courses through Open University after the Hunger Strike, and upon her release in 1986, she rejoined the IRA in progress and continued her studies at Queens University. She was an outspoken critic of the policy of strip-searching and spoke frequently on the topic. In March 1988, Mairéad Farrell was with Séan Savage and Daniel McCann in Gibraltar, Spain, where members of the Royal Anglian Regiment of the British Army was. According to published reports, the three had been under surveillance by the MI5 when a SAS team pumped them full of bullets while they walked the street—unarmed. Reportedly, keys found in Mairéad's purse opened a car in which a 100-pound bomb rested. Richard English recounts the controversy that called the "shoot-to-kill" policy into the public forum. English details that "[t]he four SAS soldiers who shot the IRA team had apparently been told that the republicans were to detonate their bomb by remote control (in fact they planned to use a timer) and that the IRA unit would be armed (which they were not)."[41]

Mairéad's death was tragic, as was her funeral. As Farrell, Savage, and McCann were to be laid to rest in Belfast's Milltown Cemetery, loyalist Michael Stone attacked the funeral attendees in a hail of bullets and grenades. Three mourners died, and later, during the funeral procession for one of those killed at the Farrell funeral, two unwitting British Army soldiers (Corporals Derek Wood and David Howes) were dragged from their car, beaten, and shot by the IRA. The tragic cycle of violence captures the fear and loss in the conflict, as well as the commitment of Republicans active in the war. Though many IRA women will remain unnamed in history, their actions—most frequently—left them in jail or on the run (OTR). Under the Good Friday (Belfast) Agreement of 1998, all political prisoners were released and OTRs allowed to return home to Ireland.

Recording Her-Story in *AP/RN*

An Phoblacht/Republican News was, and is, the weekly Republican paper that captured the heart of the Republican movement. Its contributors included smuggled communications from inside prisons, articles from legendary figures in Sinn Féin, constant coverage of the struggle of daily life in the North, and passages from reporters who sought to tell a truth that the mainstream papers in Ireland and the United Kingdom often ignored.

AP/RN, based in Dublin, was a fun, energetic (if not threatened) environment, especially in the 1980s. In addition to war-styled espionage to get stories smuggled out of Long Kesh and Armagh Jail, reporters and the entire *AP/RN* staff was subject to constant scrutiny, even death threats. During this time, Rita O'Hare was on staff, becoming editor in 1985, as she balanced her role in Sinn Féin as a party activist. She remained at *AP/RN* until 1990–91, when she was sent to the United States as an official party representative, later becoming general secretary and then treasurer for Sinn Féin in recent years. Chrissie McAuley, a seasoned Sinn Féin activist, was a Belfast correspondent. Her constant coverage of key events in the Troubles made sure to capture the human suffering and female perspective embedded in the conflict. Another young women active at *AP/RN* at this time was Treasa Quinn.

Treasa Quinn was just 15 years old when she came to work at *AP/RN*.[42] Danny Morrison was editor then; Morrison was a close friend of Gerry Adams and a chief party strategist. Treasa worked wrapping papers for delivery and was shortly moved into paper administration until becoming the general manager of the paper. In recent years, she has been serving as Sinn Féin's cotreasurer until moving into the finance department of Sinn Féin in January 2009.

The close relationship between *AP/RN* and Sinn Féin allowed for the Republican voice to be heard and Irish her-story to be recorded. Since the October 1988 British Broadcasting Ban censored Sinn Féin on the airwaves much like the 1971 Irish Republic's Section 31 ban continued to do, *An Phoblacht* was a vital component of "setting the record straight" and disseminating Republican debates across Ireland. In 2006, *AP/RN* became the first paper to be made available online in Ireland.

Social Agitation—Armalites, Ballot Boxes and *The Politics of Irish Freedom*

Eibhlín Glenholmes recalls one afternoon when Gerry Adams, who was about 19 years old at the time, stopped into her home. As he left the doorway, she inquired who he was. Her father responded that he was her future.[43] Whether prophetic or insightful, her father was right. Though the path to peace was slow, it was indeed deliberative. There would be, and still are today, those who doubt whether or not Gerry Adams's Sinn Féin made an error in calculating the British response. However, the political maneuverings of the late 1980s and early 1990s did indeed change Eibhlín's future, and that of all Northern Ireland's. In 1981, Danny Morrison delivered a speech at the Árd Fheis referencing the armalite in one hand and the ballot box in the other. The infamous speech coined the "Armalite and Ballot Box strategy" of an armed struggle with active, political engineering. The 1985–86 decision, embodied by Gerry Adams, to amend Sinn Féin's party constitution to allow elected TDs (members of the Irish Parliament) to take their seats. An electoral strategy was formulated and began being implemented in the mid-1980s. In 1988, as Gerry Adams sat down to chat with John Hume of the Social Democratic and Labour Party, electoral and political participation was a possibility for Sinn Féin. Sinn Féin women sat beside or behind Adams in each of these steps, steps that others might not have been bold enough to take (for fear of their consequences). John

Hume, and his co-recipient David Trimble, will be remembered for their 1998 Nobel Peace Prize, but Gerry Adams will be remembered in Sinn Féin for changing the future.

PROFILES IN COURAGE

- Eibhlín Glenholmes
- Martina Anderson
- Ella O'Dwyer
- Lily Fitzsimmons
- Jennifer McCann

Eibhlín Glenholmes

Eibhlín Glenholmes was born into a Republican family and grew up in a Catholic ghetto of East Belfast known as the Short Strand. Her father, IRA man Richard "Dickie" Glenholmes, who served 10 years in a British prison for trying to spring Brian Keenan from jail, was a big influence on her. Dickie Glenholmes was a steadfast Republican and ex-prisoner who had been a trade unionist prior to the armed struggle. Her political background included regular family discussions of Republican books and Irish history. She recalls many women and men, who helped to shape her political awareness, but was very impacted by local Belfast veteran Brian Keenan. Eibhlín explains that, in the height of the armed struggle, there was not much time to be shaped or molded. One was politically aware out of necessity. "I think I shaped myself the most" she offers for consideration.[44] She attended St. Dominick's school, the same school as Marion and Dolours Price, before leaving home at 17. Eibhlín had been engaged to Séanna Walsh, Bobby Sands's best friend, in the 1970s; both Eibhlin and Séanna were Short Strand natives. Séanna was a blanket man, who spent his formidable adulthood in the H-Blocks. He first met Bobby in Cage 8 of Long Kesh. In 2005, he was chosen to read the IRA statement that signals that weapons were being put beyond use.[45]

In the 1980s, she was on remand in Armagh and subject to strip-searching and interrogations. Although she was never convicted of any crime, she was accused of participating in several campaign activities and held on remand in 1983. In 1983, an article Eibhlín wrote under a pen name appeared in *An Phoblacht*.

It [strip-searching] didn't have any security benefits to it. Because the only time that anything could have been passed would have been

Eibhlín Glenholmes, national coordinator for gender equality. (Courtesy Kelly Morris)

when you had received a visit. . . . It was an exercise in bullying and an attempt to dominate the women. They didn't strip search us when we were coming back from visits with our visitors from the outside because they knew that if they did that we would refuse visits. We would have wrecked the place. We would have organized and protested. So instead they realised that the best time, the only time, they could use it was when we went to court because we had to appear in court. And they could do anything. We could not refuse to go to court, so they had us.[46]

She was hereafter released, only to receive nine warrants, including murder and various weapons charges, for her arrest in 1984. She was also wanted for questioning in connection with the 1984 Brighton bombing. In 1986, she successfully challenged extradition in the Dublin High Court, only to be rearrested by Irish Garda in a dramatic scene on the street immediately after. When she was released on a second hearing, she fled and lived as an OTR for about 15 years. A beneficiary of the Good Friday Agreement's policy on OTRs (on the runs), Ms. Glenholmes returned to Northern Ireland in 2001. Her close friend Siobhan O'Hanlon (Gerry Adams's former personal assistant) facilitated her homecoming, which came in the form of a surprise appearance to her parents' home.[47]

Eibhlín was settling into life back in Belfast when Gerry Adams called her into service in Sinn Féin. He asked her to work in the Equality Department, which would—under her direction—undergo restructuring. The new Party Development Department emerged with a renewed focus that integrated gender equality into party construction. Equality is not a gender-based concept, it was argued, and neither should be the party infrastructure. Completing her term on the Ard Chomhairle in 2009, Eibhlín Glenholmes remains committed to the Gender Equality Directive of the Party Development Department. Eibhlín Glenholmes's current role is discussed in chapter 8.

Martina Anderson

Martina Anderson was born into an interesting household in Northern Ireland. Her father was a Protestant who converted to Catholicism. Her mother was a Catholic with a strong Republican commitment. She has nine siblings, six of whom are sisters. Martina's mother campaigned and picketed the social inequalities in the 1950s and 1960s. Under the "one man, one vote" system, a house was required to vote, and most Catholics did not own houses in order to vote. Martina was deeply shaped by the community activism and commitment to equality and justice that her mother instilled in her. In her late teens, Martina met her future husband Paul who introduced her to left-wing politics in republicanism. Martina and Paul would later marry in an English prison. In 1981, she was arrested under charges of firearm possession and the intent to cause an explosion. She was held at Armagh Jail for a couple of months before going OTR to avoid an appearance before a "Diplock Court." She claims to have resided in Donegal for the next three or so years.

She was arrested in 1985 in Glasgow, along with Ella O'Dwyer, and held for 13 months on remand in the Brixton prison in England. It was an all male establishment, which made it difficult for female prisoners. In Brixton, Martina and Ella were on 23-hour lockdown as Category (Cat) A prisoners. When in 1988, Martina and Ella were moved to Durham prison, the women found that they were two of three political prisoners, the third being an alleged East German spy. There, a Cat A was on a 19/20-hour lockdown unless there was additional time for bad behavior.[48] In the British penal system, Republican prisoners were integrated into the social prison population. Martina recalls that "[i]n England, you were very much face to face with the system yourself."[49] The isolation from one's community and the irregularity of visits were particularly challenging, as they separated her from the Republican family.

Martina Anderson, director of Unionist engagement and MLA for Foyle. (Courtesy Kelly Morris)

Martina was subject to repeat strip-searching. In addition to the psychological terror of house raids, interrogation, and detainment, she soon found the strip searches to be yet another act of terror. "The British government is using women's nakedness to tyrannise them. We feel that our bodies are used like a weapon to penalize us with the intention of making us collapse under the pressure. If we haven't collapsed by now, I don't think that we will."[50] She was strip-searched roughly 400–600 (estimates differ) times in 14 months.

In July 1994, Martina and Ella won their transfer to Maghaberry prison but were held for one year on a non-Republican wing as a condition of their transfer. In a Republican wing, the POWs had an O/C to represent the petitions or complaints of the Republican women as a liaison for all POW needs. As a condition of the Good Friday Agreement, Martina Anderson was released and returned to her home of Derry. After 14 years in prison, she and her husband, also released under the Agreement, celebrated their honeymoon. She worked in Sinn Féin research, elections, and party development for a few years, then as director of the All-Ireland strands before Gerry Adams appointed her to be the director of Unionist Engagement in 2006. Her postprison work in Sinn Féin is discussed additionally in chapter 8. Among her recent accomplishments is a 2007 seat in the Northern Ireland Assembly. In 2009, she is an MLA, the Sinn Féin party spokesperson on equality and human rights, and a member of Northern Ireland Policing Board.

Ella O'Dwyer

Ella O'Dwyer is a typical Republican with anything but typical qualities. She was born in 1959 and grew up in County Tipperary with six siblings. Her grandfather Martin had sheltered IRA Volunteers in the 1920s, and her mother often accompanied her on Hunger Strike protests in 1981.[51] Ironically, she experienced little of her family's republicanism, for she grew up in the Republic somewhat removed from the movement. She attended University College Dublin where she earned a BA and did exchange studies on the continent. This is where she was first challenged to learn more about republicanism, and when she returned to Ireland, the H-Block campaigns were underway. Her involvement in the movement accelerated quickly, and by 1985, she was arrested in Scotland with Martina Anderson on conspiracy to plant explosives. She and Martina were on remand in Brixton together, and she was also transferred to Durham Jail and then Maghaberry. On a life sentence, Ella was also a Cat A prisoner and subject to heavy solitary confinement periods. During this time, she began taking graduate courses and earned an MA, from Durham University. She went on to complete a PhD from the University of Ulster.

Ella is a creative writer, and she occasionally writes pieces for *An Phoblacht*. She has received acclaim for her novel *The Rising of the Moon* published with Pluto Press in 2003. It is a political examination of language and reflects her strong commitment to republicanism. In addition to a recent academic fellowship at Boston College in the United States, her postrelease academic career reflects her sympathetic support for other former prisoners. Dr. Ella O'Dwyer occupies a visiting fellow position in Irish Literature at the University of Ulster and is a political education officer for Coiste na nIarchimí / Committee for Republican Ex-prisoners. She also recently began a two-year term on the Ard Chomhairle in January 2009.

Lily Fitzsimmons

Lily Fitzsimmons was living in the Turf Lodge area of Belfast when her son Séan was on the blanket in Long Kesh. She, along with other mothers, sisters, and partners, took to the streets to demonstrate the grueling conditions of the prisons. A key member of the Belfast community, she was often with her close friends, including the late Kathleen Holden and the late Marie Moore. She spearheaded the Anti-H Blocks/Armagh Campaign and the Relatives Action Committee.[52] She was among many of the visitors who smuggled in materials for the Long Kesh prisoners. At almost every march and public demonstration in the early 1980s, Lily Fitzsimmons was a visible voice for the prisoners, often wearing a blanket in solidarity with her son. She was tireless in her efforts, traveling abroad to speak on behalf of the Anti-H Block/Armagh Committee or simply political prisoners in general. In 1985, she became the first female Sinn Féin woman to be elected to a city council (Belfast, in her case) since the Countess.[53]

In 1996, Lily turned her passion toward writing. She published *Liberty is Strength: 30 Years of Struggle*, in which she recounted the contributions of Republican women over the last three decades. What is somewhat unique is that Lily actually *knew* and worked with them. These stories capture the solidarity of sisterhood in the movement, and, not surprisingly, how often Lily herself was a part of the mix. Unlike other reads of women in Ireland, Lily tells of the strength of women and their commitment to not simply endure, but act, and act swiftly and defiantly. An *AP/RN* review of her booklet describes it as such: "The women Fitzsimmons writes about (including herself) are quite definitely not spectators; nor are they silent or passive. They argue their case, they fight with authority, they challenge the state and defy the behavioral standards society sets them. They take up the gun when they have to—often in the face of opposition from the men on their own side—and suffer the pain of separating and other horrors which being imprisoned brings."[54] Lily continues to write and sing, another past time. In March 2009, Gerry Adams recalled how Marie Moore loved Lily's singing, especially her rendition of "Crazy."[55]

Jennifer McCann

Jennifer McCann was arrested five times before she was 18. Given the intimidation and hate that she experienced as a child, it is not tremendously surprising. Like the Sands family, the McCann family was forced to leave their home in Rathcoole for the Twinbrook estate. By 17, she was active in the IRA, and rose quickly within the ranks. At 20, Jennifer was arrested for the shooting of an RUC man and given 20 years in jail.[56] She was in Armagh and used to listen to the news on a small crystal radio, smuggled in of course, for the POWs. She was a close friend of Mairéad Farrell's, and she frequently speaks at commemoration events to honor Mairéad.

After being transferred to Maghaberry, she was released after 10 years of her sentence and began work in Sinn Féin's POW Department. Jennifer worked hard to expose the collusion of Loyalist paramilitaries with the British government by organizing An Fhirinne (the anticollusion group). She remains very committed to the community in which she was raised, volunteering at the Falls Community Council's Community Drugs Programme as well as spending time nurturing the Ógra (Sinn Féin youth). After all, Jennifer became politically active at just 14.

In 2006, Jennifer briefly served as a Sinn Féin councillor for Lisburn Council as a Dunmurry Cross councillor before, in 2007, being elected to the Northern Ireland Assembly from West Belfast. During this time, she was also serving as the party's spokesperson on Women's Issues (as well as Refugee Rights), an expert on the subject as she had been heavily involved in the Women's Department. In this capacity, she has highlighted the importance of addressing domestic abuse as a human rights issue.[57] In turn, she is committed to furthering the role of women in Sinn Féin; Jennifer has said that: "[w]e need to encourage more women to become involved in political life and we need to ensure that candidates are in winnable seats."[58] Balancing three children at home, in mid 2009, she took over Mitchel McLaughlin's chair-ship of the Finance and Personnel Committee in the Assembly.

CONCLUSIONS

In 1989, Sinn Féin was poised on the outskirts of a Northern Irish peace process. Gerry Adams's face, if not his voice—due to the Broadcasting Bans, was recognized around the world. Sinn Féin women had agitated in the streets, campaigned for justice, and endured in the darkness of the Armagh, Durham, and Maghaberry Jails. Some women picked up guns, others protest blankets and banner signs. Many of the women who spent the 1980s in jail were themselves children of the Troubles, mere teenagers when they were arrested and sentenced. Those who escaped conviction sacrificed decades with their families as OTRs or experienced rough interrogations and daily intimidation. The cataclysmic invasiveness of strip-searching violated women—in principle if not directly in practice—globally. The oppressed flowers of the 1980s did not wilt; instead, they rooted in the dirty soil in which they found themselves and bloomed. In 1981, Bobby Sands and his nine comrades had died for what they believed; and no one in Sinn Féin will ever let the world forget that. Their sacrifice laid the foundation of a shift in Irish consciousness and led to new hopes for future generations. The Troubles' atrocities of the tremendous violence and deep suffering know no owner. Life in the Six Counties devastated everyone in the 1980s.

Chapter 7

TENDING THE LILY IN AN INTERNATIONAL GARDEN, 1990s

A good nationalist should look upon slugs in a garden much in the same way as she looks upon the English in Ireland, and only regret that she cannot crush the Nation's enemies as she can the garden's, with one tread of her dainty foot.

—Countess Markievicz[1]

CHAPTER OVERVIEW

Gerry Adams, Martin McGuinness, and Mitchel McLaughlin . . . the men of Sinn Féin are known to us all. Throughout the peace process in Northern Ireland, the media has covered their daily actions, press releases, and political posturing. However, the women in Sinn Féin are often depicted in a supportive role rather than an integral front within the Republican movement. Perennially footnoted in the annals of history and contemporary news coverage, Sinn Féin women receive little to no acknowledgement for their role in crafting a peaceful strategy.

Sinn Féin women have been instrumental in the vision, negotiation, and implementation of a peace process in the North of Ireland. Who are they? What contributions have they made? How have they contributed to the development of peace in Ireland? And who was poised to tend the lily in the 21st century? As each one of these questions is explored, Sinn Féin's peace strategy reveals a keen awareness of the need to engender peace processes. Over a decade before the United Nations Development Fund for Women (UNIFEM) call for action, Sinn Féin women developed a model of multitiered participation of women in the conflict-resolution process and encouraged a gender responsive framework in conflict transformation. Recognizing the value of and need for empowered women in a conflict society, Republican women have been sowing the seeds of peace in an international garden of sisterhood.

Placing Sinn Féin within the context of a global initiative to engender the field of conflict resolution in practice (and then into politics of a transitioning, peaceful government) highlights the sophisticated development of the party's peace strategy. An overview of the 1990s Republican woman and the established initiatives for female empowerment within the modern Sinn Féin party demonstrates how Sinn Féin women have been instrumental in defining the conflict issues, in emerging as leaders in the party and in government, in fostering an environment for peace in the community, in demanding the inclusivity of all-party talks in negotiations and in society at large, and finally in assisting in the implementation of the Belfast Agreement. By accessing the network of solidarity developed in the 1980s, the women were able to focus an international spotlight on Northern Ireland. With pressure groups shoring up international interest in a peaceful solution, the capabilities of women in a conflict society were magnified for the world to see. It is, therefore, appropriate to examine the development and implementation of a peace strategy in Northern Ireland within the framework of the current global call for feminization in conflict resolution.

Although it is unwise to label Northern Ireland as a textbook example of any political theory (be it ethnic conflict, consociationalism, or conflict resolution), the context-specific dimensions of the conflict can be paired with the failures of previous attempts at conflict resolutions for some general recommendations for international application. Central to these recommendations must be the importance of inclusivity in the conflict-resolution process. Inclusivity conveys two central themes in its meaning: (1) include all the stakeholding members in a conflict society and (2) include women in particular as an overarching stakeholder to bridge sectarian or identity-based groups.

Peace carries so many meanings to different stakeholders in an entrenched conflict. Much like weeding an overgrown, neglected garden, the embedded conflict issues are often difficult to identify, classify, and eradicate. One must recognize that peace is sometimes hard won, as Sinn Féin activist Caitríona Ruane warns:

> In Belfast the women's groups, especially in the working class areas, loyalist and republican, are leading the way slowly, painfully, talking to each other, looking at all the issues and accepting that different groups have different agendas and that there is a gulf between us. That is the beginning—dealing with the issues not pretending that

they do not exist. We are going to help build a new Ireland, an Island that makes space for everyone regardless of their colour, religion, sexual orientation, gender or ethnic background.[2]

Although the concerns of Sinn Féin women in a postconflict society are most certainly heard, Northern Ireland entered into yet another round of peace negotiations with the Saint Andrews Agreement in October 2006. But at least a female Republican voice can be heard among those troubled with the prospects for real peace.

Chapter Organization

The 1990s was a time of turbulent hopes. The development of the peace process brought excitement and enthusiasm but also tension and bitter hatreds rising to the surface. The clandestine bilateral meetings of the 1980s became the foundation of a peace movement, and Sinn Féin wanted a place at the peace table. Table 7.1 details key dates and movements toward that peace table.

Table 7.1
Key Dates in the Northern Irish Peace Process

1988	Adams/Hume Talks. Gerry Adams, Sinn Féin President, and John Hume, Social Democratic and Labour Party leader, conduct secret talks from January to August.
1991	Brooke/Mayhew Talks. Secretary of state for Northern Ireland Peter Brooke begins talks with four parties (not Sinn Féin) that lead to the establishment of the Three Strand Talks (North-South, East-West, and within Northern Ireland). The Brooke/Mayhew Talks last from March 1991 to November 1992.
December 15, 1993	British prime minister John Major and Irish Taoiseach Albert Reynolds sign a joint statement, called the Downing Street Declaration, which furthers the movements toward peace.
1994	U.S. president Bill Clinton grants Gerry Adams a visa to come to the United States. The visa is seen as an acceptance of Sinn Féin as an interested party in the peace process.

(continued)

Table 7.1
Key Dates in the Northern Irish Peace Process (*Continued*)

May 10, 1995	Sinn Féin meets with the British government in Stormont for the first official meeting in over 20 years. Secret talks had been going on for years, but confirmation of those talks remained speculation, by some, at the time. The meeting is recognition of the IRA's cease-fire of August 31, 1994.
January 1996	The Mitchell Report, chaired by former U.S. senator George Mitchell, examines decommissioning and recommends that all parties must renounce violence to have a place at the peace table. This is known as the Mitchell Principles.
June 10, 1996	All party talks begin. Notably absent is Sinn Féin, which is excluded on the basis of an IRA return to violence.
September 9, 1997	Having secured an IRA cease-fire in July 1997, Sinn Féin enters the Stormont All-Party Talks. Sinn Féin is expelled in February 1998 for the RUC's assessment of their involvement in recent violence. They reenter on March 23, just in time for the agreement.
April 10, 1998	The Good Friday (Belfast) Agreement is signed. It includes the establishment of three strands for implementation, an equality platform, policing platform, decommissioning process, security force demilitarization, prisoner release programme, and police restructuring.

In order to understand the historical overview of the peace process in Northern Ireland, one must examine what it took for Sinn Féin to get there. The party had developed extensive international networks in the 1970s and 1980s, and party leaders hoped to learn from the process of ending apartheid in South Africa. Hence, looking at the development of the Northern Ireland peace process through an international lens allows us to recognize the impact of Sinn Féin's policies. To do so, we look to the United Nations for such a standard lens. The United Nations organ UNIFEM has published a key document entitled "Securing the Peace" in which the role of women in a peace process is examined. This chapter will utilize that framework as the international lens to demonstrate the significant steps Sinn Féin took to cultivate women as stakeholders, trainers, negotiators, and affirmed positions in the party.

Continuing with the UNIFEM recommendations for establishing peace in a conflict society, this chapter profiles the 21st-century Sinn Féin gardeners who tended the lily of Irish peace. The foundational soil was cultivated by Siobhan O'Hanlon, Rita O'Hare, and Michelle Gildernew, but those who helped to implement UNIFEM's typological goals for equality included Chrissie McAuley and Mairead Keane, who refined the definition of conflict issues; Marie Moore, Mary Lou McDonald, Caitríona Ruane, and Sue Ramsey, who emerged as leaders; Mary Nelis, Maura McCrory, and Carál Ní Chuilín, who fostered an environment of peace; Monica McWilliams and Bairbre de Brún, who demanded inclusivity; and those many Sinn Féin women who have and continue to push for peace in the postconflict transition.

HISTORICAL OVERVIEW OF THE PEACE PROCESS

- Leading Up to the Belfast Agreement
- 1998 Stormont Talks
- Solidarity in Sisterhood

Leading Up to the Belfast Agreement

In the late 1980s, Sinn Féin began crafting a peace strategy. In the 1987 party document titled "Scenario for Peace," the central component was a peace process in which the core issues of the conflict could be explored and resolved. This was built on the foundation of secret talks, according to Sinn Féin, since the 1970s with the British government and in 1980s with the Social Democratic and Labour Party (SDLP). By 1993, the peace process produced official, open bilateral talks between Gerry Adams and John Hume (of SDLP) and continued unofficial dialogue through back channels with the British and Irish governments. That December, the Irish and British governments signed the Downing Street Declaration in Dublin Castle. Though the men remained in the spotlight during the early 1990s, Republican women played central roles supporting, directing, and fostering the peace strategies from the 1992 party strategy entitled "Towards a Lasting Peace" (discussed later in this chapter).

The August 31, 1994, IRA cease-fire complemented Sinn Féin's early peace strategy. As the interchange over Sinn Féin's "20 Questions" to the British government transpired, Sinn Féin's delegation team emerged as sophisticated negotiators. Siobhan O'Hanlon, Michelle Gildernew, and Lucilita Bhreatnach were instrumental members of the negotiation team. The process began to falter in 1995 when decommissioning became equated with demilitarization, and the tension remained until the breach of nonviolence in 1996. During this time, Rita O'Hare, in her position as the national publicity director, was touring the United States building support for the peace process. With the break of the cease-fire on February 9, 1996, however, Sinn Féin was expelled from the multiparty talks. As 1997 came to a close, Sinn Féin entered the negotiations again, having had limited electoral success in May 1997 (which included the election of Adams and McGuinness as Westminster MPs), and Michelle Gildernew was appointed the party's representative in London. Meanwhile, as head of the International Department since 1994 and a senior negotiator for Sinn Féin since 1997, Bairbre de Brún toured the United States discussing the party's fundamental negotiation points.[3] Throughout 1998, Bhreatnach, O'Hanlon, O'Hare, de Brún, and Gildernew bolstered the implementation of Sinn Féin's peace strategy at the negotiation table. Their efforts and actions revealed that Sinn Féin women had mastered many arts, including negotiation, publicity, and history. Their approach was well thought out and crafted to appeal to an international audience.

1998 Stormont Talks

In late 1997, the Sinn Féin delegation walked into the Stormont talks to take a seat at the peace table. Flanking Gerry Adams and Martin McGuinness were Lucilita Bhreatnach, Siobhan O'Hanlon, and Bairbre de Brún, among many other Sinn Féin supporters. It was the acknowledgement that all parties must be present to resolve the conflict in Northern Ireland.

Former U.S. senator George Mitchell's International Body had a difficult task. Even though Sinn Féin publically pursued direct access to all parties, it would be another nine years before Gerry Adams would meet Reverend Ian Paisley face-to-face. As the negotiators worked toward Mitchell's April 9, 1998, deadline to resolve the issues for the agreement, many internal parties speculated that this round of peace attempts might fail too. But, in the early morning hours of April 10, 1998, the Belfast Agreement was reached. Convincing their constituency to accept the Agreement with a yes vote, however, proved to be a tall order—one that required the concerted efforts of the Sinn Féin women to appeal to their communities through established social networks in sisterhood.

Solidarity in Sisterhood

What would peace bring? And what could be lost if it failed? The women of the Sinn Féin leadership rallied behind the hope of what peace might bring for mothers, daughters, wives, and sisters. The appeal required an active network of community-rooted activists, and it was built upon the foundation of the Women's Department. The Women's Department throughout the 1980s and 1990s had developed this international network of "sisters" through the organization of International Women's Day celebrations. The Women's Department had emerged as an energetic, committed group in 1981, and it quickly set out to create opportunities for women to be heard. It had been a difficult path, especially with the divisive issues of abortion and contraception, but the peace process gave Republican women the opportunity to couch their issues in terms of equality and not just the National Question. Equality as a principle in a peaceful society was a concept that the Women's Department had been ruminating on for close to two decades. Linking an engendered voice with other women in conflict societies allowed Sinn Féin women an intellectual discourse on what true equality should mean. It is precisely this international voice that UNIFEM now seeks to advance. "Securing the Peace," a pamphlet published by UNIFEM, acknowledges the power of women to transform conflict into peace.

> The transition from war to peace opens a unique window of opportunity to address the root causes of conflict and transform institutions, structures and relationships within society. Increasingly, formal peace processes create a space for negotiation of deeper-rooted societal and political issues, such as post-war power-sharing; constitutional, electoral and legislative reform; disarmament and reintegration of combatants; and decisions relating to refugees and internally displaced persons.[4]

The modern Sinn Féin woman is multifaceted in role and in background. She might have been educated at an Irish or European university or grown up in the thick of street politics. She may have been active in the civil rights struggles in the 1960s or she may have joined after the 1994 cease-fire. She may emerge as a new Republican in the 1990s or she may come from generational, familial connections to the movement. She may be from County Wicklow in the South or County Armagh in the North. She may be balancing the roles of mother and wife or she could have a same sex partner. Of all of the qualities that Sinn Féin women possess, above all else she is a dedicated Republican with a commitment to gender parity and social equality for all and access to an international network of sisters.

INTERNATIONAL DIMENSIONS OF UNIFEM AND PEACE PROCESSES

- Growing Pains of Feminization
- Party Efforts to Cultivate Women
- Stakeholders
- Educational Training
- Negotiators
- Affirmative Action

On October 31, 2000, the United Nations Security Council passed Resolution 1325. Recognizing the special role that women play in conflict prevention, transformation, and resolution, the Security Council was "[r]eaffirming the important role of women in the prevention and resolution of conflicts and in peace-building, and stressing the importance of their equal participation and full involvement in all efforts for the maintenance and promotion of peace and security, and the need to increase their role in decision-making with regard to conflict prevention and resolution."[5] While the United Nations is just beginning to formally recognize the role of women in conflict, the women of Sinn Féin have been integral in the Northern Irish peace process for well over a decade. Whether the rhetoric of the party is real or based on an imagined community of equality, Sinn Féin has demonstrated a lasting commitment to the principles of gender equality and parity. As the party entered the 21st century, it was poised to promote women in the party as an institution, the party in the electorate, and the party in government.

The Governance, Peace, and Security Forum of the United Nations Development Fund for Women (UNIFEM) targeted increased female participation in four strategic areas. They are (1) framing new laws promoting gender equity; (2) promoting the recruitment, training, and integration of female political candidates; (3) building a new government with women at the peace table and in leadership roles; and (4) pursing gender justice by eliminating inequality.[6] Since the conflict in Northern Ireland included disputes over equality of national identity as well as gender, the first and fourth UNIFEM goals seem to be an ensuing focus of postagreement transition; that is, laws concerning equality, and hence the elimination of inequality for gender justice, are dependent on institutions that recognize equality first. Therefore, the principle points that Sinn Féin identified early on seem to be promoting female recruitment and training, including but not limited to standing women in elections, and integrating women into the negotiation process and in party leadership during the conflict-resolution process.

Growing Pains of Feminization

Although Sinn Féin has been focusing tactical emphasis on gender empowerment in the past decade, the principle that Sinn Féin was comprised of articulate, dedicated, and active women was not new. The decision to purse a female membership or support base could be a logical outgrowth of century-old Sinn Féin values, but the changes in Northern Irish society made it wise to strategically target an agenda appealing to the feminist mind. A snapshot of sociodemographic data from 1961–2001 allows one to see a net increase in a female population, in a Catholic population, and in a youthful population.

Across the span of the past 40 years, the population of Northern Ireland has increased over 26,000 or 15.4 percent of the 2001 population. Since 1961, there has been a net growth in *estimated* Catholic population of just over 23,000 or 31.8 percent of the *estimated* Catholic population in 2001.[7] There is also a net increase of *self-identified* Catholics when the population is broken down by religious affiliation, but since the census has allowed respondents to identify "other" since 1991, it must be viewed with statistical uncertainty. The biggest increase seems to be the *estimated* Catholic population, which rose from 35.3 percent in 1961 to 36.8 percent in 1971, to 38.5 percent in 1981, to 41.5 percent in 1991, and to 43.76 percent in 2001.[8]

Since presumably the target audience for Sinn Féin recruitment and policies would be the Catholic women, one should also examine the cumulative population increase of women. Investing in the future is a political party strategy manifested across the globe; thus, the youth age demography should be examined as well.

In 2001, the estimated female population was calculated to be 863,818, spanning the age of female infants to elderly women. This is 51.26 percent of the population of Northern Ireland. Considering most interest in political activism is formed during late childhood and early adulthood, this percentage captures the political viable female statistic. When narrowed down to those females over the age of 16, the percentage increases: 670,023 of 1,287,211 over the age of 16 or 52.05 percent female.[9] However, this number captures all females without isolating religion (or ethnic identity). Mindful that the number of respondents who do not identify religion has been on the increase since the 1991 census, the census results should be viewed with appropriate suspicion.[10]

The significant female population was of strategic importance to Sinn Féin. Combined with a youthful national population, the party could tactically increase membership and electoral support, while influencing the political socialization of youths in the home, in the community centers, in the party's youth movement (Ógra Sinn Féin), and in the schools. Since its creation in 1997, Ógra Sinn Féin has been targeting the 15–25 age demographic by infusing an awareness of street politics and international solidarity with other youth movements. At its inception, Deirdre Feehan, a Sinn Féin youth activist, noted that "[w]hat we are trying to develop is a movement of young republicans which not only addresses the needs and concerns of young people today, but also sets an example for the broader movement, to bring new ideas, new experiences, a more up-to-date approach to politics."[11]

Given the high rate of civic engagement in the North of Ireland by women, the Center for the Study of Conflict at the University of Ulster in Coleraine, Northern Ireland, has identified female volunteerism as an important area of study. In "The Company We Keep: Women, Community and Organisations," Valerie Morgan and Grace Fraser explore the ways in which women are engaged in the Northern Irish community and identify their contributions within a conflict society. Although the study was cross-sectarian, it curiously did not include Republicans. Broadly surveying the role of women in the Northern Irish conflict, the authors concluded that the politics of the conflict are permeated with national and religious identity issues intertwining an odd gender history of marginalization and idealized power, especially within the nationalist and Catholic community. Morgan and Fraser further note that "[f]or many Unionists, feminism has been conflated with socialism and nationalism, even republicanism, and thus regarded as an object of suspicion."[12] The study offers a cumulative assessment of issues that challenge the civic mindedness of Irish women: a lack of cross-sectarian female engagement, a disenfranchisement of rural and poor women in political efficacy, a conflicting set of traditional family values and gender roles, and a general confusion about stopping perpetual violence. In light of these conclusions, it appears that the Republican tradition of the actively engaged female might be enshrined in "sinn féin" values and national identity, but calculated party decisions maximized the appeal for potential party members and electoral support for Sinn Féin.

Party Efforts to Cultivate Women

Paving the road for the peace process in the 1990s, Republican women in Sinn Féin had set forth a dynamic and brash agenda in the 1980s. Based on initiatives and policies developed in the 1980s, Sinn Féin was poised to maximize its female voice. Captured so eloquently by Republican martyr Mairéad Farrell, the female voice was intertwined with the National Question: "I'm oppressed as a woman, but I am also oppressed because

I'm Irish. Everyone in this country is oppressed and we can't successfully end out oppression as women until we first end the oppression of our country."

Like gardeners tending their flowers, the women in party leadership cultivated an environment where women could flourish. National identity and the drive for republicanism anchored all their efforts. The most significant party initiatives, and those which other conflict society can also benefit from, were: (1) the recognition of women as conflict stakeholders; (2) the creation of both formal and informal educational training programs for women; (3) the emergence of women in peace negotiations; and (4) the adoption of the policy of affirmative action (known as co-option) within party leadership.

Stakeholders

Although there are some who would portray women in conflict societies to be the archetypal peace activists, it is equally important to recognize the Republican archetype of a warrior-queen. Whether on the front lines of the conflict or conflict resolution, the valued point is that Republican women were and are stakeholders in Northern Ireland. To mobilize them and give them a voice in Sinn Féin was not just a good political decision for the party, it was an opportunity to open cross-sectarian dialogue by way of a gender linkage. The UNIFEM policy document "Securing the Peace" underpins this message: "As victims, survivors and even wagers of armed conflict, women are major stakeholders in the resolution of conflict and the course that is set for future development." As both targets of and tactical agents in political violence, a woman and her child are not immune to the games of war. Whether as an innocent civilian or as an armed fighter, the psychological impact of death, destruction, and loss alters the ability of a woman to establish a peaceful domicile for her family and makes the value of life numbingly void. Women are now specific targets in a combat, and certain tactics such as rape, molestation, and strip-searching are implemented in order to leave a victim as testimony for future targets and to break the foundation of a community. "Whether as victims or combatants, women often shoulder an additional burden due to traditional gender roles: their labour, strength and determination maintain their families and communities during war and throughout the long, slow process of rebuilding the peace."[13]

Women in Ireland had been directly affected by the conflict. One often thinks first of the women impacted by the reality that their husbands, fathers, and sons were on the front lines of the Troubles, but their mothers, sisters, and daughters were too. As Una Gillespie, Sinn Féin councillor and Belfast Rape Crisis Centre employee, pointed out:

Republican women have been shot, beaten, abused and imprisoned as a result of their participation in the struggle. They form the nucleus of the campaigns being waged on behalf of our prisoners, and mother, sisters and partners have had their lived dominated by the endless round of prison visits. Many of them have had to shoulder full responsibility in the rearing of children because of their partners' imprisonment. To claim that women have only played a supportive role would be totally inaccurate, yet equality both within our republican communities and wider society is still something that these politically active women have yet to achieve.[14]

The British Army and the RUC did not just detain or intern males. Strip-searching was not a male prisoner policy. Poor access to medical care and systematic terror did not just target men. Housing and educational inequalities did not just disfavor Catholic men. The women understood this, and the leadership of Sinn Féin did as well. While some of the aforementioned issues were embedded in conflict issues presumed to be based on identity inequalities, some of the gender experiences of the Troubles provided an overarching commonality that could transcend the sectarian divide. That is, a Republican mother and a Unionist mother shared the same hopes and fears for their families in terms of safety, security, education, and prosperity (even though the causes of the concerns in these hopes and fears might have been oppositionally defined). To identify the possible areas of potential overlap between communities from a gender perspective thus became an important component of Sinn Féin's peace strategy in the 1990s.

Educational Training

In the midst of a patriarchal society fraught with inequality based on ethnic identity, Republican women became a resource for change. A Republican woman in the 1980s had been educated, trained, and engaged in social and political action. The "classrooms" for a Republican woman were often informal since university education was not the norm for Republican women in the North during the 1980s. Some Republicans were schooled in the prisons. Many women learned from educational programs held at community centers, and even more honed their political skills on the streets. Street politics in the North combined social activism, political goals, and community awareness into a highly visible platform for a female Sinn Féin voice.

Although the extent that Sinn Féin women were allowed into the backroom of the boys club is suspect, there is little doubt that female involvement was more welcome than in most conflict societies. The politics of Irish freedom—at least publicly—acknowledged the discrimination based on Irish identity and gender. Unlike many political parties (in Ireland or elsewhere), the power of women was harnessed and organized in Sinn Féin. By the early 1990s, Republican women spoke with the clear voice of the Sinn Féin Women's Department. Many had been female Republican prisoners who had served time in the Maghaberry, Mountjoy, or Armagh prisons. They had refined knowledge, from the prisons, streets, and community centers, of Irish history, culture, and language. They had been a cornerstone of the No Wash and hunger strikes in the 1980s. Women were being actively recruited for political office in local city councils and for internal party activist posts. Women were trained in community activism and party issues. Women's issues were presented to annual Árd Fheis conferences and incorporated into the party platforms.

Eventually, these party documents would culminate in the 1992 "Women in Ireland" and subsequently the 2004 "Women in an Ireland of Equals" documents. In 1992, the Women's Department put a document to the Sinn Féin Árd Fheis (party conference) for discussion. Revealing a frank assessment of social issues of serious concern for the women of Ireland, these issues included pornography, rape, strip-searching at Armagh and Maghaberry prisons, sexual harassment, domestic violence, fertility, women and children in poverty, workplace concerns, and family law.[15] Councillor Una Gillespie explains that the elevation of an engendered perspective of conflict issues enriched the national party platform: "The presenting of a second women's policy document to the 1992 Árd Fheis is evidence of the continued development of women's politics within Sinn Féin. The "Women in Ireland" document is not only a comprehensive outline of our policy on women, but also defines our demand for an Ireland which recognized the full and equal role of women in all aspects of its society."[16]

Going beyond the obvious conflict issues inherent in a pre–cease-fire Northern Ireland signaled that Sinn Féin women were not simply conflict activists, they were capable of party governance. Furthermore, women's issues were on the agenda, although Sinn Féin women in the 1990s were keenly aware of Hanna Sheehy-Skeffington's warnings that feminists should not be buried under the national question. Of some interest, therefore, is the point that the initial draft of "Towards a Lasting Peace" was also being considered at the 1992 Árd Fheis. "Towards a Lasting Peace" was conceived in a postabstentionist, pre–cease-fire climate. It defined Sinn Féin's peace strategy and embedded, much like feminist issues had been so many times before, the low status of women into the partition: "Peace is not just the absence of war but is also establishing conditions which will ensure a lasting peace. This means eradicating the root cause of the conflict by gaining national self-determination, which in turn lays the foundation for justice, democracy and equality—the safeguards of lasting peace."[17]

Negotiators

Recognizing the need for women to participate in decision-making and, in particular, in the negotiation process, a few Republican women, notably Bairbre de Brún, Lucilita Bhreatnach, and Michelle Gildernew, began to accompany the men to negotiation talks throughout the 1990s. By demonstrating the capabilities and impact of an engendered perspective on the prospects for peace, Sinn Féin helped to define paradigm shift within negotiation practices. Many recent studies on the influence of gender in negotiation reveal that the style, approach, and articulation of interests can contain gender perspectives and influence negotiation performance.[18] The creation of UNIFEM institutionalized these conclusions in the international community's commitment to both recognizing and facilitating the involvement of women in conflict resolution.

The women of Sinn Féin understood the power of a collective female voice to affect social and political change. Accordingly, the Women's Department coordinated community conferences that were open to all communities throughout the 1980s and 1990s. By participating in the 1994 National Forum for Peace and Reconciliation (NFPR) in Dublin, Sinn Féin initiated the development of community linkages based on commonalities not differences. Held in the wake of the historic IRA cease-fire that August 31, the forum met regularly throughout 1995 and into February 1996. Rita O'Hare, Siobhan O'Hanlon, and Lucilita Bhreatnach regularly accompanied Gerry Adams, Pat Doherty, and Caoimhghín Ó Caoláin to the standing meetings of the forum.

In the wake of the 1994 IRA cease-fire, several women were poised in prominent leadership roles in the early negotiation process, notably Lucilita Bhreatnach and Siobhan O'Hanlon. As Annie Taylor, spokesperson for the Council for the Status of Women delegation to the NFPR, commented in 1995: [Sinn Féin is] "the only party leading into the peace process that has shown they have women involved in key areas of negotiation, the only party where women are key players in the peace process."[19] Approximately half of Sinn Féin's delegation to the NFPR were women (including Mary Nelis and Dodie McGuinness); eight women were serving on the 30-person party executive; and key party positions like the education, foreign affairs, and general secretary were headed by women. Lucilita Bhreatnach had been serving as the party's general secretary since 1987. Under her direction, the party developed an electoral strategy and peace strategy that empowered a female voice. Among the significant peace documents developed during this time were "Scenario for Peace" (1987) and "Towards a Lasting Peace" (1992). In 2002, she assumed the helm of the newly created Equality Department after 15 years as a highly visible party activist.

Affirmative Action

Recognizing women as an integral part of the Republican movement, Sinn Féin had long recommended a policy of co-option where at least on quarter of its Ard Chomhairle (National Executive) should be female. In 2000, when a quarter was not nominated, Republican feminists sprung into action. After an internal commission reviewed the matter, motion 189 was submitted to the 2001 Árd Fheis as a solution to the gender crisis. Motion 189 recommended a policy mandating that at least 30 percent of the executive should be female.[20] Motion 189 was supported by the Ard Chomhairle, but it failed to receive the required two-thirds support to change the party constitution.

With a tradition of Maeve-like, warrior-queen leadership epitomized by Constance Gore-Booth, Mary McSwiney, Margaret Buckley, Bernadette Devlin McAlliskey, and Máire Drumm, Sinn Féin understood the potential power of the so-called fairer sex. Creating a Women's Department in 1980 had allowed for the women to channel their collective efforts into an organizational punch. "The women's department came out of a realization that women had to have an organized political voice within the party. Women came together from all over Ireland to discuss their work within Sinn Féin, the problems they faced in fulfilling their roles as political activists and the need for Sinn Féin to have strong, progressive policies on issues important not just for women but to society as a whole."[21] The policy of expanded co-option was viewed as a guaranteed voice for women in a leadership role and demonstrated a visible party commitment to equality. It was important to the National Executive that there was a transparent legitimization of the policies it was pushing at the negotiation table. Simply put, Sinn Féin needed to walk the walk and talk the talk of equality.

The creation of the Equality Department in 2002 would further advance these principles. With Lucilita Bhreatnach as its head, the department set out to develop a specific, effective policy to advance women in the party. "Targeting various sections within the party, these seminars have been specific to those developing policy, at leadership levels in comhairlí ceantair, election directorates, elected reps and party spokespersons. Participants have indicated that equipping them with tools appropriate to their role in the organisation, eg. gender impact assessment and gender proofing, has been very useful."[22] The Ard Chomhairle additionally held a gender impact seminar and requested papers on how to advance gender equality. Combined with training workshops that following February (2003) on media training, negotiation, presentation skills, and Irish language and history, a hands-on approach to eradicating gender inequalities was implemented. The results were concrete and real.

At the 2003 Árd Fheis, Bairbre de Brún opened debate on the co-option policy once again with a proposal that Rule 21 be amended to require a 50 percent female membership on the National Executive. The debate over co-option was heated, but narrowly passed with 104 for and 52 against.[23] A mere two years after a motion to increase the female presence to 30 percent failed, Sinn Féin agreed to support a 50 percent female leadership in its National Executive. The reversal indicated an awareness of the commitment to equality. Again and again, Sinn Féin was trying to prove that a commitment to equality had to be demonstrated not just advocated. Inequality, no matter what institution was harboring it, violated the principles of the party itself. Lucilita Bhreatnach explains that:

> [i]f we are truly committed to achieving an Ireland of Equals, we have to start with ourselves. Our role is to try to tackle inequality wherever it may exist. That is a responsibility for us all. We want a sea change in the political culture. We will play our part by empowering women republicans and by educating everyone in Sinn Féin to recognise and reject gender inequality. It is about promoting awareness of genderproofing and making it the norm in our daily work. As in all areas of the Equality Agenda, this is about redressing the balance. This is about a culture of change that will benefit all of society, men and women. This is an integral part of our vision of an Ireland of equals.[24]

TWENTY-FIRST CENTURY GARDENERS

- Foundations
  - Siobhan O'Hanlon
  - Rita O'Hare
  - Michelle Gildernew
- Five Steps to Equality
  - Conflict Issues
    - Chrissie McAuley
    - Mairead Keane
  - Building Leadership
    - Marie Moore
    - Mary Lou McDonald and Caitríona Ruane
    - Sue Ramsey

- An Environment of Peace
  - Mary Nelis
  - Maura McCrory
  - Carál Ní Chuilín
- Demanding Inclusivity
  - Monica McWilliams
  - Bairbre de Brún
- Postconflict Transition

Foundations

The female facets of Sinn Féin reveal a political party with an awareness of inequalities in Irish society. The portraits and miniatures of Republican women both reinforce and shatter the archetypes of female power and gentility in Ireland, but most importantly, Republican women are committed to a political process of peace and of equality. As picture frames displayed on the mantle of a family home, these modern Sinn Féin women share features and values while standing apart as strong individuals.

Siobhan O'Hanlon

Siobhan O'Hanlon is a part of a generational commitment to the Republican cause. Her uncle was Joe Cahill, a founding member of the Provisional IRA (including rising to the rank of IRA Chief of Staff) and an honorary vice president of Sinn Féin. He had been convicted of killing a police officer in 1942 and importing explosives from Libya in 1973. Cahill additionally served as a Republican negotiator during the 1990s peace process, until his death in 2004.

Holding up her uncle's legacy, O'Hanlon had played as an important component of the 1998 historic Sinn Féin negotiation team. A close advisor to Gerry Adams and former political prisoner, O'Hanlon served Sinn Féin in a number of different capacities—head of the South Africa desk, liaison with the British and Irish governments, and Féile an Phobail coordinator.[25] Having spent eight years in the Armagh jail, O'Hanlon brought a keen understanding of Republican politics to her positions. Nonetheless, despite prominent women like O'Hanlon capably functioning at the highest levels within the party and external party politics, many still doubted the sincerity of their access to power within Sinn Féin. Accusations of "tokenism" concerning the co-option of female Ard Chomhairle members abounded, even in a climate of negotiating equality. Siobhan was a trusted friend within Sinn Féin. When she was diagnosed with breast cancer in 2002, her friends rallied to her side as she fought it with the tenacity of her spirit. She succumbed to the fight in April 2006, leaving a four-year-old baby behind. Gerry Adams delivered her eulogy, in which he described the quintessential Siobhan style: "She had her own unique way of working. I overheard her once in animated telephone conversation talking about babies and teething and pregnancies and all of that. When I asked her out of curiosity who she was talking to she said that was so and so from Downing Street."[26]

Lucilita Bhreatnach

Lucilita grew up in Dublin in a prominent Republican family. She joined Sinn Féin at the age of 16, going to work on the Stop the Strip-Searching Campaign affiliated with the Anti-H Block Movement. Her publicity skills were soon apparent, as she served in the Foreign Affairs department and worked for *AP/RN* in the 1980s before becoming the party's general secretary in 1988. Her work as a Sinn Féin negotiator was a valuable contribution to the 1997 Downing Street meetings with the British and the preparation of the reports to the International Body during the Belfast Agreement negotiations. She recalls the impact of these vital years: "I had the opportunity to play a key role in the development of the party's Peace Strategy and be involved in negotiations leading up to the Good Friday Agreement. Also central to my role during this period has been the ongoing development of the party both internally and in helping to advance our electoral growth."[27] She was a driving force in the creation, negotiation, and implementation of the peace strategy.

After an unsuccessful bid for the EU seat from Leinster in 1994, Lucilita began focusing more on the equality movement in Sinn Féin, from 2000 to 2002. She resigned as general secretary in 2003, working on gender equality issues and party development structure until she moved quietly into private life as a contributing journalist and member of the Foras na Gaeilge (Irish language group) in association with RTE (Ireland's Radio and Television Broadcaster).

Rita O'Hare

Rita O'Hare has held many high-level positions within Sinn Féin as she amassed significant political experience. Among her personal experiences include that she reportedly jumped bail while awaiting trial for the death of a British soldier, and professionally, she was a reporter for *An Phoblacht/ Republican News* then *AP/RN* editor from 1985 to 1991. During the negotiation of the Belfast Agreement, she was a publicity director for Sinn Féin working, among many roles, as a liaison between then secretary of state for Northern Ireland Mo Mowlam and Sinn Féin chief negotiator Martin McGuinness. While serving as the publicity director in the United States, O'Hare became the focus of many Americans "invested" in the Northern Irish peace process. She went on to become the formal Sinn Féin representative and lobbyist to the United States, until she was temporarily barred from the United States for apparently violating the terms of her visa in 2005. Her work in the United States involved developing networks with Congress, not limited to but especially with Senator Ted Kennedy and Congressman Peter King. By combining the official role of lobbying with her experience as a publicity director, O'Hare targeted winning the hearts and minds of Americans. Reiterating the need for inclusive talks in the peace process, Rita O'Hare mobilized support for third-party intervention and the successful implementation of Sinn Féin's role at the peace table. In 2007, Rita O'Hare became the general secretary for Sinn Féin; in 2009, she became one of the party's treasurers and sits on the Ard Chomhairle.

Michelle Gildernew

Michelle Gildernew is evidence of hereditary, familial traditions within Sinn Féin. Michelle's mother was a prominent community activist in Derry during the 1960s. Deeply impacted by the issues of discrimination embedded in the civil rights campaign of 1968–69, Michelle represents a strong commitment of republicanism to defend and protect the community since the outbreak of the Troubles. Much like Gerry Adams, Michelle's family has been fully engaged on the front lines for generations. Thus, she was selected to be the party's representative to London in 1997 and served as a member of the first Sinn Féin delegation to 1997 talks with the British prime minister. Her high-level access on Track One formal negotiations also included negotiations with the Irish Taoiseach (prime minister) on issues of demilitarization and North-South cooperation.[28]

University educated and well traveled, Michelle balances family with a blooming political career. Having served as a Sinn Féin member of the Assembly in 1998, a member of the Ard Chomhairle, a member of the party's subcommittee on equality and women's forum, and party spokesperson on housing, Michelle was then elected MP for Westminster Parliament for Fermanagh/South Tyrone in 2001 and MLA to the Northern Ireland Assembly in 2003. She was reelected to Westminster in 2005. She is also the party spokesperson on housing, a fitting post for her family legacy. In May 2010, she was narrowly reelected MP for Fermanagh/South Tyrone and maintains a position on the Northern Ireland Executive as the minister for agriculture and rural development.

Five Steps to Equality

A political party is defined as a group of people seeking to influence government policy through becoming elected. The interesting history of the North has challenged some of the traditional functions of a political party. The 1986 shift away from the policy of abstentionism, for example, allowed for Sinn Féin candidates to officially fulfill this normal party function. It is, therefore, in the context of a recent history of political party roles that we see women becoming more actively involved. Within the past decade in particular, Sinn Féin women have been integral in *defining conflict issues, establishing party and community leadership, building an environment for peace, demanding inclusivity in the peace process, and attempting to implement a postconflict transition.*

Conflict Issues

Issues of structural inequality and political disenfranchisement permeated all of Northern Ireland, but for Republican women, the added dimension of a gender perspective highlighted a lack of gender parity in government, policy, and society at large. Among the multitude of engendered conflict concerns were the strip-searching of female political prisoners, sacrificing family commitments to battle inequality and injustice, the demands of single parenthood as widows or partner commitments to the Republican cause, equal access to social policy institutions like health care and education, and comprehensive discrimination within employment. However, as Republican women raised their voices in Sinn Féin, their issues were later placed on the agenda for all-party talks in the late 1990s.

Chrissie McAuley
Throughout the 1980s, Sinn Féin's Women's Department was a locus of activist voices and a civic culture of sorts within the party. Women such as Chrissie McAuley and Mairead Keane (who was the head of the department at the peak of activities from 1987 to 1993) were among the members of the Women's Department at this time.

A founding member of the Sinn Féin Women's Department, Chrissie McAuley understood the dimensions of conflict issues in Northern Ireland. Arrested in Cork in 1975 for possession of explosives, McAuley served time as a political prisoner including four years in Mountjoy prison in Dublin. Later released, McAuley became a reporter for *An Phoblacht/Republican News* (*AP/RN*) and a tireless activist for political prisoner rights, including a dedicated role in the campaign to end stripsearching. As a Sinn Féin councillor in the Belfast City Council, McAuley worked to highlight community development programs that would regenerate the West Belfast and Skankill communities.

In 2005, while serving as the Equality and Human Rights political manager, McAuley's home was attacked; she remained undeterred in her commitment. The mother of three (and grandmother of seven), Chrissie is a daily fixture on the streets of Belfast, where she works nonstop to serve her community. She is articulate, direct, and clear. In her clarity for Sinn Féin, she sets the tone of the postconflict issues of paramount importance for the party. Her advice is well-sought, and she has provided consultation for the Sinn Féin negotiators during the peace process and now to the Party Development core.

Mairead Keane

Mairead Keane's Sinn Féin career took form across the Atlantic Ocean. Having joined Sinn Féin in 1984, she quickly rose to the helm of the Women's Department by the end of the decade. In this role as the Director of the Women's Department in 1992, she undertook a prolonged publicity tour across the United States. Her talents were clearly recognized, for the party nominated her to be the first Sinn Féin representative to the United States. Throughout the 1990s, Keane was often addressing prominent crowds such as the 1997 speech to the United States Naval Academy. A single mother balancing diplomacy with family, she stood as a 2002 Sinn Féin candidate in Wicklow for the 28th Dáil but was not elected.

The Women's Department that Mairead Keane once headed was a duplicitous environment of sisterhood empowerment and power marginalization in the early 1990s. Concerns about the volume of the female "voice" and the controversies perceived to be the imprint of ranting feminists often led to the department being portrayed as radical. And there was perhaps nothing a Unionist feared more than a radical feminist Republican. Thus, gently shaping and guiding the concentrated efforts of the department became a necessary nuance to advance the movement. The activities focused on informational awareness and empowerment through active demonstrations concerning embedded conflict issues. By exposing and highlighting the latent issues, the women were identifying issues for future negotiators. But in a short-term, day-to-day reality, these women provided hope for the Republican community, for organizing discontent is a first step for social and political change. On the eve of a historic IRA cease-fire and eventual admission into all-party talks, Sinn Féin women were identifying a gender perspective in institutionalized ethnic and gender identity based policies.

Building Leadership

In 2000, historian Margaret Ward wrote a policy analysis paper for Democratic Dialogue, Northern Ireland's first think tank. Entitled *The Northern Ireland Assembly and Women: Assessing the Gender Deficit*, the summary report notes that the gender parity concern within government institutions is very real. Although there had been a substantial increase in female members in the Assembly (elected MLAs)—from 3 to 14 members since the 1980s, the Welsh and Scottish equivalency was approximately triple the percent of gender parity than in Northern Ireland.[29] Sinn Féin, it is noted, emerged as the party with the most successful female candidates for all parties in the Northern Irish Assembly. In short, Sinn Féin has been selecting a higher percentage of their female membership base to support in their candidacy for election. Furthermore, these women were more successful than their Unionist counterparts.

The platform of the equality of citizenship serves as a cornerstone of feminist interest. "Sinn féin" is self-sufficiency, which serves an electoral appeal across identities and communities. The manifesto reverberates in the application of internal party measures to compensate for the lack of external inequalities facing women, and this demonstrates good faith and transparent intentions to, as a party in government, apply similar principles for Irish society. The policy of internal affirmative action (co-option) in female leadership and party candidates is based on an acceptance that "women suffer from '*institutionalised sexual discrimination*' and the party has practiced positive discrimination on behalf of women by use of a quota system for its national executive. In terms of public visibility, the Sinn Féin leadership has consistently included women within its most senior positions. Party policy, which includes detailed policies on a wide range of issues affecting women, has been reflected in the numbers of Sinn Féin women elected to the Assembly."[30] The institutional solution, therefore, is to put forth a high ratio of female candidates to solidify a female presence in governance. The electoral strategy produced 21.6 percent female candidacy for the 1998 Assembly and 27.8 percent female membership—5 MLAs of 18 Sinn Féin MLAs in the Assembly were women.[31]

Although the commitment to female participation within the party has also been evidenced by two female party presidencies (notably Margaret Buckley from 1937 to 1950 and Máire Drumm as acting president in 1973), today the prominent female faces in Sinn Féin include a larger delegation of women in a much more public realm. International travelers and articulate speakers, they can frequently be seen at press conferences in Dublin, Belfast, London, Washington, D.C., and Strasbourg. With a female vice president, female European Parliament member, female general secretary, female party treasurer, female director of publicity, many female elected members of the Northern Ireland Assembly, many female city councillors, and general party activists, Sinn Féin has been fulfilling its paper commitment to gender equity and enfranchisement internally. Each woman represents a facet of Irish history and the political experience of Republicans north and south of the border.

As with any organization, each member within Sinn Féin brings personal qualities and character to the political party. Their backgrounds could be described as divergent, crossing a partitioned Irish border and society, but their commitment to a Republican cause is what links these women together. A few select women have emerged in front of the photographers as they enter government buildings or community centers. There are even more Republican women working behind the scenes. They should not go unnoted, for it is their strength that has been implementing and securing change—perhaps the most daunting task of all. As the international community continues to advocate for the advancement of women in politics and society, it is truly the community activists who are the foot soldiers for peace. Those women in front of the camera are held up by those behind the camera. As the women in Sinn Féin emerge onto the front lines of the political stage, each lady demonstrates finely tuned skills sets of leadership honed in the arenas of community centers, universities, party activism, and international networks.

Marie Moore

Marie Moore was a lifelong Republican. Involved in Belfast politics since 1969, she wore many party hats and shaped the direction Sinn Féin took in the 1990s. Having served as head of the POW Department during the prison protests, she was launched into politics and served 13 years as an elected councillor of the Belfast City Council. While a councillor, Moore worked closely with many archetypal legends such as Vice President Máire Drumm. In 1999, she served as the first Sinn Féin deputy mayor of Belfast. Along with Rita O'Hare, she assisted in the first drafts of the Women's Department policy papers.[32] Her commitment to Republican goals spanned four decades of active political involvement, highlighting the perpetual need for equality for women in Ireland. Marie's experience served to inspire other young women into Republican activism and public service. Her death in March 2009 was a great loss to Sinn Féin.

Mary Lou McDonald and Caitríona Ruane

Two young women who entered public service in 1990s Sinn Féin were Mary Lou McDonald and Caitríona Ruane. Both mothers of young children when they were called to duty, Mary Lou and Caitríona are daily faces

in Irish news. Mary Lou McDonald grew up in the middle-class Dublin
suburbs, and she holds a degree from University College Dublin in English
literature. Though her previous Fianna Fáil party membership and clas-
sical university education are a far cry from Marie Moore's life, she was
inspired to join Sinn Féin on the front lines of the peace implementation.
Often portrayed dismissively as a "she Shinner" or "Shinner Spice" by the
media, McDonald has proven her Republican ideals are just as tough as
the men she stood beside during the ups and downs of Belfast Agreement
implementation. Her command of language and Republican history has
made her a frontline negotiator, champion of liberties, and Sinn Féin vice
president (Jennie Wyse-Power, Margaret Buckley, and Máire Drumm pre-
cede her).

Caitríona Ruane was with Mary Lou McDonald and Gerry Adams when
the Sinn Féin delegation met with Irish prime minister Bertie Ahern in December 2005. Ruane's background shares some qualities with that of Mc-
Donald (university education, mother, commitment to equality), but her
Northern residence and expansive international experience sets her apart.
Ruane was born in County Mayo and grew up primarily in West Ireland.
As a champion tennis player, she settled in the North in the late 1980s to
head up the Human Rights Centre, Centre for Research and Documentation in Belfast. An experienced negotiator, Ruane has served as the party
spokesperson on equality and is currently serving as the minister of education in the Northern Irish Executive. Both Caitríona and Mary Lou stand
on the shoulders of Máire Drumm, Marie Moore, and the women who lead
before them. Their shared passion for gender equality inspires them to be
committed to nurturing young women as future leaders in Sinn Féin.

Sue Ramsey

Representing a more traditional evolution of female republicanism is Sue
Ramsey. Ramsey's political experience is a prototype for growing a political activist. In her mid-thirties, she became engaged in Sinn Féin after the
1980 hunger strikes. Her Republican education is a mixture of "community
activism, electoral organization and front line street politics."[33] A Belfast
native, Ramsey first joined Sinn Féin through the Youth Department and
by 1992 was participating in the Women's Department. During the peace
process, Sue supported the negotiation team, working side by side with the
late Siobhan O'Hanlon. In 1998, she was selected for electoral politics and
elected as a Member of Legislative Assembly (MLA) for West Belfast. She
served as the party spokesperson on health and children's issues, until recently becoming the spokesperson on trade unions. She continues to work
with the Connolly House constituency office and helped to set up the Just
Us theatre with Brian Kennan's widow Chrissie.

An Environment of Peace

An environment of peace must be supported by nation and state building simultaneously, and in Northern Ireland, this means fostering a new sense of community that does not conflict with deeply rooted histories and ethnic identities. According to UNIFEM, "ensuring women's *effective* participation involves a range of actions. Even before peace processes officially begin, the international community can support diverse women's peacebuilding activities at local and national levels, facilitating their development of a common agenda for peace, and strengthening their capacity as leaders to prepare them for the negotiating table and the post-conflict transition."[34] Therefore, providing a gendered perspective for peace and reconciliation is integral to community building.

Mary Nelis

Building on the work of female community activists in the 1960s, among whom was Derry resident and former Sinn Féin city councillor Mary Nelis, Republican women continued to prioritize feminist issues that all women—regardless of politics—could identify with in Ireland. From access to health care, education, and housing to strip-searching and spousal abandonment, being a woman in Ireland provides a link to all communities. Although there have been numerous community relations groups in Northern Ireland, the one receiving notable attention during the peace process was the Community Relations Council (CRC). Founded as an independent charity institution formally established in 1990, the CRC houses the Belfast Interface Project, orchestrates Irish Studies conferences, and provides hands-on training and support to community relations organizations, such as Survivors of Trauma in North Belfast, for fighting sectarianism.

Maura McCrory

A conflict society often entrenches a heightened need for highly localized, community responsiveness. In an environment where trust is in short supply, the immediate community could be a proximate lifeline. Maura McCrory is a seasoned activist who had been engaged in the Relatives Action Committee (RAC) during the 1980s H-Block campaigns and hunger strikes with Bernadette McAliskey (Devlin). She tirelessly accessed the scarce resources of the Republican community to identify and support women's issues throughout the 1980s and 1990s. As the chair of the Falls Women's Center in West Belfast, she has overseen the development of comprehensive programs targeting the needs of women in their community. These programs include but are not limited to educational courses, child care, special needs information, homework club for children, and support groups. As the chair of a panel at the 1995 Belfast Women's Conference with a focus on "The Role of Women in the Peace Process," she presided over a discussion on the role of Republican women in the peace process. Seated beside Mary Nelis and Máire Quigery of Clan na mBan (a Republican anti-imperialist feminist group that held a prominent, controversial conference in Belfast in 1994), a statement from the Maghaberry women political prisoners was read to the conference attendees:

> The peace process offers an apparatus within which we, as republican feminists, can promote and build upon the awareness evident from your presence here. Issues like British disengagement from Ireland need contributions from women and men. From the republican delegation in talks with civil servants, to the organised activities on the streets, there are places for us all.[35]

Sinn Féin has long understood the power of female solidarity. The link of international sisterhood can transcend identity in that the struggles of womanhood are often quite similar. By committing to a structural element of equality and gender in party initiatives, Sinn Féin has expanded the scope of its voice.

In addition to the Women's Conference, Sinn Féin's Women's Department began publishing *Women in Struggle* in 1995. The magazine explored issues affecting women in a changing society and Republican feminism.[36] This public dialogue allowed for Republican women to explore their role in a changing Ireland and in a new Irish society. Mary Nelis summarized the sentiment of many Republican women at the 1995 conference when she concluded, "A country run by women would be no better than that run by men, if the system remains brutal and repressive . . . This is not the kind of power we want in a New Ireland."[37] But the channels for Republican women to engage in discourse with government were not completely open in the 1990s. As the public faces of Sinn Féin—Gerry Adams, Pat Doherty, and Martin McGuinness—lobbied for all-party talks (the inclusion of Sinn Féin into peace talks post-1994 cease-fire), the women of Sinn Féin accompanied them and assisted in the development of an international network to pressure for Sinn Féin's inclusion. This network took many forms, some formal relationships and many informal ones, but the fruits of this effort are still visible today. One such output is the role that the Women's Support Network (WSN) plays in Northern Ireland. Interestingly, one of the key actors in the WSN is Maura McCrory.

Founded in 1989, the Women's Support Network is an international NGO with approximately 40 cross-sectarian organizations. Since the Good Friday (Belfast) Agreement in 1998, the WSN has been working in Northern Ireland to implement the agreement's goals of human rights and equality and develop community linkages with the government called "partnerships for change."[38] One example that these policy goals address is the cross-sectarian issue of domestic violence. Whether Republican or Unionist, all women in Northern Ireland can readily identify with the need for a nonsectarian police response to domestic violence situations. By identifying to someone as a woman not as a Unionist or as a Republican, women were able to cooperate together to push a common agenda in this, and other issues. As other gender issues continue to bubble to the surface, and other small community-building measures are developed, a partnership of all women invested in a common goal secures a channel for resolution dialogue.

Carál Ní Chuilín

Carál Ní Chuilín was born in the New Lodge community of North Belfast, where she still resides. She was apprehended in 1989 for a failed IRA bomb plot and, while in prison, received her BA from Open University. Upon her release, Carál began her work with Tar Anall, an ex-prisoners group and family center, and worked on the North Belfast Partnership Board. She recently earned a master's in management while serving as the MLA from North Belfast. She is the chief party whip in the Northern Ireland Assembly, where she maintains her commitment to the welfare of ex-prisoners, human rights, Irish language promotion, and children. Speaking out against the persistence of youth-based sectarian violence, she has said: "Violence is a legacy of the conflict, and is rooted in sectarianism. That is the case regardless of where or how the violence occurs, whether it is petrol-bombing or someone being beaten unconscious, and whether the damage is physical or emotional. We must make sectarianism history."[39] Despite her recent activist work on Sinn Féin's fuel poverty campaign, she is rumored to be on the fast track for a more political future. Many regard Carál as a future candidate for Lord Mayor of Belfast.

Demanding Inclusivity

The United Nations (UNIFEM) focuses upon the power of gender to transcend issues in conflict societies. It recommends that "[d]uring the negotiations, women from various backgrounds must be brought forward in official and informal capacities so that the voices and experiences of women throughout the country will be considered during decision-making that will affect all of society."[40] The utilization of both Track One—official negotiations—and Track Two—or unofficial dialogue—was what mediators, under the direction of former U.S. senator George Mitchell, were able to deploy in 1998. However, in reality, many of the purported successes of the Belfast Agreement had been facilitated by the work of the Northern Ireland Women's Coalition.

Monica McWilliams

Monica McWilliams, a self-proclaimed Republican, founded the Northern Ireland Women's Coalition (NIWC) in 1996. A professor of women's studies and social policy at the University of Ulster in Belfast, McWilliams has also served as a MLA before recently being named chief commissioner for human rights in the Northern Ireland Human Rights Commission in 2005 and in 2008. As a delegate to the Multi-Party Peace Negotiations in 1998, she was a critical part of the development of the Belfast Agreement. Her work in the peace process was recognized with the honor of the John F. Kennedy Leadership and Courage Award in 1998. Currently, she also serves as an MLA for South Belfast in the Assembly, as a member of the Northern Ireland Women's Coalition party. She is not a member of Sinn Féin, but her efforts to establish dialog across the sectarian divide deepened the efforts of the Sinn Féin. Any discussion of gender politics, especially domestic violence, in the Six Counties is incomplete without recognizing her work in the NIWC.

The differences between NIWC and the Sinn Féin Women's Department were intensely clear—the role of the physical force tradition in republicanism, an intertwined relationship of anticolonial and gender oppression, and the constitutional question of a partitioned Ireland.[41] Redefining republicanism as it did, the NIWC was not embraced by Sinn Féin, although McWilliams and Kate Fearon were able to bridge a communication gap between the Republican and Unionist woman. Providing a theatre for conflict transformation proved to be challenging for the NIWC, but nonetheless, allowed for a dialogue to emerge between Sinn Féin and the Progressive Unionist Party (PUP). As this external zone of conflict transformation developed, internal shifts within Sinn Féin were thrusting women to the front of the peace lines.

While Sinn Féin pushed for all-party talks in the 1990s, several prominent Republican women cut their political teeth on much-needed political experience. Demanding inclusivity and transparency in conflict resolution reinforced Sinn Féin's general commitment to equality. This platform for change facilitated the party's interests in engaging, training, and deploying female representatives to the negotiation table. As negotiators, Sinn Féin women represented a different perspective involved in the conflict. In addition to identifying women's issues in particular, female negotiators were embedding a gender perspective in peace. This is evidenced in the institutions created by the Agreement. For example, Sinn Féin argued for an institutionally separate Department of Equality during the Good Friday (known in Ireland as the Belfast) Agreement talks. Reflecting the party's deepening commitment to equality, Sinn Féin itself had an Equality Department. However, even though an engendered perspective highlighted issues for the negotiation table, it did not regularly translate into the Agreement, as the Equality Department for Northern Ireland was set up as junior ministries within the Offices of the First and Deputy First Ministers under the Belfast Agreement.[42] Despite the roller-coaster ride of successes, failures, and compromises normally associated with any conflict-resolution process, Sinn Féin's peace strategy incorporated an active female presence throughout the 1990s. Along with Lucilita Bhreatnach, Siobhan O'Hanlon, and Michelle Gildernew, the most visible women were Rita O'Hare (in the United States) and Bairbre de Brún (in Ireland and Europe).

Bairbre De Brún

Bairbre de Brún is currently one of the top Sinn Féin negotiators, one of the MEPs for Northern Ireland, and the MLA for West Belfast (1998–2004). Born in Dublin in 1954, Bairbre became active in Republican politics through the H-Blocks/Armagh campaign in the late 1970s. A graduate of both University College Dublin and Queens University Belfast, she is a former teacher and fluent Irish speaker (as well as speaker of French and German). Her initial involvement in Republican politics brought her in close contact with the female prisoners in Armagh Jail, a cause still dear to her. She joined Sinn Féin in 1982.

During the 1980s and 1990s, she worked in the cultural and international departments, becoming head of the International Department in 1994. In 1996, she was selected to be the party spokesperson on policing and justice while also serving as a part of the negotiation team to the Northern Ireland Forum.[43] During the negotiation of the Belfast Agreement, de Brún accompanied Martin McGuinness and Gerry Adams for much of the Stand negotiations. She served in these positions until her election in 1998 to be an MLA for West Belfast.

Having demonstrated a genuine concern for women's issues such as access to social services for all women and children, Sinn Féin selected de Brún for nomination to the Northern Ireland Executive. As the minister of health and social services (1999–2002) in the short-lived, often suspended, Northern Ireland Executive, she insisted on the creation of a new Royal Maternity hospital and midwife-led maternity care center in Belfast City. In 1999, she additionally oversaw the release of the Sinn Féin policy document *Women in Ireland,* which had been based on work previously undertaken by the Women's Department while she was a member. *Women in Ireland* eventually evolved into, in various incarnations, *Women in an Ireland of Equals,* published by the Sinn Féin Election Directorate Women's

Committee in 2004. In the recent 2009 European Union elections, in which she was overwhelmingly reelected, Bairbre de Brún announced her hope to make Irish an official language of the EU.

Postconflict Transition

According to the recommendations from UNIFEM, "[O]nce the agreement is signed, women must continue to participate in implementation and monitoring mechanisms, ensuring that the priorities of half the population are allocated resources and attention in the post-conflict environment."[44] A paper peace alone is never successful. Since the Belfast Agreement was signed in 1998, the peace process in Northern Ireland has sputtered, coughed, and stalled. The role of women in the postagreement North includes negotiating the further implementation of the accord at Saint Andrews, monitoring the implementation process, assuming roles in government through the electoral process, and rising to new roles within the party.

In October 2006, Sinn Féin negotiators—including Mary Lou McDonald and Caitríona Ruane—went to Saint Andrews, Scotland, for yet another round of talks concerning the implementation of the Belfast Agreement. The Belfast Agreement had created three strands of relationships, constitutional reforms in the South of Ireland, and a couple of institutions, notably the Northern Ireland Assembly and Northern Ireland Executive. Both bodies were suspended on October 14, 2002, when terms of the 1998 agreement were not implemented. The ensuing elections in the North demonstrated a polarized community, with electoral support for the moderate Social Democratic and Labour Party (Catholics) and Ulster Unionist Party (Protestants) was fading in favor of Sinn Féin (Republicans) and Democratic Ulster Party (Loyalists). Interestingly, the political parties heralded for the Agreement and to which the Nobel Peace Prizes (John Hume of SDLP and David Trimble of UUP) were awarded in 1998 have suffered after the Agreement. However, during that brief time, the women in Sinn Féin had enjoyed much electoral success. The female voices in Sinn Féin had been heard in the midst of the quagmire of an increasingly polarizing political polity.

As women in Sinn Féin stood for various elections in 1998, 2003, 2004, and 2005, popular support continued to rise for the party and for their candidacy. In 1998, Sinn Féin won 17.65 percent of the vote for the Northern Ireland Assembly and took 18 seats of which 5 members were women. By 2003, Sinn Féin held 24 seats, 6 of which were women, in the assembly. It was an increase in Sinn Féin seats but a decrease in female parity—the proportion of female MLAs in the Sinn Féin delegation decreased slightly from 27.8 percent in 1998 to 25.0 percent in 2003. With two seats on the Northern Ireland Executive, Bairbre de Brún and Martin McGuinness were selected. In the 2005 Westminster elections, Sinn Féin won 5 seats (up from 4 seats in 2001 when Gildernew was first selected as a MP for Fermanagh/South Tyrone) and increased their vote share to 24.3 percent (from 21.7 percent of the vote in 2001), reelecting Michelle Gildernew in 2005.[45] The May 2010 Westminster elections saw an additional increased Sinn Féin vote (to 25.5 percent) with five seats earned. In turn, the European Parliament elections of 2004 were very important for Sinn Féin, as they increased their vote share from 17.3 percent in 1999 to 26.3 percent in 2004. In an interesting electoral development, in the same election that Bairbre de Brún was elected in the Six Counties, Mary Lou McDonald was elected in the Dublin district in the South with 11.3 percent of the vote. And so it was, in 2007, that two of the four Sinn Féin candidates for the European Parliament (EP) were women, and both women were elected. North and south of the border, Sinn Féin was picking up support for its female candidates. However, the loss of McDonald's seat in 2009 provided a setback in this advancement.

In addition to the feminized electoral strategy following the Belfast Agreement, Sinn Féin continually promoted the role that its female members could play in the implementation phases as well. Since implementation rested on monitoring key policy areas for promoting peace, Sinn Féin appointed the first female chief education and training inspector in the Education Department of the Northern Ireland Assembly. Furthermore, the party promoted policies centered on new family-friendly work policies, career planning for women, domestic violence awareness, and health care. The sustainability of peace must be fostered in unofficial government arenas as well, a principle that Sinn Féin women prioritized by supporting community programs that identify the promise of women and children in conflict transformation programs. Within the party, women's issues emerged not as conflict issues but as government issues.

In the Republican transformation from paramilitaries to parliamentarians, Sinn Féin has leaned on the lessons learned by the African National Congress (ANC) in South Africa, one of the important networks developed by both men and women of Sinn Féin during the conflict. One lesson gleaned from the ANC is to be a political party that delivers to the needs of the conflict-torn society. This seems to have emerged in Sinn Féin's postagreement political experience. Fraught with issues of dissident Republicans, decommissioning, and allegations of insincerity, Sinn Féin appears to be conducting itself as a functioning, democratic socialist political party. The election manifestos were based on policy creation and innovation.[46] Among the platform issues of universal health care access, paid parental leave based on the Swedish system, and free breast and cervical cancer screening (for women over 40 and all women respectively), there lies the heart of a political party—a group of people seeking to collectively influence policy through the mechanism of elections and governance.

CONCLUSIONS

Republican women have been actively engaged in the formal and informal tiers of peace processes across the Northern and Southern counties of Ireland since the early 1990s. Whether in the glare of the camera lights or in the face of community scrutiny, the women of Sinn Féin faced the political challenges with intelligence, compassion, and fortitude. Throughout the 1990s, Sinn Féin women engaged in the party's transformation from a conflict society voice into a political party engaging in a democratic process. Reaping the benefits of key party decisions in the 1980s, notably the creation of the Women's Department in 1980 and the "Scenario for Peace" document in 1987, Republican women in the 1990s were integrated into the collective Sinn Féin voice. Collaborating side by side with their male counterparts engendered peace. Bringing a female perspective and skills into the patriarchal fray empowered a community and directed change both internally and externally. Sinn Féin women helped to define the conflict issues, emerged as leaders in the party and in government, fostered an environment for peace in the community, demanded inclusivity in negotiations and in society, and assisted in attempts to implement the Belfast Agreement. The concerns about equality voiced by Sinn Féin women in a postconflict society demonstrate a lasting commitment to a peaceful solution to ensure that equality, evidenced concretely by the election manifestoes from the 2005 elections.

The re-creation of the Northern Ireland Assembly, and its executive, was constituted in the Belfast Agreement of 1998, but distrust and speculation concerning the decommissioning of IRA weapons, policing reforms, and intermittent paramilitary activities led to its suspension in 2000 for three months, in August and September 2001 for 24-hour suspensions, and from October 2002 to May 2007.

In October 2001, the IRA began to decommission its weapons under the watchful eye of the International Independent Commission on Decommissioning (IICD), chaired by Belfast Agreement mediator General de Chastelain of Canada, and the International Monitoring Commission (IMC). The process was declared complete in September 2005, when the IRA issued a statement declaring that its weapons had been put beyond use (and the IICD verified this). Simultaneously, Sinn Féin concerns about the lack of progress to reconstructing an equal opportunity police force absent of Loyalist/British collusion abounded. From the perspective of Irish Republicans, the lack of anticollusion implementation was the impediment to IRA decommissioning. Once the IRA's decommissioning statement was issued in September 2005, efforts to revamp the Assembly quickly gained speed, and the political parties convened in October 2006 in St. Andrews, Scotland.

Even as Northern Ireland entered into the Saint Andrews Agreement in October 2006, the women were tending the lilies in the garden of peace. By cultivating themselves in the 1980s, these women were harvesting a generational flourish for the 21st-century Irish garden. When the Northern Ireland Assembly elections were held on March 7, 2007, Sinn Féin emerged as one of the two largest parties in the Assembly (the Democratic Ulster Party or DUP was the other). The once-marginalized parties were now set center stage in the power-sharing assembly. On March 26, 2007, Gerry Adams met Ian Paisley (of the DUP) for the first time, after so many years of conflict, to establish a legislative assembly and ministerial council (the Executive). On May 8, 2007, the new 108-member, Northern Ireland Assembly elected Reverend Ian Paisley of the DUP as first minister and Martin McGuinness of Sinn Féin as deputy minister. In March 2008, Paisley resigned his position as first minister of the Northern Ireland Executive, and Peter Robinson of the DUP assumed the seat. Currently, in 2010, the Northern Ireland Executive additionally includes 11 ministerial positions. The next scheduled Assembly elections are in 2011.

Chapter 8

MODERN SINN FÉIN WOMEN IN THE 21ST CENTURY

And I know that that the daily grind of work and organising and building and campaigning can be challenging, and indeed, at times, it is hard to see where the piece that you're working on fits into the bigger picture. But that's not how Bobby Sands saw it. Bobby Sands understood better, and earlier than most of us, the critical importance of campaigning and working on behalf of people. He threw himself into his community activism, after he was released from his first prison sentence . . . he was creating the template for the later Sinn Féin activists of today.

—Bairbre de Brún[1]

CHAPTER OVERVIEW

In the 21st century, the question of gender parity in political representation is of heightened focus in the international community. Many scholars identify gender quotas as a mechanism to achieve gender equity in party leadership, nominations, and elections. This chapter explores the dominant forms of gender quotas and gender parity data in international context and then seeks to demonstrate how a qualitative case study of a political party in Western Europe might offer some insight into gender equity. Through primary party documents and personal interviews with high-ranking elected women and female party officials in Sinn Féin in Ireland, this chapter demonstrates that while structural reforms took place in the British electoral system and the Irish electoral institutions embody characteristics most favorable to gender equity, the gender gap remains. Thus, in order to achieve gender parity in Irish politics, Sinn Féin embarked on an internal party directive to recruit, train, and promote women as leaders in the party and in government.

Chapter Organization

In July 2009, Sinn Féin received the largest vote share of any political party in the Northern Ireland elections to the European Parliament. In May 2010, Sinn Féin garnered the largest vote share (25.5 percent) of the parties in Northern Ireland for the Westminster Parliament election. It is a fitting point in the overview of a centenary review of the little party founded in 1905 by Arthur Griffith. A solid electoral strategy, combined with community organizing and party development, reached the people of Northern Ireland and swelled into a solid showing at the polls. The Sinn Féin political party of the 21st century is poised to usher in freedom and equality for a new generation of Irish girls and boys.

This chapter will place the recent developments of party development in a global context of party parity and electoral politics. First, an introduction to "party parity" will examine the global initiatives to engendered politics worldwide. Sinn Féin is on the cutting edge of party-system to structure party-based education, to mobilize, and to retain female Republicans. A brief overview of the various political and electoral systems in the Republic of Ireland and Northern Ireland will provide a glimpse into the electoral strategies that Sinn Féin has been promoting in order to demonstrate its commitment to an Ireland of equals.

The women at the helm of Sinn Féin have established clear goals of party parity and equality, both in front of and behind the cameras shining on the new era of peaceful politics in Ireland. In addition to examining the nature of (gender) party quotas on the ballot and in leadership posts, Sinn Féin has established a Gender Equality Directive (discussed here within). Finally, a profile of three high-ranking Sinn Féin women discusses the challenges of balancing work, home, and activism in light of a passionate call to service.

AN INTRODUCTION TO "PARTY PARITY"

- Global Movement to Gender Parity and Equality
- Irish Electoral System(s)

Why are there so few women in politics? Many explanations focus on structural explanations that identify institutional barriers to gender participation in politics, specifically in elected politics. According to the prevailing theories, if institutional obstacles exist, then gender parity in politics hinges on advocating systemic reforms, across various methodologies. But can the reform be driven from within the political parties themselves rather than the electoral or political systems? Furthermore, is it possible that the party can serve as a vessel for cultural reformation? Since institutional constructs embedded in a political system reflect cultural values, cultures with a strong female archetype and/or social system seem to correspond with higher female representation in government. By enhancing or modifying the gender policy of a political party, can that party, when in government, pursue gender parity from the inside out?

In order to explore the answers to these questions, this chapter will begin by establishing a baseline of gender parity in politics and reveal the systemic factors that favor female representativeness in government. Looking at aggregate data on women in high-level politics around the world, one finds a high level of female representatives in the Nordic zone. Of particular interest to scholars is the Scandinavian model of quotas, specifically the "zipper" or "zebra" ballot where alternating candidates on a party list are women. In the Nordic countries of Sweden, Denmark, Finland, Norway, and Iceland, women have achieved the highest levels of participation in parliamentary legislators, ranging from 36.1 percent to 47.0 percent.[2] In comparative perspective, the Nordic region boasts a 41.4 percent female representation compared to 19.3 percent across Europe, excluding the Nordic countries, and 18.4 percent of parliaments worldwide.[3] Overall, the net gender representation is higher in single or lower house assemblies (18.6 percent) than in upper houses of legislatures (17.5 percent). Globally, this reflects a net increase of 6.7 percent in female representatives in national parliaments since 1997. Many scholars attribute this increase to the globalizing adoption of gender quota systems.[4]

In comparative perspective, there are a record number of American women in Congress. In 2009, there are currently 74 female members of the House of Representatives and 17 female senators. Even so, the gender gap in the United States Congress falls short of the international norm—17 percent of the United States Congress is female. This is 1.4 percent less than the international mean.

Sinn Féin has made steps toward gender equity in politics since 2000 in party quotas, party structure, and gender communities. The author interviewed four high-ranking Sinn Féin members in the spring of 2007: Mary Lou McDonald (then member of European Parliament), Caitríona Ruane (member of Northern Ireland Assembly), Martina Anderson (former-POW and newly elected member of Northern Ireland Assembly) and Eibhlín Glenholmes (former OTR (on the run) and new gender equality director—an initiative of the Party Development Department).

Placing the Sinn Féin case in the context of globalizing gender empowerment allows one to examine the foundation of constitutionalism, political
and electoral systems, party ideology, and party mechanisms employed to
facilitate gender parity in politics.

Global Movement to Gender Parity and Equality

In order to establish the goals of the advancement of women in politics,
a few key terms related to *parity* must be established. Gender parity in politics is defined as the premise that men and women should share equally in
the political system. It may represent an inherent break with assimilation
to male logic in patriarchy. A method employed by a number of political
parties, including Sinn Féin, to achieve gender parity has been gender quotas. Gender quotas encompass a similar ideology to that of affirmative action, where either a government or a political party sets quotas for female
candidates to correct inequality.

There are many forms of gender quotas; among them are legislative quotas, party quotas, and reserved seats. Reserved seats are when seats are held
for only female nominees or appointees. This strategy is not applicable in
this case study, but legislative and party quotas do impact the advancement
of women in Irish politics. Legislative quotas attempt to reform the gender
gap in politics by promoting systemic and institutional reforms. Among
these would be: legislating positive discrimination, requiring candidate
quotas, establishing women-only short-lists for nomination, and designat-
ing separate districts for women. In 2002, positive discrimination in election candidacy lists was legalized in the United Kingdom; this development
impacts the case study selected here within. Party quotas are often adopted
internally and might impact the platform issues, the nomination pool, the
candidate selection, and the development of nominees and candidates. It is
the later method of gender quotas—party quotas—with which this study is
primarily concerned. Such strategies are hoped to increase the number of
women in politics and are designed not to exceed the levels of inequality.
By establishing gender parity (or equity) in politics, a society can pursue an
engendered discourse within the political system.

Feminists have been urging the embrace of structural and cultural
mechanisms to bridge the divide. Notably, in 1995, the Beijing Process
set a goal of 30 percent representation of women in national legislatures.
Only 24 countries, including Rwanda, Sweden, Cuba, and Finland, have
met or maintained that goal. For more information on national legislative
gender parity totals, please consult the Quota Project under the direction
of International IDEA, Stockholm University, and the Inter-Parliamentary
Union.[5]

Unicameral legislatures are more reflective of a homogeneous society. Bicameral legislatures often appeal to countries with a diversity in population and provide different avenues for representativeness. Not all legislative chambers are elected; many are appointed. In turn, the relative power of women in legislative chambers is not fully depicted by the statistics. Some chambers enjoy purely ceremonial functions, and in many cases, women do not enjoy full privileges as an MP. However, examining the comparative data does provide a minimum threshold goal of gender representativeness and highlight those countries that have designed, or redesigned, their electoral systems to encourage gender parity.

Some of the measures designed to establish gender parity in political representation have focused on gender quotas, perhaps due to the widely established success of quotas in Scandinavian politics. However, a few essential points concerning the applicability of the measures have been swept under the proverbial carpet in favor of decisive action. In order to fully establish the model's universality (or lack thereof), one should pause to consider the following elements: implementation duration, electoral system, party platforms, and political system.

Political System

Feminist literature draws upon both cross-national statistical studies and qualitative case studies. Consistently, explanations embodying a political-structural approach hold constant in both analyses. According to the dominant supply-and-demand argument, political systems that foster pluralism and equality produce female candidates more readily than autocratic ones. The evidence identifies structural barriers for educational attainment as a key element for reducing or eliminating females from the pool of eligible or desirable candidates.[6]

Furthermore, governments that are firmly committed to female representation in politics have adopted "held seat" models. In such cases, a certain number of appointed seats are to be designated for female officeholders. The constitutional status of women directly impacts the social expectations for/on women. In societies where women enjoy political rights, the public better receives female candidates.

Electoral System

An important element of female representation in politics is the form of electoral system. Studies consistently reveal that a proportional representation system assists women in elections.[7] The single-member district system, used in the United States, makes it such that a female candidate is "costing" the party a male seat. In a proportional representation system, the level of support for the party is directly reflecting the support for the party, not the candidates themselves directly. In such cases, a party may feel the need to balance the delegation in a manner that represents their level of gender support and can bridge gaps among other parties with a gendered perspective. This can be particularly useful in coalition governance. In party list systems, candidates can be packaged or paired with a male counterpart to enhance or soften the party's image without compromising a man's "place" on the ticket.

Proportional representation systems and multiparty list systems are the most conducive to the adoption of gender quotas. Although quotas can exist on a number of phases in the election phase, there are three placements for establishing a quota of a certain number of women: in the pool of candidates, in the nominee list, and in the elected offices. The most common is the gender quota for the nominees.[8]

Party Platforms

While electoral systems can be a tool for gender equity in politics, certain ideological values can be embedded in the political structures to prevent the advancement of women in politics. The obstacles can be as simplistic as an unwillingness of the party to accept women as candidates. Such an argument emerges in societies with lower levels of democracy scores. As democracy takes root and begins to flourish, the institutions that once confined women are reformed, notably universal suffrage and women's rights legislation. Therefore, autocratic traditions may be reformed, but it is possible that the social and ideological principles of inequality remain embedded in the party ideologies.

A subordinate position on the ballot may reveal a subordinate position of a gender in society or simply within the party. As pluralism increases, so will the diversity of parties with gender equality. Thus, the political parties begin to reflect the commitment to a pluralistic society and absorb the values onto their political platforms.

With a party-list electoral system, the political party has an opportunity to publicly reflect its internal commitment to gender equality and parity by promoting female candidates. Driven to produce a gendered party-list of candidates, political parties have employed a party-enforced quota for female candidates.

Implementation Duration

In Scandinavian experience, there has been close to 90 years of implementation of gender quotas. Scholars must recognize that in the rush to promote gender quotas the lessons in policy evaluation will directly impact policy implementation. Party quotas gained popularity in the United Kingdom in the 1990s and were combined with the creation of Women's Departments for oversight. Interestingly, the first-past-the-post systems, in which those who earn a plurality of votes needed to win the seat earn a seat, worked counter to the party quotas, producing little national female representatives. Perhaps normative reforms assumed a tone of institutional restructuring.

In turn, government institutions must be examined within the appropriate sociocultural contexts. In societies where women hold distinct social roles and are empowered in local governance, political quotas may be more readily received. Cultures with a strong social welfare system embrace quotas better than those with a weak welfare state. Thus, the duration of the dynamic interaction of legislative public-policy process and party-driven quotas must have time to seep into the fabric of the culture and the institutions.

Irish Electoral System(s)

Sinn Féin is a registered political party in both the Republic of Ireland and in Northern Ireland. Its candidates stand for elections to local governments, where the representatives are called councillors; national elections in the Republic and Northern Ireland; elections to Westminster Parliament (as an abstentionist party); and in European Union elections in both the Republic of Ireland and Northern Ireland. The many layers of government have led to a complex electoral strategy, one that must be carefully described on each "national" front.

Figures 8.1 and 8.2 detail the different layers of elections that a citizen can participate in within the Republic of Ireland and within Northern Ireland respectively. The arrows indicate direct popular elections and the chambers are organized (left to right) in proximity to local governance.

Figure 8.1.   Elections in the Republic of Ireland

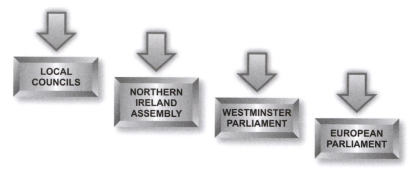

Figure 8.2.   Elections in Northern Ireland

In the South

The Republic of Ireland was established in 1949, after 28 years of Free State status. It is a constitutionally Roman Catholic country with a strong commitment to Irish political values and a traditionally patriarchic system. It is a republic in the truest sense, as throwing off the yoke of British colonialism revealed a strong strain of nonmonarchical tendencies. The ensuing Government of Ireland Act (1920) established a Free State of 26 counties and partitioned the northern 6 counties in full union with the United Kingdom. This arrangement remains to date.

The Republic of Ireland has a two-fold bicameral parliament. The lower chamber, Dáil Éireann, currently has 22 female members with a gender representativeness of 13.25 percent of the chamber. In the most recent election in May 2007, Sinn Féin received four seats, but none of the current TDs are women. Elections to the upper chamber, the Seanad Éireann, are indirect. Currently, there are 13 women senators with a representativeness of 21.67 percent.

Politics of irredentism, national liberation, and armed resistance persisted for the next 88 years. Sinn Féin employed political tactics and electoral strategies. Throughout the conflict and the Troubles, Sinn Féin maintained an electoral strategy both north and south of the border, hence the need for the discussion of British, Irish, Northern Irish, and European political and electoral systems. Table 8.1 depicts an overview of each tier with recent results from elections through July 2009.

In the South, Sinn Féin participates in European Parliament elections (since 1979), Irish Dáil elections, and nominations or indirect elections to the Irish Seanad.[9] Since there are no direct elections for the Seanad (Senate), this chapter focuses upon the Dáil elections and European Parliament elections. The method for selecting EP members is the same as in

Table 8.1
Data on Female Representativeness in Sinn Féin Elections

	Ireland	Northern Ireland	British (UK)	European Union
Party System	Multiparty	Multiparty	Two-party Dominant	Multiparty
Electoral System	Single Transferable Vote (STV)	Single Transferable Vote (STV)	First Past the Post (FPTP)	(Proportional Representation)
Number of Female Members (All Parties)	22/166 in Dail 13/60 in Seanad	27/108 Total	126/646 Total	3/12 for Ireland; 2 (NI) of 33/78 for UK
Number of Female Members (Sinn Féin)	0/4 of 166 in Dail 0/1 of 60 in Seanad	8/27 of 108	1/5 Sinn Féin Delegation	0 of 3 Ireland; 1 of 2 UK
Sinn Féin Uses Party Quotas	Yes	Yes	Yes	Yes

the United Kingdom. Mary Lou McDonald served as the lone Sinn Féin female representative, until she lost her seat in the spring of 2009. In the Dáil Éireann, Sinn Féin does not have any female members, though the single transferable (STV) multi-party system functions similar to the Northern Ireland Assembly elections. Certainly, the impact of ideology (nationalism in favor of republicanism) and generational divide between Fianna Fáil and Sinn Féin has impacted the voter turnout in the South.

In the North

As a political party in the North, Sinn Féin participates in European Parliament elections (since 1979), House of Commons (Westminster Parliament) elections, and Northern Ireland Assembly elections (since 1998).[10] European Parliament elections for the Six Counties are based on a multiparty PR system. Bairbre de Brún currently serves as the female MEP for Sinn Féin. The elections for Westminster Parliament allow constituencies for Northern Ireland as well, held in the first-past-the-post method. Michelle Gildernew currently serves as the sole female MP for Sinn Féin; Gerry Adams, Martin McGuinness, Pat Doherty, and Conor Murphy round out the Sinn Féin MP delegation newly elected in May 2010. Finally, the newly created Northern Ireland Assembly is based on a single transferable vote (STV), multiparty system. The devolved authority has 26 percent women, with Sinn Féin holding the largest number of female representatives of all political parties.

For those unfamiliar with the STV system, a brief explanation might be necessary. The Single Transferable Vote system (STV) allows voters to rank their preferred candidates in a multimember district. A threshold quota is calculated based on the electoral turnout; any candidate who receives first-order preference votes above the threshold is automatically elected. The "elected" candidates' surplus first-preference votes are redistributed to the second-preference candidates, and so on until the maximum members for the district are filled. A party-list vote is available, but voters usually vote for candidates.

Despite structural reforms in the British electoral system in 2002 and the implementation of favorable electoral system characteristics, the Irish and Northern Irish gender gap, excepting the whole UK delegation to the European Union, remains below the international norms and Beijing Process goals. Thus, Sinn Féin decided to aggressively pursue internal policies to foster gender parity within its own party and in government. The decision signaled a reinforcement of the party's ideological commitment to equality, and it should be recognized that Sinn Féin's 21st-century gender policy is a reincarnation or perhaps an evolution of its party history. That said, Sinn Féin's platform commitment to gender equality and parity has not translated into meeting international goal levels either. However, the ideological "conduciveness" to gender equality may be a strong variable in the ease of implementing party quotas, structures and policies.

The role of the political party can be to serve as the gatekeeper of nominations.[11] This may be what motivated parties in the UK and Ireland to adopt party-driven quotas. Despite legislation allowing, but not mandating, positive discrimination for female candidates, female candidates for the 2007 elections to the Northern Ireland Assembly and the Irish Dáil seem to have declined. In the case of Sinn Féin, the decision to focus on the quality of the candidate and not simply the gender, as well as the sophisticated networking/mentoring programs, identifies a long-term solution for gender inequality rather than a short-term fix.

This data mirror aggregate conclusions found when quotas are implemented systematically without institutional configuration, according to Monica Krook.[12] Her research suggests that while some countries have experienced a dramatic increase in gender parity in politics since the adoption of quotas, other countries have not shared this experience. The conflicting information seems to be the result of a mismatch of quota form and institutional structures. In order to reconcile the divide, one must examine the systemic and party reforms that Sinn Féin developed, including new programs, departments, and policies internally to advance gender equality in politics.

SINN FÉIN WOMEN IN POLITICS

- The Nature of Party Quotas
- Gender Equality Directive
- Balancing Work, Home, and Activism
  - Caitríona Ruane
  - Mary Lou McDonald
  - Martina Anderson

Returning to the birth of Sinn Féin in 1905, Sinn Féin's early Ard Chomhairle (National Executive) and First Dáil Éireann were comprised of many of the leading women of their day. Among these were Countess Markievicz, Kathleen Clarke, Dr. Ada English, Mary MacSwiney, Margaret Pearse, Kathleen O'Callaghan, Caitlin Brugha, and Dr. Kathleen Lynn. Chapter 1 demonstrated that Sinn Féin was a progressive party that allowed women a foray into the world of patriarchal politics. Though true gender equality may have been an errant goal of the early 20th century, elements of parity filtered into the Easter Proclamation of 1916, the ideological foundation of the Irish Republic to which Sinn Féin swore allegiance. Principles of equality can be found in the Easter Proclamation: "*The Republic guarantees religious and civil liberty, **equal rights and equal opportunities to all its citizens**, and declares its resolve to pursue the happiness and prosperity of the whole nation and of all its parts, cherishing all the children of the nation equally, and oblivious of the differences carefully fostered by an alien government, which have divided a minority from the majority in the past* [emphasis by the author]."

The late Marie Moore, the first Sinn Féin deputy mayor of Belfast, is often referred to by her comment that the saying "women are the backbone of Sinn Féin" was annoying. Sinn Féin gender equality director Eibhlín Glenholmes explains that Marie's disgust was over the fact that the backbone of the organization means you are at the rear, while the brains of the organization are at the front. Glenholmes reiterates the sentiment: "We are political animals. We've a right to express them. We don't have to nor should we feel the need to conform to any male stereotype image or to present ourselves as anything other than what we are. We are about the business of changing the political future of our country."[13]

In 2007, Sinn Féin won the most female seats to the Northern Ireland Assembly of any political party. Those who were reelected from 2003 increased their vote share.[14] There were two female Sinn Féin members seated in the European Parliament, and one female MP in the House of Commons. In turn, there were significant numbers of women elected onto the party's National Executive and many serving as heads of the party's departments. In 2010, Sinn Féin's National Executive included, once more, a female vice president, Mary Lou McDonald. One hundred years after a progressive beginning, Sinn Féin now approaches gender inequalities pragmatically. It is particularly interesting to note that Sinn Féin has developed gender policies that target the education of women *and men* regarding gender parity in society and politics.

Within the context of globalizing gender initiatives and national legislative quota movements in Ireland and Northern Ireland, Sinn Féin found that Irish women were still dramatically underrepresented by both international goal norms and internal party goals. Thus, at the dawn of the 21st century, Sinn Féin developed a party directive on gender parity in politics built on its party history and ideological commitment to equality. Below, the nature of party quotas and party restructuring, the development of a Gender Equality Directive, and recruitment and training efforts are examined.

The Nature of Party Quotas

Since 1998

In 1998, former American senator George Mitchell announced the signing of the Good Friday (Belfast) Agreement. Sent as a part of an international mediating body, Mitchell and his team interacted with numerous parties in the Northern Irish conflict, including the negotiating team from Sinn Féin. Chockfull of seasoned Republican strategists and political novices, the Sinn Féin team was headed by Gerry Adams and Martin McGuiness and flanked with a couple of unnamed, frequently unacknowledged women. Bairbre de Brún, Chrissie McAuley, Lucilita Breathnach, and Michelle Gildernew were among them.

The women of Sinn Féin had been a collective force of resistance throughout the Troubles, but in 1980s they organized internally. In 1980, a Women's Department had been created to train, educate, and promote women's issues to the front of the party's agenda and the national stage. The result had been to channel street politics into the ballot box. Numerous women's documents circulated among party members, and briefly, abortion, domestic violence, and contraceptives made it onto the party platform in 1985. However, the women began to notice that a Women's Department isolated women from the men in the party. The department became associated with radical feminism. Then, in the midst of a civil conflict, women from the streets were drawn to the negotiation and press rooms. Sinn Féin, long an advocate for equality in a society they felt oppressed in, began to see the dichotomy of isolating women in a political party in order to empower them. Why not, the party leadership supposed, empower all Irish Republicans—regardless of gender—to equality? A pragmatic approach to party strategy commenced with the implementation of the peace agreement.

Party Quotas?

Sinn Féin adopted an internal party quota for female representativeness very early on in its history. In the 1990s, discussion began to emerge over whether the quota level should be raised from 25 percent. At the annual party meetings (the Árd Fheis), proposals would circulate proposing a rise to 40 percent or even 50 percent. However, the internal party leadership quotas did not seem to be translating into candidacy quotas. Furthermore, party leaders became concerned that the root causes of gender imbalance were being overlooked.

There are three aspects of the Irish/Northern Irish electoral systems that might assist in correcting gender imbalance in elected offices. The types of quota measurement are 1) district magnitude—how many elected representatives per district; 2) formula—the decision of how a seat is won; and 3) ballot structure—whether a voter picks a candidate or a party and whether they get to identify a spectrum of political opinion.[15] Recent studies suggest that district magnitude might be less successful than effective party quotas guaranteed by the party.[16] Within a STV system, voters have multimember districts, threshold formulas with preference rounds, and a mixed-candidate/party-list ballot. Thus, since elections to the Dáil Éireann and Northern Ireland Assembly are structurally favorable, one would expect to find more party-driven quotas. In fact, this is precisely what Sinn Féin concluded in 2002–03—to focus of the supply of its candidates and party leaders vis-à-vis quotas.

A December 2002 article in *An Phoblacht* recounted the initial strategies to redefine the methods Sinn Féin employed. In "What SF Is Doing," Lucilita Breathnach, then director of the Equality Department, explains the purpose of the gender impact assessment seminars. She states: "Our role is to try to tackle inequality wherever it may exist. That is a responsibility for us all."[17]

Party strategies included the development of a local approach, of party policy papers, and of targeted training programs for women. Bringing the strategy local was a significant shift in Sinn Féin gender strategy. It had been assumed that political participation was the onus of the individual. However, as Sinn Féin's internal party leadership recognized, there was an internal party barrier for gender parity in membership, leadership, and candidacy. Lucilita Breathnach announced, after years of serving as the party's general secretary and then head of the Equality Department, that she would be stepping down. The opportunity for leadership change allowed for a reformulation of the internal party strategy.

Sinn Féin president Gerry Adams has long been viewed as a proponent of gender equality. Consistent with the current paradigm in feminist literature,[18] Sinn Féin employed a party elite driven approach to party parity in membership, leadership, nomination, and candidacy. In an effort to connect the membership and elections elements, Adams recommended the creation of a new party department that would serve as a link between the Election, Equality and fledgling Women's Department. The Árd Fheis (party conference) embraced the idea, and so in 2006, the Party Development Department was created. Its first task was to build a local field study at the *cuige* (district) level to study the sources of gender inequality within the party.

Gender Equality Directive

The Recognition of the Four Cs

Shortly after the Belfast Agreement, Sinn Féin's Ard Chomhairle (National Executive) had disbanded the Women's Department. When the

Equality Department was launched, the medium of transmitting equality became educating women. Later, this approach was broadened to include men as well. Explaining the disbandment of the Women's Department, Sinn Féin (former) Ard Chomhairle member Eibhlín Glenholmes says that "my sense of the Women's Department was that any department that was called the women's anything had two effects on male comrades. One was that it allowed those who had no interest in gender equality to abdicate responsibility. And the second was that it also, to a degree, denied male comrades who were proactive on the issue and believed in the necessity to gender balance the party and it denied them an opportunity. They felt that they were excluded."[19]

In 2006, the party announced the creation of an initiative for equality, housed within the Party Development Department. Sinn Féin president Gerry Adams personally asked Ms. Eibhlín Glenholmes to steer a special program on gender equality. She prioritized the following areas to promote women in politics—recruitment, retention and promotion, leadership, and overall gender-equality policies. "Women alone cannot solve this . . . It is a global issue. We need to look, and learn, from other modules and people who have addressed this problem before us and learn from both their successes and from their mistakes. We look at the Nordic and Scandinavian modules. We look at what France has done. We applaud the positions that women are taking up globally."[20]

Committed to a grassroots data collection, Ms. Glenholmes decided to take the party to the people. The Party Development Department set up five to six meetings in each *cuige* (district). The requirements for the meetings were that they would be held separately from any normal party business or function, that they would start on time and last one hour, and that there could not have a single-gender audience. "We were keen to avoid the perception that it was 'a women's issue' and so insisted on meetings mixed by gender."[21] The purpose of the decentralized approach, Glenholmes states, was to establish a dialogue and build a community upon it. She explains the role that the department played in the process: "The Party Development Department is an umbrella. It is a generic term for the recruitment department, because we need to bring more women into Sinn Féin, gender equality, because we need to see this as an issue but it doesn't stand alone. It's not just for bringing women into the party; it's about future leadership figures, bringing women through, creating them space that allows them, looking at the tools they need."[22]

An internal party document, stemming from the September 2006 study, revealed that activists felt four central components served as barriers to gender parity in Sinn Féin: cash, culture, confidence, and child care. These components became known as the four Cs. Cash refers to the inequality in pay and poverty levels. The resulting financial burden serves as a barrier to those who cannot afford to travel to meetings or events. Culture draws on the assumptions about what it takes to emerge as a leader within the party—being pale, male, and stale. The image of a middle-aged man of leadership required a change in mind-set. Confidence refers to the insecurity of cosmetic judgments that the women felt were applied to them unequally, especially regarding their age and appearance. It was noted that recruitment of female leaders at the senior level would have to reflect a systemic commitment party-wide to build internal confidence. Child care was the final C. Unlike their male counterparts, female activists who could be groomed for candidacy often had children. The cost of child care and the time commitment away from family and work provided layers of challenges for recruitment of female candidates. At present, the Ard Chomhairle is examining recommendations to provide child care, or to subsidize it through the Election Department, to facilitate more female participation.

The four Cs strategy required a comprehensive party understanding. Thus, members of the Ard Chomhairle, Assembly teams, and Dáil leaders were engaged to address the issue directly. Each *cuige* was asked to designate a gender-balanced team of four to serve as a pipeline for communication and education at the grassroots level. In addition to the grassroots communication pipeline, the party established a core group of approximately 30 women who are brought together, at party cost, every three months for educational training, networking, unofficial mentoring, and party building. All teams are also trained by professional gender-equality trainers based on curriculum developed by two professional experts, who donated their time to develop a tailor-made program for each *cuige*.

Harnessing the energy and drive has been quite easy, Eibhlín explains, as they were eager to learn the tools of leadership. The group spans age, marital status, and backgrounds. Groomed for future candidacy or core activists, the women have a networked friendship and support even in an e-mail, format. The peer mentoring process has been so engaging that when European MP Mary Lou McDonald came to inaugurate the opening meeting, she was engaged for hours! Among the tools with which these women have been provided is a media relations program, which fine tunes interview techniques and focuses on the ability to articulate Sinn Féin positions.

Furthermore, specific representative goals were adopted by the Party Development Department. In compliance with the constitutional mission of the party to uphold party quotas in leadership and candidates, the "Gender Equality Program" established a minimum 30 percent goal within 5 years (by 2011), a critical mass of 40 percent representation within 10 years (by 2016), and a full gender parity of 50 percent from 2016 on. The report concludes in the spirit of optimistic creativity: "This project is both a political and moral imperative, and it is achievable. It will not happen over-night, but it cannot be delayed."[23]

The Evolution of the Party Platform Documents

The restructuring of the party infrastructure was complemented by the development of party papers. Recorded under the direction of the Women's Department and the Elections Department, three key party papers signaled the direction of women's issues: *Women in an Ireland of Equals (2002) revised in 2004; Equality for Women 2005; Women's Manifesto 2007*.

In 2002, Sinn Féin had been in the midst of the peace process, establishing baselines for entry into the negotiations and sustaining their involvement. While the primary focus of the party leadership was conflict resolution, it was clear that in creating peace Sinn Féin saw the opportunity to create new opportunities for equality. *Women in an Ireland of Equals* tied the issues of gender inequalities in legislation, funding for women's groups, affirmative action programs in employment and education, and gender proofing and gender mainstreaming to the core mission of the party to build an Ireland of equals.

Gender proofing refers to combing through legislation to expose gender bias embedded in it. Gender mainstreaming refers to centralization of women's rights into the party's agenda and into government on behalf of society. "Women's rights are basic human rights. We cannot have a just and free society without equality for women," the document reads. Sinn Féin then reiterated the National Women's Council of Ireland (NWCI) call for a 60/40 quota for management boards and policy-making arena. It is worth noting that supporting and achieving the implementation are two different pledges. However, the 2004 revision to the party document references the Ard Fheis motion put forth by MEP Bairbre de Brún to change party rules to ensure that 50 percent, up from 30 percent, of the Ard Chomhairle are women. It also reveals that compulsory party seminars of gender inequality had been conducted by the Equality Department, under Breathnach's leadership, for the Ard Chomhairle, party officers and regional officers. A commitment to women's issues was renewed on the party's platform, specifically in the areas of reducing female poverty, protecting women from domestic violence, and increasing female access to affordable and accessible health care, education, child care, housing, and employment.

Sinn Féin: Equality for Women (Elections 2005) incorporated women's issues specifically into the election campaign. Equality of women "is the guiding principle that directs our [Sinn Féin's] policies, the structure of our party and the campaigns in which we are involved."[24] The campaign for women in the economy centered on advocacy for paid parental leave, protection of social security benefits, increased minimum wage, antidiscrimination in employment, reduction of the gender gap in employment, and so on. The party document connects the needs of women in health care, education, child care, domestic violence, female pensioners, rural women, and female participation in politics to its campaign platforms. The results were clear—two of the primary Sinn Féin candidates, both women, were elected to the European Parliament: Bairbre de Brún for the Six Counties and Mary Lou McDonald for Dublin. "Sinn Féin wants to build an Ireland of Equals and we recognise the vital need for gender balance, gender proofing and gender equality in the decision making process."[25]

At the Árd Fheis in March 2007, a draft of *Sinn Féin Women's Manifesto* was introduced. In addition to reiterating the previous documents, the manifesto couches its gender policies in the calls by the United Nations Convention on the Elimination of All Forms of Discrimination Against Women (CEDAW) and calls for the direct implementation of European Union antidiscrimination legislation and the party's Gender Equality Directive. In Irish, the directive can be summarized as: *Nil saoirse gan saoirse na mban* (no freedom without freedom for women) and is reflected in the following key points, echoing the *Women in an Ireland of Equals* document.

> We advocate the use of all possible mechanisms for advancing gender equality including:
>
> - Equality and other legislation
> - Funding for women's groups
> - Affirmative action (measures to actively promote women and thereby redress the legacy of discrimination and exclusion of women on the basis of gender)
> - Gender-proofing (checking to ensure that proposals, policies, practices, laws or budgets do not disadvantage women as a group)
> - Gender mainstreaming (ensuring that women's equality is not ghettoized, but instead becomes fully integrated as everyone's concern and responsibility).[26]

Reflecting on the progress toward gender parity in politics, the draft document reveals the party's frustration at the lack of substantial progress. "These statistics are an indictment of our society. They are unacceptable and Sinn Féin intends to work both within our party and at local, national and European levels to make the necessary changes."[27] In addition to the

60/40 recommendation by the NWCI, Sinn Féin calls for the achievement of 50/50 parity in political representation.

According to the 2007 report, the internal party quotas have been somewhat successful. Fifty percent of the Ard Chomhairle is female, and more than 50 percent of the party's officer board is female. In 2007, both the general secretary and the national party chair were female. More than 40 percent of the party's department heads were female. In the previous Northern Ireland Assembly (before the collapse that served as a hiccup in the peace process), the Ministerial Council was allotted on a 50/50 gender parity (Bairbre de Brún and Martin McGuinness). Twenty percent of the Westminster delegation was female. Twenty-seven percent of the local councillors in the Twenty-Six Counties (the Republic) and 25 percent of the MLAs (members of the Northern Ireland Assembly) were female prior to the 2007 elections. Twenty-two percent of the Leinster House (Dáil Éireann) candidates and 24 percent of the Assembly candidates in the 2007 elections were women. "These levels represent a general improvement on past performance. However, we [Sinn Féin] recognise that women are still under-represented at the level of elected office."[28] Even so, both candidacy levels and elected officers to the Dáil and the Assembly fell short of the 30 percent Beijing Process levels of gender parity goals.

In the 2009 European Parliament elections, Sinn Féin MEP (Belfast) Bairbre de Brún became the only candidate to be elected on a first-order preference. The electoral success was dampened by the loss of Mary Lou McDonald's MEP seat in the Republic.

Balancing Work, Home, and Activism

A central tenant of the Sinn Féin strategy to achieve gender equity in politics is the recruitment and training of female party activists and candidates. Three women that were nudged into the national and international spotlight were Caitríona Ruane, Mary Lou McDonald, and Martina Anderson.

Caitríona Ruane

Caitríona Ruane is an activist at heart. She credits this to the strong sense of social justice that her parents raised her with and her uncle who is a progressive priest who has served in India and Brazil. Her early childhood memories include a pervasive level of censorship in the West of Ireland on Sinn Féin and playing *The Men behind the Wire* on record player. The internment song shaped her political consciousness: "Armoured tanks and cars and tanks and guns came to take away our sons," she begins to recite until she corrects the song's gender bias, "they forgot about the daughters!"[29] She is married to a Sinn Féin life member and is the mother of two politically aware teenage girls. In the early part of her political career, she was active in international human rights organizations in Latin America and established a human rights organization in West Belfast. She coordinated inquiries into RUC police human rights abuses and then raised the bar by bringing in international inquiry into British Army practices, specifically the shoot-to-kill and collusion policies. Her human rights activism also included being an international elections monitor in South Africa and participating in the Beijing Women's Conference.

She remained outside Republican politics for some time, but her connection to Sinn Féin largely came through the West Belfast Féile and her husband (the child of Republican internees). The West Belfast Féile is a festival fighting for protecting Irishness in a community where cultural identity was oppressed. "That festival, it showed me that you can fight for people's rights but you also have to show people the dream, show people what things can be."[30] Sinn Féin president Gerry Adams served on the Féile board, and Caitríona saw Sinn Féin as a powerful group of people who were taking on the state. Her husband's support was a key factor in her decision to heed the call to duty for Sinn Féin. He understood the time

Caitríona Ruane, Northern Ireland Assembly minister for education. (Courtesy Kelly Morris)

commitment, she explains, in that Sinn Féin is a way of life, not just a job. During the crisis of the Colombia Three in 2001, she was chosen to represent Sinn Féin in Colombia to bring international attention to the men's plight. The Colombia Three were three Sinn Féin men who were held by the Colombian government for allegedly training FARC guerrilla fighters. It was a precarious assignment, especially for the mother of two young girls, but her husband's support allowed Caitríona to be a continent away in the face of immediate danger in order to advocate for the Three's release.

When Caitríona returned to Ireland, she was approached to consider running for elected office. Having experience in running an election campaign, she considered it seriously before committing. "As a woman, I was always reluctant to join a political party because does any political party fully fit all your ideas and policies? Can you agree with every policy? What happens if you don't support the party line? There is a discipline in being a member of a party, but I am glad that I have joined and I have made the right decision. You have to be a part of something to change something."[31] Today, Caitríona Ruane serves as an elected member of the Northern Ireland Assembly and is the Minister of Education in the Northern Ireland Executive. She is also one of the 30 women engaged in the equality program for peer mentoring within the party.

Though her experienced background, education, and internationalization may not be typical of the average Sinn Féin member, Ruane represents the increasing power of women within Sinn Féin, Ireland, and the world.

Mary Lou McDonald

By contrast, Mary Lou McDonald came to politics after the Belfast Agreement. A young university graduate from the South, Mary Lou was a fresh face in the wake of the peace process. She was attracted to Sinn Féin for the opportunities it offered women, not simply because of its commitment to social activism alone. From a Fianna Fáil family background, Mary Lou was deeply moved by the Republican Hunger Strikes in 1980–81. It, she recounts, inspired a generation of Irish children to a republican consciousness.

As a core member of Sinn Féin's negotiation team throughout the implementation phases of the Good Friday Agreement, Mary Lou McDonald often went unacknowledged in media coverage. She recalls the frustration as "there are times that you would go to particular meetings and do particular jobs of work and it was almost an automatic assumption by some elements in the media that you were there for decoration, just to take the bad look off the delegation. And to this day, certain people still struggle to accept the fact that yes, I actually am part of this team, I am the chairperson of the party; that's why I'm there."[32]

Mary Lou McDonald, vice president of Sinn Féin. (Courtesy Kelly Morris)

In 2005, Sinn Féin recruited her to stand for election in the Dublin area for the European Parliament. She won. She remained an MEP, while also serving as the national party chair (2007–2008), until the recent electoral loss in July 2009. Running for electoral politics is hard on the family, she admits. "Your whole family sort of runs for public office. This is where it is a different type of job or way of life. You cannot neatly divide your working life and your family, simply because it is so erratic at times. I know from talking to colleagues of mine that it is a big decision to say 'right, I'm going to run for election. I'm going to put myself out there.' "[33] Now, she is balancing being vice president of Sinn Féin (2009–2010 Ard Chomhairle) with mothering her two small children.

McDonald acknowledges that the way that the media portrays Republicans, and Sinn Féin women in particular, is a challenge for the women who may be considering coming forward into politics. The negative coverage serves as a disincentive. "It is interesting. When I emerged as a candidate, a whole media conversation emerged. 'My God, what's this woman running? Image—she's running for Sinn Féin, breaking stereotypes of what people understood as a republican, in particular, to be . . . to be northern, to be male, to be rough and tough' . . . so, I did not conform to all of that."[34] The stereotype trivializes the female candidates, in her opinion, or creates an alternative stereotype of being a "dolly bird," and this can be very off-putting for a women considering bridging the gender gap in political representation. It has not impacted the party's decision to engage Sinn Féin activists on the Party Executive, however. In 2009, there were 10 women on the 19-person executive—that is 52.6 percent of the national party core.

Martina Anderson

For Martina Anderson, the decision to run for office was a call to duty. Newly elected to the Northern Ireland Assembly in March 2007, Martina represents a traditional Republican element of Sinn Féin. A convicted POW—the term that Sinn Féin uses to designate Republicans who served time for terrorist offenses, Martina Anderson endured years of strip searches. She estimates that she was searched over 600 times during her imprisonment. The female ex-prisoners, post–Belfast Agreement, have been integrated into electoral politics. Their contribution is valuable for a democratic transition where a female voice will formulate equality policies for the 21st century.

Martina was released under the terms of the Good Friday (Belfast) Agreement on November 11, 1999, and shortly after became active with the Assembly team as a party researcher. Moving into the Assembly business committee, whose purpose is to facilitate organization of weekly activities, and the ministerial team who liaised and coordinated with the two Sinn Féin ministers.

When the Assembly collapsed, Martina took up work on the Strand Two (All Ireland agenda) until Gerry Adams personally asked her to head up the Unionist Outreach campaign in 2006. She understood the importance of the role immediately.

> It was a particular Ireland that was going to involve shaping the form of Ireland that needed to be discussed: a new constitution, a new system of governance. The brown envelope of politics in the Twenty-Six Counties would just be transferred here. That we wanted an Ireland of equals—an inclusive Ireland that regardless of their religious denomination or the color of their skin would feel welcome and would be a part of, and would be involved in the shaping of it, and I realized that we need to have an engagement with the Unionist community around all that.[35]

The common ground includes a common humanity and a common experience. There is a great amount of poverty across both communities that united Unionist and Republican communities in a challenge to overcome it. Among her initiatives have been discussions where she has engaged with a group of women from the Shankill during the West Belfast Féile and the organization of public meetings through the Protestant churches. The commonality of gender and poverty has served as an overarching link between the communities, and Martina feels that there is a trust among the Shankill and Falls Road women when it comes to the need to overcome deprivation. She calls them brave and courageous in their fight against the impact of poverty on their community and commends their consciousness to lead as women.

Newly elected to the Northern Ireland Assembly for Derry, Martina recalls that, until recently, she did not distinguish between elected and non-elected activists. Everyone simply made their contribution in the way they could, she reflects, but now she has risen to the call to use the elected arena to address community-based politics and republicanism: "[I]t's about changing the lives of people in the here and now," she feels. As a candidate, Martina was supported by a great network of activists in her campaign and, she muses that, in contrast to some of the other political party candidates in the area, was quite relaxed going into the March 2007 elections because of the hard work of her election team. Having served as a director of elections during her career as an activist, she understands that this is where the heart of the organizational effort is. As the candidate, and not an activist on staff, it is busy but not overwhelming. She laughs as she says, "[T]his is the most relaxed I've been since I got out of prison!"[36]

The most important lesson that Martina has learned as a Republican activist is to make sure that it does not happen again. "We want a society in which we can all be proud of what we have been able to build. Because coming out of the tragedy and the heartache and the pain that has been across the board, both inflicted on us and we have inflicted on others, for me the lesson that I have learned is to work my heart out to make sure that another generation never has to go through that."[37] A Sinn Féin woman in the 21st century, she ponders, has been empowered by the women who were involved in the war. "War is a terrible thing. It is how you get out it that is important. And how you build conflict resolution . . . I wouldn't be where I am today as an individual, and I don't mean in status, I just mean me as a person, in growth as a person, if it hadn't been for the Republican movement."[38]

The results of the 2007 elections offer some interesting anecdotal evidence. Though the Social Democratic and Labour Party, a rival for party support of Catholic voters, pushed more female nominations (40 percent of SDLP candidates) in 2007 but did not win but 4 of those 14. Sinn Féin slated 9 of 37 women on their nominee list (only 24 percent) but won 8 female seats. This was a drop, however, in the number of women nominated

In 2003 for Sinn Féin (12 of 38 nominees or 32 percent). Since the implementation of the Equality and Party Development Departments, Ireland has risen in the world standings of female representativeness in governance. Though there has been little movement in Dáil Éireann data, there has been more success in the Northern Irish Assembly and in the European Parliament. That point noted, the 2009 European Parliament elections have demonstrated how big the gender gap can get—and quickly. Ireland recently dropped from 7th to 21st in terms of highest female representativeness in European Parliament (38.5 to 25 percent).

If Sinn Féin cannot control the electoral outcome, it certainly can demonstrate its commitment to gender parity internally. The Ard Chomhairle, which is a 12-person elected officer board, now includes a female vice president, Mary Lou McDonald; General Secretary Dawn Doyle; Director of Publicity Rosaleen Doherty; and Treasurer Rita O'Hare. Among the female members selected by the local party districts (three members per *cuige*) are Bairbre de Brún, Noeleen Mac Poilin, Mary McArdle, Shannonbrooke Murphy, Áine Ní Gabhann, and Ella O'Dwyer. Once again, over half of the national party executive is currently female!

CONCLUSIONS

Sinn Féin's postagreement party development has targeted gender parity in political representativeness and equality as a whole in Ireland. By focusing upon the case of Sinn Féin, one finds that it ideological complementarity for gender equity can enhance structural reforms at the national and party level. Though Ireland and Northern Ireland use the electoral systems that are good fits for producing an advancement of women into politics, the legislative quotas and general political system characteristics have not been able to produce systematic results. This evidence reinforces the dominant conclusions in feminist theories that party quotas drive higher levels of gender equity in politics.

Even so, party quotas can be meaningless or meaningful depending on the level of enforcement and social willingness to embrace female candidates and party leaders. Efforts to internally reform the party can employ party platform development, department restructuring, affirmative action programs for party officer boards and party management, educational programs, and peer mentoring programs.

Levels of inequality can persist. By identifying key elements of both institutional and cultural barriers to gender parity in politics, one can redress each individual element in a directive to retrain the gender-biased system. The most meaningful reforms treat gender inequality as a systemic social problem, not simply a political representation issue.

Furthermore, evidence of the party elite argument is clear. Case after case reveals a strong personal commitment of the Sinn Féin president to establishing and developing a gender equality program. Gerry Adams personally selected two of the women interviewed by the author and asked them to take on key elements of the party's strategy to overcome gender inequality in the party and in government. In turn, the Ard Chomhairle's (National Executive) recommendation to link the Elections, Women's, and Equality Departments amounts to visionary party infrastructure reflecting party ideology and strategy. Thus, the impact of leadership must be noted in a best-practices approach to gender equality in party development.

The overlap of the Northern Irish peace process with the development of a 21st-century gender policy should also be recognized. It is clear that Sinn Féin has a pragmatic approach to the contradiction that peace between the Nationalist and Unionist communities centers on equality of ethnicity while a vast level of inequality between men and women across the ethnic divide persists. The women's issues of poverty transcend ethnicity. Thus, it is an opportunity for radical, progressive change in both the government and the society. It is an opportunity for the advancement of women in Irish politics, and, the beginning of the recognition of the role Sinn Féin women have played in the realization of Republican politics.

NOTES

ACKNOWLEDGMENTS AND INTRODUCTION

1. http://womenshistory.about.com/od/quotes/a/s_d_oconnor.htm.

2. Mulholland, Marie. 2002. *The Politics and Relationships of Dr. Kathleen Lynn*. Dublin: Woodfield Press; Litton, Helen, ed. 1991. *Kathleen Clarke, Revolutionary Woman*. Dublin: O'Brien Press; Ward, Margaret. 1993. *Maud Gonne: A Life*. Ontario: Pandora Press; Ward, Margaret. 1997. *Hanna Sheehy-Skeffington: A Life*. Cork: Attic Press; O Duigneanin, Proinnsios. 1991. *Linda Kearns: A Revolutionary Irish Woman*. Cork: Cork University Press, 342.

3. Ward, Margaret. 2001. *In Their Own Voice, Women and Irish Nationalism*. Cork: Attic Press; Taillon, Ruth. 1996. *When History Was Made: The Women of 1916*. Belfast: Beyond the Pale Publications; McCoole, Sinéad. 2003. *No Ordinary Women*. Dublin: O'Brien Press.

4. Nelis, Mary. 2006. Interview in *Slí na mBan*. http://www.tallgirlshorts.net/thewayofwomen/.

5. Sinn Féin. 2006. *History*. http://www.sinnfein.ie/history.

6. Farrell, Mairéad. 1980s. Quoted in "Mairéad." *Relatives for Justice*. http://www.relativesforjustice.com/mairead-farrell.htm.

7. McDonald, Mary Lou in Joanne Corcoran. May 19, 2005. "Women Demand Welfare Rights—11,000 Letters of Protest to Department of Finance." *AP/RN*. http://www.anphoblacht.com/news/detail/9618.

8. Rafter, Kevin. 2005. *Sinn Féin: 1905–2005—In the Shadow of Gunmen*. Dublin: Gill and Macmillan.

CHAPTER 1

1. Butler, Mary. 1906. *The Ring of Day.* London: Hutchison and Company.

2. The term "sinn féin" describes an ideological movement. When "sinn féin" is capitalized as Sinn Féin, it refers to the political party.

3. For more information on the 1798 Rebellion, please consult: Keogh, Daire, and Nicholas Furlong, eds. 1998. *Women of 1798.* Dublin: Four Courts Press.

4. For more information on the Young Irelanders and *The Nation,* please consult: Anton, Brigitte. Autumn 1993."Women of The Nation." *History Ireland* 1 (3): 34–37; and Davis, Richard. *The Young Ireland Movement.* 1987. Dublin: Gill and Macmillan Ltd.

5. Excerpts from "The Objects of Inghinidhe na h-Eireann" in *United Irishman,* October 13, 1900.

6. For additional information on the history of Sinn Féin, please consult: Feeney, Brian. 2002. *Sinn Féin: A Hundred Turbulent Years.* Dublin: O'Brien Press; Laffin, Michael. 1999. *The Resurrection of Ireland: The Sinn Féin Party 1916–1923.* Cambridge: Cambridge University Press; Rafter, Kevin. 2005. *Sinn Féin 1902–2005: In the Shadow of Gunmen.* Dublin: Gill & MacMillan; MacDonncha, Michael, ed. 2005. *Sinn Féin: A Century of Struggle.* Dublin: Republican Publications; and Malliot, Agnes. 2004. *New Sinn Féin: Irish Republicanism in the Twenty-first Century.* New York: Routledge Press.

7. Butler, Mary. 1920s. "When the Sinn Féin Policy Was Launched." In *The Voice of Ireland,* ed. W. G. Fitzgerald, 105–109. Dublin and London: Virtue and Company.

8. Maud Gonne married Séan MacBride, one of the martyrs of the Easter Uprising in 1916. She is often referred to as Maud Gonne MacBride as well as by her maiden name.

9. Griffith, Arthur. 1904. *The Resurrection of Hungary: A Parallel for Ireland.*

10. Molony, Helena in Margaret Ward. 1995. *Unmanageable Revolutionaries.* London: Pluto Press, 66.

11. Biletz, Frank. 2002. "Women and Irish-Ireland: The Domestic Nationalism of Mary Butler." University of St. Thomas, *New Hibernia Review* 6 (1): 59–72.

12. For more information on the early revolutionaries, please consult: McCoole, Sinéad. 2003. *No Ordinary Women: Irish Female Activists in the Revolutionary Years 1900–1923.* Madison, WI: University of Wisconsin Press.

13. Wyse-Power, Jennie in W. G. Fitzgerald, ed. 1920s (exact date uncertain). *The Voice of Ireland.* Dublin and London: Virtue and Company, 158–161.

14. For more information on Mary Butler, please consult: Butler, Mary. 1906. *The Ring of Day.* London: Hutchison and Company; and Biletz, Frank. 2002. "Women and Irish-Ireland: The Domestic Nationalism of Mary Butler." University of St. Thomas, *New Hibernia Review* 6 (1): 59–72.

15. Butler, Mary. 1901. "Women and Nationhood." *United Irishman* (Dublin).

16. Butler, Mary. 1901."Women's Role in Sustaining Gaelic Culture." *United Irishman* (Dublin); and Biletz, Frank. 2002. "Women and Irish-Ireland: The

Domestic Nationalism of Mary Butler." University of St. Thomas, *New Hibernia Review* 6 (1): 59–72.

17. For more information on Maud Gonne, please consult: Ward, Margaret. 1990. *Maud Gonne: Ireland's Joan of Arc.* London: Pandora Press.

18. Gonne, Maud in Margaret Ward. 2001. *In Their Own Voice, Women and Irish Nationalism.* Cork: Attic Press, 5.

19. Ibid., 14.

20. For more information on the membership requirements of the Daughters of Ireland, please consult: Ward, Margaret. 1995. *Unmanageable Revolutionaries.* London: Pluto Press, 40–87.

21. Séan MacBride would later be awarded a Nobel Peace Prize in 1974.

22. For more information on Constance Gore-Booth, please consult: Marreco, Anne. 1967. *The Rebel Countess: The Life and Times of Constance Markievicz.* New York: Phoenix Press.

23. Markievicz, Constance in Margaret Ward. 2001. *In Their Own Voice, Women and Irish Nationalism.* Cork: Attic Press, 51.

24. Molony, Helena in Margaret Ward. 2001. *In Their Own Voice, Women and Irish Nationalism.* Cork: Attic Press, 80.

25. Milligan, Alice in Margaret Ward. 2001. *In Their Own Voice, Women and Irish Nationalism.* Cork: Attic Press, 11.

26. For more information on Hanna Sheehy-Skeffington, please consult: Ward, Margaret. 1997. *Hanna Sheehy-Skeffington: A Life.* Cork: Attic Press.

27. Sheehy-Skeffington, Hanna in Margaret Ward. 2001. *In Their Own Voice, Women and Irish Nationalism.* Cork: Attic Press, 30.

28. For more information on Kathleen Clarke, please consult: Litton, Helen, ed. 1991. *Revolutionary Woman: My Fight for Irish Freedom: Kathleen Clarke.* Dublin: O'Brien Press.

29. For more information on the Easter Rising, please consult: Ryan, Anne. 2005. *Witnesses: Inside the Easter Rising.* Dublin: Liberties Press; and Tallion, Ruth. 1999. *When History Was Made: The Women of 1916.* Belfast: Beyond the Pale Publications.

30. Unknown. May 3, 1916, article in the *London Times*.

31. Skinnider, Margaret. 1917. *Doing My Bit For Ireland.* New York: Century Co.

32. For more information on Linda Kearns, please consult: O Duigneain, Proinnsios. 2003. *Linda Kearns: A Revolutionary Irish Woman.* Manorhamilton, County Leitrim: Drumlin Publications.

33. Taillon, Ruth. 1996. *The Women of 1916: When History Was Made.* Belfast: Beyond the Pale Publications, 110.

34. For more information on Grace Gifford Plunkett, please consult: Plunkett, Grace. 1919. *To Hold as Twere.* Dundalk, Ireland: Tempest Dundalgan Press. For more information on Sidney Gifford Czira, please consult: Hayes, Alan, ed. 2007. *The Years Flew By: The Personal Recollections of Madame Sidney Gifford Czira.* New York: Syracuse University Press.

35. Plunkett, Grace. March 15, 1922. "The White Flag of 1916" in *Poblacht na h-Éireann* 1 (12).

36. Price, Leslie in Ruth Tallion. 1996. *When History Was Made: The Women of 1916*. Belfast: Beyond the Pale Publications, 25.

37 Markievicz, Countess in Margaret Ward. 1997. *Hanna Sheehy-Skeffington: A Life*. Cork: Attic Press, 227.

CHAPTER 2

1. MacSwiney, Mary in "50 Years Ago—Margaret Buckley, President of Sinn Féin." *Saoirse—Irish Freedom,* July 1998.

2. For more information on Mary MacSwiney and other postrevolutionary women, please consult the following: Sigillito, Gina. 2007. *Daughters of Maeve: 50 Irish Women Who Changed the World*. New York: Citadel Press; Sawyer, Roger. 1993. *We Are But Women: Women in Irish History*. London: Routledge Press; and Fallon, Charlotte. 1986. *Soul of Fire: A Biography of Mary MacSwiney*. Dublin: The Mercier Press.

3. Ó Brádaigh, Ruairí. February 28, 2007. Interview with the author. Dublin: Republican Sinn Féin headquarters.

4. For more on Ruairí Ó Brádaigh, please consult: White, Robert W. 2006. *Ruairí Ó Brádaigh: The Life and Politics of an Irish Revolutionary*. Bloomington: Indiana University Press.

5. Centre for Advancement of Women in Politics. http://www.qub.ac.uk/cawp/.

6. Unknown. October 30, 1922. "Proclamation by the I.R.A. 'To maintain the Republic.'" *Irish Times*.

7. Ward, Margaret. 1995. *Unmanageable Revolutionaries*. London: Pluto Press, 203.

8. Unknown. May 12, 1937. "Women and the Constitution." *Irish Press*.

9. Ward, Margaret. 1995. *Unmanageable Revolutionaries*. London: Pluto Press, 244.

10. Sheehy-Skeffington, Hanna. 1943."Women in Politics." *The Bell* 7 (2): 143–148. Ward, Margaret. 1995. *Unmanageable Revolutionaries*. London: Pluto Press, 192.

11. MacSwiney Brugha, Maire Óg. 2005 *History's Daughter: A Memoir of the Only Child of Terence MacSwiney*. Dublin: O'Brien Press, 13.

12. Eichacker, Joanne Mooney. 2003. *Irish Republican Women in America*. Dublin: Irish Academic Press, 99.

13. MacSwiney, Mary in Joanne Mooney Eichacker. 2003. *Irish Republican Women in America*. Dublin: Irish Academic Press, 219–220.

14. Eichacker, Joanne Mooney. 2003. *Irish Republican Women in America*. Dublin: Irish Academic Press, 109.

15. MacSwiney Brugha, Maire Óg. 2005. *History's Daughter: A Memoir of the Only Child of Terence MacSwiney*. Dublin: O'Brien Press, 20.

16. *Daily Sheet*. November 19, 1923. No. 22.

17. MacSwiney, Mary. November 12, 1923. "Civil War Prisoners, General Strike 1923." Unknown.

18. McCoole, Sinéad. 2003. *No Ordinary Women*. Dublin: O'Brien Press, 185.

19. "50 Years Ago—Margaret Buckley, President of Sinn Féin." July 1998. *Saoirse—Irish Freedom.*

20. Rafter, Kevin. 2005. *Sinn Féin 1905-2005.* Dublin: Gill & Macmillan, 72.

21. Ó Brádaigh, Ruairí. February 28, 2007. Interview with the author. Dublin: Republican Sinn Féin headquarters.

22. Buckley, Margaret. 1938. *The Jangle of the Keys.* Dublin: James Duffy and Co. Ltd., 30.

23. Ibid., 31.

24. Ibid., 33.

25. Ibid., 53.

26. Ó Brádaigh, Ruairí. February 28, 2007. Interview with the author. Dublin: Republican Sinn Féin headquarters.

27. Buckley, Margaret. 1938. *The Jangle of the Keys.* Dublin: James Duffy and Co. Ltd., 108–112.

28. Ibid., 113.

29. Ibid., 50.

30. McCoole, Sinéad. 2003. *No Ordinary Women.* Dublin: O'Brien Press, 97.

31. Comerford, Marie in Margaret Ward. 1995. *Unmanageable Revolutionaries.* London: Pluto Press, 108.

32. McCoole, Sinéad. 2003. *No Ordinary Women.* Dublin: O'Brien Press, 151.

33. Ministry of External Affairs, Saorstat Éireann. 1923. "Report on Activities of Miss O'Brennan in Switzerland."

34. McCoole, Sinéad. 2003. *No Ordinary Women.* Dublin: O'Brien Press, 190–191.

35. Ward, Margaret. 1997. *Hanna Sheehy-Skeffington: A Life.* Cork: Attic Press, 250.

36. "O'Callaghan from Prison Bars." July 1937. In Ward, Margaret. 1995. *Unmanageable Revolutionaries.* London: Pluto Press, 186.

37. Ibid.

38. Association of Old Cumann na mBan. May 18, 1937. Letter to de Valera.

39. Ward, Margaret. 1995. *Unmanageable Revolutionaries.* London: Pluto Press, 245.

40. Sinn Féin. May 7, 1938. "The Anglo-Irish Pact Denounced by Sinn Féin."

41. MacSwiney, Mary. May 11, 1938. "Editorial." *Irish Independent.*

42. Ó Brádaigh, Ruairí. February 28, 2007. Interview with the author. Dublin: Republican Sinn Féin headquarters.

43. Ibid.

CHAPTER 3

1. MacSwiney, Mary. Saturday, January 7, 1922. *DÁIL EIREANN PUBLIC SESSION.* http://www.ucc.ie/celt/online/E900003-001/text010.html.

2. MacEoin, Uinseann. 1997. *The IRA in the Twilight Years: 1923–1948.* Dublin: Argenta Publications, 709.

3. Buckley, Margaret. 1938. *The Jangle of the Keys.* Dublin: James Duffy and Co. Ltd., 1–2.

4. Irish High Court. 1948. Ruling.

5. Goulding, Seamus in Uinseann MacEoin. 1997. *The IRA in the Twilight Years: 1923–1948.* Dublin: Argenta Publications, 709.

6. Ibid., 708.

7. Buckley, Margaret. 1956. *A Proud History Gives Confidence of Victory.* Dublin: Sinn Féin.

8. *Irish Press.* March 4, 1939.

9. Ibid.

10. Feeney, Brian. 2002. *Sinn Féin: A Hundred Turbulent Years.* Dublin: O'Brien Press, 177.

11. MacSwiney, Mary. March 20, 1940. "Private Letter to Mrs. De Valera."

12. Josephine Mary Plunkett. March 15, 1940. "Letter to de Valera."

13. Cavan County Council Meeting. January 16, 1940. "Minutes."

14. Feeney, Brian. 2002. *Sinn Féin: A Hundred Turbulent Years.* Dublin: O'Brien Press, 189.

15. Comerford, Marie. May 5, 1950. *Irish Times.*

16. Ó Brádaigh, Ruairí. February 28, 2007. Interview with the author. Dublin: Republican Sinn Féin headquarters.

17. Ibid.

18. Ibid.

19. Feeney, Brian. 2002. *Sinn Féin: A Hundred Turbulent Years.* Dublin: O'Brien Press, 199.

20. Unknown. November 8, 2001. "Volunteer Jimmy Drumm." *An Phoblacht/Republican News.*

21. Ó Brádaigh, Ruairí. February 28, 2007. Interview with the author. Dublin: Republican Sinn Féin headquarters.

22. Ibid.

23. Adams, Gerry. January 1, 2007. "Speech by Gerry Adams, then President of Sinn Féin, at an Event to Commemorate Seán Sabhat and Feargal Ó hAnnluain, County Fermanagh, 1 January 2007." http://cain.ulst.ac.uk/issues/politics/docs/sf/ga010107.htm.

24. Ó Brádaigh, Ruairí. February 28, 2007. Interview with the author. Dublin: Republican Sinn Féin headquarters.

25. Sinn Féin. 1958. Pamphlet.

26. Ó Brádaigh, Ruairí. February 28, 2007. Interview with the author. Dublin: Republican Sinn Féin headquarters.

27. Unknown. July 8, 1957. "63 Held in Garda Round-Up." *Irish Press.*

28. Unknown. November 25, 1957. "Sinn Féin Ard Fheis." *Irish Press.*

29. Feeney, Brian. 2002. *Sinn Féin: A Hundred Turbulent Years.* Dublin: O'Brien Press, 206.

CHAPTER 4

1. Glenholmes, Eibhlín. February 22, 2007. Interview with the author. Belfast.

2. Ibid.

3. Padraig Mac Logain. November 7, 1960. "Arrests Are Continuing: S.F. leader." *Irish Press.*

4. Unknown. February 21, 1961. *Irish Times.*

5. Ibid.

6. Mules, Daisy in Kathleen Kane and Karen Steele. 1999. "Sinn Féin and the Educative Process: An Interview with Daisy Mules." *Jouvert: A Journal of Postcolonial Studies* 4 (1).

7. Feeney, Brian. 2002. *Sinn Féin: A Hundred Turbulent Years.* Dublin: O'Brien Press, 222.

8. Ó Brádaigh, Ruairí. February 28, 2007. Interview with the author. Dublin: Republican Sinn Féin headquarters.

9. McCafferty, Nell. August 10, 2000. *An Phoblacht/Republican News.*

10. Moore, Marie in Claire Hackett. 2004. "Narratives of Political Activism from Women in West Belfast." *Irish Women and Nationalism: Soldiers, New Women and Wicked Hags*, ed. Margaret Ward and Louise Ryan. Dublin: Irish Academic Press, 153.

11. McAuley, Chrissie. 1988. "Nationalist Women and the RUC." Sinn Féin Women's Department, 7.

12. McAuley, Chrissie. 1988. "Nationalist Women and the RUC." Sinn Féin Women's Department, 10.

13. Nelis, Mary in Chrissie McAuley. 1989. *Women in a War Zone: Twenty Years of Resistance.* Dublin: Republican Publications, 14–15.

14. Keane, Mairead in Laura Lyons. 1992. "At the End of the Day: An Interview with Mairead Keane." *Boundary 2* 19 (2): 269.

15. McAuley, Chrissie. 1989. *Women in a War Zone: Twenty Years of Resistance.* Dublin: Republican Publications, 11.

16. Ibid.

17. Devlin, Bernadette. 1969. *The Price of My Soul.* New York: Random House, 3.

18. Devlin McAliskey, Bernadette. October 22, 1980. "Speech Delivered to the District Council 37 American Federation of State, County and Municipal Employees in New York." www.irelandsown.net/bernadette1.html.

19. Nelis, Mary. "A Diary from Derry." 1996. Derry: *Beyond the Wire.* http://irelandsown.net/Wire.htm.

20. Nelis, Mary in Chrissie McAuley. 1989. *Women in a War Zone: Twenty Years of Resistance.* Dublin: Republican Publications, 14.

21. Nelis, Mary. "A Diary from Derry." 1996. Derry. *Beyond the Wire.* http://irelandsown.net/Wire.htm.

22. Ibid.

23. Adams, Gerry. March 26, 2009. "Our Friend Marie." http://leargas.blogspot.com/2009_03_01_archive.html.

24. Friel, Laura. March 26, 2009. "Veteran Republican Marie Moore Dies." *AP/RN.* http://www.anphoblacht.com/news/detail/37908.

25. For addition reading on this period, please consult: Purdie, Bob. 1990. *Politics in the Streets: The Origins of the Civil Rights Movement in Northern Ireland.* Belfast: Blackstaff Press. Northern Ireland Civil Rights Association (NICRA). 1978.

"We Shall Overcome" . . . *The History of the Struggle for Civil Rights in Northern Ireland 1968–1978.* Belfast: Northern Ireland Civil Rights Association (NICRA); McKittrick, David. 2000. *Making Sense of the Troubles.* Belfast: Blackstaff Press; Ó Dochartaigh, Niall. 1997. *From Civil Rights to Armalites: Derry and the Birth of the Irish Troubles.* Cork: Cork University Press; and Dooley, Brian. 1998. *Black and Green: The Fight for Civil Rights in Northern Ireland and Black America.* London: Pluto Press.

CHAPTER 5

1. Breen, Suzanne. December 7, 2004. "Old Bailey Bomber Ashamed of Sinn Féin." *The Village.* http://irishfreedomcommittee.net/NEWS/december_2004.htm #Marian_Price_interviewDec04.

2. Corcoran, Mary. 2006. *Out of Order: The Political Imprisonment of Women in Northern Ireland 1972–1998.* Devon, UK: Willan Publishing, 126.

3. Fitzsimmons, Lily in Chrissie McAuley. 1989. *Women in a War Zone: Twenty Years of Resistance.* Dublin: Republican Publications, 18.

4. McAuley, Chrissie. 1988. "Nationalist Women and the RUC." Sinn Féin Women's Department, 3–4.

5. Fitzsimmons, Lily. 1996. *Women in Ireland: The Unsung Heroes of Conflict in Ireland's Six North-east Counties.* Belfast: Sinn Féin, 15–16.

6. McAuley, Chrissie. 1989. *Women in a War Zone: Twenty Years of Resistance.* Dublin: Republican Publications, 17.

7. Irish National Congress. 1993. "Congressional Briefing Paper, April 1993. The Use of Plastic Bullets in Northern Ireland." http://www.irishnationalcaucus. org/pages/ArticlesUndated/Congressional%20Briefing%20Paper%20April%20 1993.htm.

8. Moore, Marie in Claire Hackett. 2004. "Narratives of Political Activism from Women in West Belfast." In *Irish Women and Nationalism: Soldiers, New Women and Wicked Hags,* ed. Margaret Ward and Louise Ryan. Dublin: Irish Academic Press, 150.

9. Ibid., 152.

10. Bloody Sunday Charitable Trust 2001. http://www.bloodysundaytrust.org/ edureaction.htm.

11. Hoggart, Simon. January 1973. "Woman Nationalist is New Leader of Provisional Sinn Féin." *Guardian.*

12. Ibid.

13. Coogan, Tim Pat. *The Troubles: Ireland's Ordeal 1966–1995 and the Search for Peace.* Hampshire, UK: Palgrave Macmillan, 217.

14. Murray, Father Raymond. 1998. *Hard Time: Armagh Gaol 1971–1986.* Co. Cork, Ireland: Mercier Press, 10.

15. Ibid., 33.

16. Corcoran, Mary. 2006. *Out of Order: The Political Imprisonment of Women in Northern Ireland 1972–1998.* Devon, UK: Willan Publishing, 21.

17. Ibid., 25.

18. McKeown, Laurence. 2001. *Out of Time: Irish Republican Prisoners Long Kesh 1972–2000.* Belfast: Beyond the Pale Publications.

19. Corcoran, Mary. 2006. *Out of Order: The Political Imprisonment of Women in Northern Ireland 1972–1998.* Devon, UK: Willan Publishing, 21, 132–134.

20. Nic Giolla Easpaig, Áine and Eibhlín. 1987. *Sisters in Cells: Two Republican Prisoners."* Translated by Nollaig O Gadhra, Foilseachain Naisiunta Teoranta, Co. Mayo, Ireland: Westport Press.

21. Talbot, Rhiannon. 2004. "Female Combatants, Paramilitary Prisoners and the Development of Feminism in the Republican Movement." In *Irish Women and Nationalism: Soldiers, New Women and Wicked Hags,* ed. Margaret Ward and Louise Ryan. Dublin: Irish Academic Press, 136–137.

22. McGuffin, John. 1973. *Internment.* Vancouver, BC: Anvil Books Ltd.

23. McAuley, Chrissie. 1989. *Women in a War Zone: Twenty Years of Resistance.* Dublin: Republican Publications, 27.

24. Moore, Marie in Pol Wilson and Rosaleen Walsh. 2001. *A Rebel Heart: Maire Bn Ui Dhroma.* Republican pamphlet.

25. Ó Brádaigh, Ruairí. February 28, 2007. Interview with the author. Dublin: Republican Sinn Féin headquarters.

26. Glenholmes, Eibhlín. February 22, 2007. Interview with the author. Belfast.

27. Friel, Laura. August 10, 2000. "One Woman's Dream." *AP/RN.*

28. http://www.troopsoutmovement.com.

29. http://www.troopsoutmovement.com/bloodysunday.htm. For more information on Peggy Deery, please consult: Nell McCafferty 1988. *Peggy Deery: A Derry Family at War.* Dublin: Attic Press.

30. Price, Marian. March 13, 2003. *Guardian.* http://irelandsown.net/price5.html.

31. Cowan, Rosie. March 13, 2003. "I Have No Regrets." *Guardian.* http://www.guardian.co.uk/world/2003/mar/13/gender.uk.

32. Price, Dolours. July 17, 2004. "Once I Knew a Boy." *The Blanket.*

33. Price, Marian in Susanne Breen. December 4, 2004. "Old Bailey Bomber Ashamed of Sinn Féin." *The Village.* www.villagemagazine.ie.

34. Gerry Adams. June 29, 2002. " 'A First Class Mayor for First Class People'—Adams." Sinn Féin Press Release. http://www.sinnfein.org/releases//02/pr022906b.html.

35. Devlin McAliskey, Bernadette. 1983."What Price Reunification?" *Counterspy* 8 (2): 41.

36. Beckwith, Barbara. 1979. "Pope John Paul II: Memories to Cherish." *The Pope in Ireland—A Salute to Irish Faith.* http://www.americancatholic.org/Features/JohnPaulII/2-Ireland-1979.asp.

CHAPTER 6

1. Fitzsimmons, Lily in Chrissie McAuley, ed. 1989. *Women in a War Zone: Twenty Years of Resistance.* Dublin: Republican Publications, 44.

2. Sands, Bobby. 1997. "Flowers, My Friends, Flowers." *Writings from Prison.* Landham, MD: Rinehart Publishers, 100–101.

3. Glenholmes, Eibhlín. February 22, 2007. Interview with the author. Belfast.

4. For more information of the hunger strike, please consult: Morrison, Danny, ed. 2006. *Hunger Strike: Reflections on the 1981 Hunger Strike.* Co. Kerry, Ireland: Brandon / Mount Eagle Publications Ltd; O'Hearn, Denis. 2006. *Nothing but an Unfinished Song.* Nation Books; and Beresford, David. 1987. *Ten Men Dead: Story of the 1981 Irish Hunger Strike.* HarperCollins Publishers Ltd.

5. Farrell, Mairéad. August 30, 1980. In McAuley, Chrissie. 1989. *Women in a War Zone: Twenty Years of Resistance.* Dublin: Republican Publications, 13.

6. Sands, Bobby. 1997. *Writings from Prison.* Landham, MD: Rinehart Publishers, 219.

7. McCrory, Maura. Autumn 1994. "Women Took the Lead." *Women in Struggle.* Dublin: Sinn Féin Women's Department,15.

8. Foley, Aran. June 15, 2006. "Remembering 1981: Two H-Block prisoner TDs Elected."*AP/RN.* http://www.anphoblacht.com/news/detail/14653.

9. Thomspon, Melissa, ed. and producer. 1998. "Interview with Mary Nelis." *Sli na mBan.* www.tallgirlshorts.net/thewayofwomen.

10. Armstrong, Maeve. October 13, 1983. "Armagh Women Suffer Further Cruelties: Repression Intensifies." *AP/RN,* 2.

11. Talbot, Rhiannon. 2004. "Female Combatants, Paramilitary Prisoners and the Development of Feminism in the Republican Movement." In *Irish women and Nationalism: Soldiers, New Women and Wicked Hags,* ed. Margaret Ward and Louise Ryan. Portland, OR: Irish Academic Press.

12. Rafter, Kevin. 2005. *Sinn Féin 1905–2005—In the Shadow of Gunmen.* Dublin: Gill & Macmillan, 133.

13. Coogan, Tim Pat. 1994. *The IRA: A History.* Lanham, MD: Roberts Rinehart Publishers, chapters 19 and 20.

14. English, Richard. 2003. *Armed Struggle.* Oxford: Oxford University Press, 289–292.

15. Adams, Gerry. 1986. *The Politics of Irish Freedom.* Co. Kerry, Ireland: Brandon Press, 167.

16. Incore, Cain. "Friday 3 November 1989–Events." http://cain.ulst.ac.uk/events/index.html.

17. McAuley, Chrissie, ed. 1989. *Women in a War Zone: Twenty Years of Resistance.* Dublin: Republican Publications, 16.

18. Tully, Jo. August 1990. "Women and National Liberation: Reports from around the World—Ireland." *SpareRib,* 49.

19. Sinn Féin. January/February 1989. "Sinn Féin Women's Conference." *A Woman's Voice* 4: 3.

20. Sinn Féin. January/February 1989. "Sinn Féin Women's Conference." *A Woman's Voice* 4: 4.

21. Sinn Féin Women's Department. February 24, 1991. "Revised Report on Women's Department & Recommendations."

22. Morgan in McAuley, Chrissie, ed. 1989. *Women in a War Zone: Twenty Years of Resistance.* Dublin: Republican Publications, 31.

23. Anderson, Martina. February 22, 2007. Interview with the author. Derry.

24. Glenholmes, Eibhlín. February 22, 2007. Interview with the author. Belfast.

25. McCafferty, Nell. 1995. "It Is My Belief That Armagh is a Feminist Issue." *Ireland's Women,* by Katie Donovan et al. New York: W.W. Norton and Company, 19–22.

26. Sinn Féin. January/February 1989. *A Woman's Voice,* 5–6.

27. Anderson, Martina. February 22, 2007. Interview with the author. Derry.

28. Ibid.

29. Ibid.

30. Ibid.

31. Unknown. September 22, 1983. "A Personal Account by Caitríona." *AP/RN,* 7.

32. Glenholmes, Eibhlín. February 22, 2007. Interview with the author. Belfast.

33. Ibid.

34. Anderson, Martina. February 22, 2007. Interview with the author. Derry.

35. Ibid.

36. Ibid.

37. Fitzsimmons, Lily. 1996. *Women in Ireland: The Unsung Heroes of Conflict in Ireland's Six North-east Counties.* Belfast: Sinn Féin.

38. Glenholmes, Eibhlín. February 22, 2007. Interview with the author. Belfast.

39. Dillon, Martin. 1999. *The Dirty War: Covert Strategies and Tactics Used in Political Conflicts.* London: Routledge, 211–225.

40. Lyons, Laura. Summer 1992. "At the End of the Day: An Interview with Máiread Keane, National Head of Sinn Féin Women's Department." *Boundary 2,* 273.

41. English, Richard. 2003. *Armed Struggle.* Oxford: Oxford University Press, 256.

42. O'Dwyer, Ella. "Interview: Treasa Quinn, Sinn Féin Joint National Treasurer." July 6, 2006: *AP/RN.* http://www.anphoblacht.com/news/detail/14994.

43. Glenholmes, Eibhlín. February 22, 2007. Interview with the author. Belfast.

44. Ibid.

45. Denis O'Hearn. 2006. *Nothing but an Unfinished Song.* New York: Nation Books, 100–110.

46. Glenholmes, Eibhlín. February 22, 2007. Interview with the author. Belfast.

47. Ibid.

48. Thompson, Melissa, ed. and pr. 1999. "Interview with Martina Anderson." *Sli na mBan.* http://www.tallgirlshorts.net/thewayofwomen.

49. Anderson, Martina. February 22, 2007. Interview with the author. Derry.

50. McAuley, Chrissie, ed. 1989. "Martina Anderson, Prisoner in Durham Jail, 22 April 1987." *Women in a War Zone: Twenty Years of Resistance.* Dublin: Republican Publications, 75.

51. Unknown. February 28, 2008. "Le ChÉile MUNSTER Honouree: Ella O'Dwyer." *AP/RN*. http://www.anphoblacht.com/news/detail/25064.

52. Whelan, Peadar. February 15, 2001. "Memories of '81 Stirred. Hunger Strike Office Opens." *AP/RN*. http://republican-news.org/archive/2001/February15/15hung.html.

53. Weinstein, Laura. 2006. "The Significance of the Armagh Dirty Protest." *Éire-Ireland* 41 (3&4): 11–41. http://www.belfastmedia.com/features_article. php?ID=879.

54. Lane, Fern. September 25, 2002. "Setting the Record Straight." *AP/RN*.

55. Adams, Gerry. March 28, 2009. "Our Friend Marie Moore." http://leargas. blogspot.com/2009_03_01_archive.html.

56. McCann, Jennifer. March 11, 2007. " 'Bobby Sands Was a Great Role Model—He Was Never Arrogant.' " *Sunday Tribune*.

57. Unknown. September 13, 2007. "McCann and Anderson Challenge PSNI on Domestic Violence." *AP/RN*. www.anphoblacht.com/news/detail/20672.

58. McCann, Jennifer. March 26, 2007. "Women Rally for Role in Politics." PeaceWomen.org. http://www.peacewomen.org/news/NorthernIreland/Mar07/RallyforRole.html.

CHAPTER 7

1. Markievicz, Countess. June 1909. "Woman with a Garden." *Bean na hÉire-ann*.

2. Ruane, Caitríona in Niamh Reilly, ed. 1997. "Cultural Rights and Social Inclusion." *Strategies and Analyses from the ICCL Working Conference on Women's Rights as Human Rights in Dublin March 1997*. http://members.tripod/~whr1998/documents/icclruane.htm.

3. Arney, Megan. May 18, 1998. "Sinn Féin Negotiator Speaks in New York." *The Militant* 62 (19). http://www.themilitant.com/1998/6219/6219_14.html.

4. UNIFEM. 2005. *Securing the Peace*. United Nations.

5. United Nations Security Council. 2000. Resolution 1325. United Nations.

6. UNIFEM. 2006. http://www.unifem.org/gender_issues/governance_peace_security/at_a_glance.php.

7. Melaugh, Martin, and Fionnuala McKenna. Last Update 2009. "Background Information on Northern Ireland Society: Population and Vital Statistics." (Compiled Data). Belfast: CAIN: Conflict Archive on the Internet. http://cain.ulst. ac.uk/ni/popul.htm.

8. Ibid.

9. Ibid.

10. Osborne, Bob. December 19, 2002. "Fascination of Religion Head Count." BBC. http://news.bbc.co.uk/1/hi/northern_ireland/2590023.stm.

11. Feehan, Deidre. August 28, 1997. *AP/RN*. http://republican-news.org/archive/1997/August28/28you2.html.

12. Morgan, Valerie, and Grace Fraser. 1994. *The Company We Keep: Women, Community and Organisations*. University of Ulster, Coleraine. http://cain.ulst. ac.uk/csc/reports/company.htm.

13. UNIFEM. 2005. *Securing the Peace.* United Nations.

14. Gillespie, Una. Autumn 1994. "Women in Struggle 1969–1994." *Women in Struggle.* Sinn Féin Women's Department.

15. Sinn Féin. 1992. *Women in Ireland.* Dublin: Sinn Féin.

16. Gillespie, Una. Autumn 1994. "Women in Struggle 1969–1994." *Women in Struggle.* Sinn Féin Women's Department.

17. Sinn Féin. 1994. *Towards a Lasting Peace.* Dublin: Sinn Féin.

18. Kray, Laura, et al. 2004. "Stereotype Reactance at the Bargaining Table: The Effect of Stereotype Activation and Power on Claiming and Creating Value." *Personality and Social Psychology Bulletin* (Sage Publications) 30 (4): 399–411; and Curhan, Jared R., and Jennifer R. Overbeck. 2008. "Making a Positive Impression in a Negotiation: Gender Differences in Response to Impression Motivation." *Negotiation and Conflict Management Research* 1 (2): 179–193.

19. Taylor in Seth Linder. February 19, 1995. "Sinn Féin's Sisterhood." *Independent* (London).

20. Ward, Margaret, and Louise Ryan, eds. 2005. *Irish Women and Nationalism: Soldiers, New Women and Wicked Hags.* Dublin: Irish Academic Press.

21. Sinn Féin Women's Department. April/May 1989. "Partition: A Woman's Issue" in *An Irish Voice.* www.etext.org/Politics/INAC/partition.and.women.

22. Sinn Féin. December 12, 2002. "What Sinn Féin Is Doing." *AP/RN.* http://republican-news.org/archive/2002/December12/12what.html.

23. ni Bhrian, Aine. 2003. "A Future of Equals." *AP/RN.* http://republican-news.org/archive/2003/April03/03equf.html.

24. Sinn Féin. December 12, 2002. "What Sinn Féin Is Doing." *AP/RN.* http://republican-news.org/archive/2002/December12/12what.html.

25. Adams, Gerry. April 12, 2006. "Gerry Adams Pays Tribute to Siobhan O'Hanlon." Sinn Féin. http://sinnfein.ie/news/detail/13832.

26. Ibid.

27. Unknown. July 25, 2002. "Bhreatnach Takes on Cultural Brief." *AP/RN.* http://www.anphoblacht.com/news/detail/24643.

28. Sinn Féin. 2001. "Debating the Ard Chomhairle's Gender Imbalance 4 October 2001." *AP/RN.* http://republican-news.org/archive/2001/October04/04af7.html.

29. Ward, Margaret. December 2000. *The Northern Ireland Assembly and Women: Assessing the Gender Deficit.* Belfast: Democratic Dialogue. http://cain.ulst.ac.uk/dd/papers/women-assembly.html.

30. Ibid., 7.

31. Ibid., 8–9.

32. Clifford, Kieran. November 11, 1999. "Maire Moore to Open Women's Conference." *AP/RN.* http://republican-news.org/archive/1999/November11/11mari.html.

33. Sinn Féin. 2005. www.sinnfeinonline.com/representatives/382; www.sinnfeinonline.com/representatives/373; http://sinnfein.ie/assembly/candidate/262.

34. UNIFEM. 2005. *Securing the Peace.* United Nations.

35. Shilton, Francis. March 4, 1995. "Maghaberry Women Political Prisoners' Statement at 'The Role of Women in the Peace Process' Conference." *AP/RN.*

Belfast: Whiterock College of Further Education/ Belfast Women's Conference. http://www.hartford-hwp.com/archives/61/012.html.

36. Hoffman, Mark. 2000."Perspectives on the Northern Ireland Women's Coalition." *SIT Occasional Papers Series: Addressing Intercultural Education, Training & Service* 3: 69–84. http://www.sit.edu/publications/docs/ops03csnireland.pdf.

37. Nelis, Mary in Francis Shilton. 1995. *AP/RN*. http://www.hartford-hwp.com/archives/61/012.html 1995.

38. British Association for Central And Eastern Europe. 2002, 5. http://www.bacee.org.uk/downloads/BACEE%20July%2002.pdf.

39. Ní Chuilín, Carál. April 22, 2008. "Carál Ní Chuilín Addresses Assembly on North Belfast Interfaces." Northern Ireland Assembly. http://www.nbin.info/index.

40. UNIFEM. 2005. *Securing the Peace*. United Nations.

41. Hoffman, Mark. 2000. "Perspectives on the Northern Ireland Women's Coalition" in *SIT Occasional Papers Series: Addressing Intercultural Education, Training & Service* 3: 69–84. http://www.sit.edu/publications/docs/ops03csnireland.pdf.

42. Sinn Féin. 2006. http://sinnfein.ie/assembly/news/detail/2233.

43. Elliott, Sydney, and W. D. Flackes. 1999. *Northern Ireland: A Political Directory 1968–1999*. Belfast: Blackstaff Press.

44. UNIFEM. 2005. *Securing the Peace*. United Nations.

45. Whyte, Nicholas. 2005. "Northern Ireland Elections." ARK. http://www.ark.ac.uk/elections/.

46. Sinn Féin policy documents include: the 2003 *Educate That You May be Free* document, the 2004 *Women in an Ireland of Equals* document, and the 2006 *Health in an Ireland of Equals* document.

CHAPTER 8

1. De Brún, Bairbre. May 6, 2009. Bobby Sands Memorial Lecture. http://www.youtube.com/watch?v=Tz5iMWDg—4&feature=channel_page.

2. Inter-Parliamentary Union. 2009. "Women in Parliaments." http://www.ipu.org.

3. Inter-Parliamentary Union. 2009. "Women in Parliaments." http://www.ipu.org.

4. Dahlerup, Drude and Freidenvall, Lenita. 2005. "Quotas as a 'Fast Track' to Equal Representation for Women: Why Scandinavia is no Longer the Model." *International Feminist Journal of Politics* 7.1; Krook, Mona. 2006. "Gender Quotas, Norms, and Politics." *Politics and Gender* 2 (1): 110–118.

5. Inter-Parliamentary Union. 2009. "Women in Parliaments." http://www.ipu.org.

6. Norris, Pippa. 1997. *Passages to Power: Legislative Recruitment in Advanced Democracies*. Cambridge: Cambridge University Press.; Rule, Wilma. 1981. "Why Women Don't Run: The Critical Contextual Factors in Women's Legislative Recruitment." *Political Science Quarterly* (Sage Publications); and Matland, Richard.

1998. "Women's Representation in National Legislatures: Developed and Developing Countries." *Legislative Studies Quarterly* 23 (1): 109–125.

7. Lovenduski, Joni, and J. Hills. 1981. *The Politics of the Second Electorate: Women and Public Participation.* London: Routledge; and Rule, Wilma. 1987. "Electoral Systems, Contextual Factors and Women's Opportunity for Election to Parliament in Twenty-Three Democracies." *Political Science Quarterly* (Sage Publications).

8. Dahlerup, Drude. 2002. "Using Quotas to Increase Women's Political Representation." In *Women in Parliament: Beyond the Numbers.* Stockholm: International IDEA.

9. It is important to note in passing that the relative depression of Sinn Féin's electoral success in the South can be tied to its association with the IRA and years of being an illegal organization in the Republic. The stronghold of Sinn Féin throughout the Troubles was the northern Six Counties.

10. Previous incarnations of devolved assemblies in Northern Ireland prior to the Good Friday (Belfast) Agreement in 1998 are not recounted here. For additional explanation, please consult information on the Stormont Assembly.

11. Dahlerup, Drude. 2002. "Using Quotas to Increase Women's Political Representation." In *Women in Parliament: Beyond the Numbers.* Stockholm: International IDEA.

12. Krook, Mona. 2006. "Gender Quotas, Norms, and Politics." *Politics and Gender* 2 (1): 110–118.

13. Glenholmes, Eibhlin. February 22, 2007. Interview with the author. Belfast.

14. http://www.qub.ac.uk/cawp/UKhtmls/electionNIMarch07.htm.

15. Schmidt, Gregory D. 2004. "The Election of Women in List PR Systems: Testing the Conventional Wisdom." *Comparative Political Studies* 37 (6): 704–734.

16. Glenholmes, Eibhlin. February 22, 2007. Interview with the author. Belfast.

17. Breathnach, Lucilita. 2002. "A December 2002 Article." *AP/RN.*

18. Krook, Mona. 2006. "Gender Quotas, Norms, and Politics." *Politics and Gender* 2 (1): 110–118.

19. Glenholmes, Eibhlin. February 22, 2007. Interview with the author. Belfast.

20. Ibid.

21. Sinn Féin. 2006. *Internal Sinn Féin Report.*

22. Glenholmes, Eibhlin. February 22, 2007. Interview with the author. Belfast.

23. Sinn Féin. 2006. *Internal Gender Equality Report 2006.* Sinn Féin Party Development Department, 13.

24. Sinn Féin. 2005. *Sinn Féin: Equality for Women (Elections 2005),* 2.

25. Sinn Féin. 2005. *Sinn Féin: Equality for Women (Elections 2005),* 6.

26. Sinn Féin. 2007. *Women in an Ireland of Equals,* 1.

27. Sinn Féin. 2007. *Women in an Ireland of Equals,* 2.

28. Sinn Féin. 2007. *Women in an Ireland of Equals,* 3.

29. Ruane. Caitríona. February 23, 2007. Personal interview with author. Warrenpoint.

30. Ibid.

31. Ibid.

32. McDonald, Mary Lou. February 21, 2007. Personal interview with the author. Dublin.

33. Ibid.

34. Ibid.

35. Anderson, Martina. February 22, 2007. Personal interview with author. Derry.

36. Ibid.

37. Ibid.

38. Anderson, Martina. February 22, 2007. Interview with the author. Derry.

INDEX

ABOUT THE AUTHOR

MARGARET KEILEY-LISTERMANN is an assistant professor of political science at Georgia Gwinnett College. She serves on the executive board of the Georgia Political Science Association and the Junior League of Atlanta. Her doctoral dissertation was on the role of Sinn Féin in the Northern Irish peace process, and her publications include "Conflict Resolution Evaluation—Constructing a Disputant Guide for Formative Feedback" (2007) and "How Has the Political Conflict in Northern Ireland Impacted Daily Life?" (2010).